LIBRARY OF NEW TESTAMENT STUDIES

645

formerly the Journal for the Study of the New Testament Supplement series

Editor
Chris Keith

Editorial Board
Dale C. Allison, John M.G. Barclay, Lynn H. Cohick,
R. Alan Culpepper, Craig A. Evans, Robert Fowler, Simon
J. Gathercole, Juan Hernández Jr., John S. Kloppenborg,
Michael Labahn, Matthew V. Novenson, Love L. Sechrest,
Robert Wall, Catrin H. Williams, Brittany E. Wilson

Constructing Ethnic Identity in 1 Peter

Who You Are No Longer

Janette H. Ok

LONDON • NEW YORK • OXFORD • NEW DELHI • SYDNEY

T&T CLARK
Bloomsbury Publishing Plc
50 Bedford Square, London, WC1B 3DP, UK
1385 Broadway, New York, NY 10018, USA
29 Earlsfort Terrace, Dublin 2, Ireland

BLOOMSBURY, T&T CLARK and the T&T Clark logo are trademarks of Bloomsbury Publishing Plc

First published in Great Britain 2021
This paperback edition published 2022

Copyright © Janette H. Ok, 2021

Janette H. Ok has asserted her right under the Copyright, Designs and Patents Act, 1988, to be identified as Author of this work.

For legal purposes the Acknowledgments on pp. ix-x constitute an extension of this copyright page.

Cover design: Charlotte James

All rights reserved. No part of this publication may be reproduced or transmitted in any form or by any means, electronic or mechanical, including photocopying, recording, or any information storage or retrieval system, without prior permission in writing from the publishers.

Bloomsbury Publishing Plc does not have any control over, or responsibility for, any third-party websites referred to or in this book. All internet addresses given in this book were correct at the time of going to press. The author and publisher regret any inconvenience caused if addresses have changed or sites have ceased to exist, but can accept no responsibility for any such changes.

A catalogue record for this book is available from the British Library.

Library of Congress Cataloging-in-Publication Data
Names: Ok, Janette H., author.
Title: Constructing ethnic identity in 1 Peter : who you are no longer / Janette H. Ok.
Description: London ; New York : T&T Clark, 2021. | Series: Library of New Testament studies, 2513-8790 ; 645 | Includes bibliographical references and index. | Summary: "Janette Ok argues that 1 Peter characterizes Christian identity as an ethnic identity, as it holds the potential to engender a powerful sense of solidarity for readers who are experiencing social alienation as a result of their conversion. In order to help construct a collective understanding of what it means to be a Christian in contrast to non-Christians, Ok argues that the author of the epistle employs "ethnic reasoning" or logic"– Provided by publisher.
Identifiers: LCCN 2020054768 (print) | LCCN 2020054769 (ebook) | ISBN 9780567698506 (hardback) | ISBN 9780567698513 (pdf) | ISBN 9780567698537 (epub)
Subjects: LCSH: Bible. Peter, 1st–Criticism, interpretation, etc. | Ethnicity in the Bible. | Identification (Religion) | Identity (Psychology)–Religious aspects–Christianity.
Classification: LCC BS2795.52 .O3 2021 (print) | LCC BS2795.52 (ebook) | DDC 227/.9206–dc23
LC record available at https://lccn.loc.gov/2020054768
LC ebook record available at https://lccn.loc.gov/2020054769

ISBN:	HB:	978-0-5676-9850-6
	PB:	978-0-5676-9854-4
	ePDF:	978-0-5676-9851-3
	ePUB:	978-0-5676-9853-7

Series: Library of New Testament Studies, volume 645
ISSN 2513–8790

Typeset by Integra Software Services Pvt. Ltd.

To find out more about our authors and books visit www.bloomsbury.com and sign up for our newsletters.

For S. Scott Bartchy
teacher, mentor, and friend

Contents

Acknowledgments		ix
Abbreviations		xi
1	Introduction: What Do Ethnicity and Identity Have to Do with 1 Peter?	1
	Defining the Terms	2
	Ethnic-Religious Composition	10
	Conclusion	11
2	Defining and Defying Ethnicity in the Ancient World	13
	Introduction	13
	Framing the Study of Greek Ethnic Identity	15
	The Emergence of Panhellenism and the Concept of the Barbarian	17
	Imagining Persia and Constructing Greekness	20
	The Proof Is in the Stock: Defining Greek Ethnicity	23
	Greek Ethnicity under Roman Rule	26
	Rome's Civilizing Mission	27
	Remaining Greek while Becoming Roman	30
	Conclusion	33
3	Common Blood: Establishing a New Patrilineage through the Blood of Christ	35
	Introduction	35
	Establishing God as Father	37
	"As Obedient Children"	43
	Connecting New Birth with Christ's Ransoming Blood	45
	Employing the Logic of Patrilineal Descent	48
	Not Sons, but Children of God	52
	Appropriating Israel's Identity-Defining Designations for a Dislocated People	54
	Elected Group Identity	58
	Conclusion	59

4	Constructing Boundaries and Contesting Stigma in the Making of Ethnic Identity in 1 Peter	61
	Introduction	61
	Barth on Ethnic Boundaries	62
	Constructing Social Boundaries in 1 Peter	65
	Disidentifying from "The Futile Conduct Inherited from Your Ancestors"	71
	Constrained Christian Identity	72
	Construing the Gentile "Other"	73
	Goffman on Stigma	74
	Contesting and Subverting Christian Stigma in 1 Peter	78
	"Faith Information Control"	82
	Stigma Reversal	84
	Honorary Ethnics	86
	Conclusion	87
5	Conclusion: Reinforcing Christian Distinctiveness through Bonds of Blood	89
	Further Implications of This Study	92
	Asian American Studies	92
	Canonical Studies	93
Bibliography		96
Scripture Index		106
Subject Index		113

Acknowledgments

This book would not have been possible without the investment and support of many significant people, organizations, and communities. Ross Wagner initially encouraged me to consider working in 1 Peter and helped forge a path into this nuanced and pastorally sensitive letter as my dissertation project. I would like to thank the members of my dissertation committee at Princeton Theological Seminary, George Parsenios, Dale Allison, and Clifton Black, for your time, expertise, and help getting to the finish line. I also extend thanks to Kenneth Appold and Rose Ellen Dunn, who were instrumental in the final stages of my doctoral program, and my anonymous reader, whose thoughtful comments helped to clarify my thinking. I will always be thankful for the mentorship, encouragement, and guidance I have received from Brian Blount, Leong Seow, Shane Berg, Loren Stuckenbruck, Benny Liew, and Gale Yee during various stages of my development as a scholar and teacher. I am also grateful to Scott Bartchy and Joel Green for generously taking the time to read portions or versions of this book and give substantive feedback at various stages.

Many friends and colleagues have been my conversation partners in enriching and life-giving ways. From PTS, in particular, I want to thank Lisa Bowens, Mary Schmitt, Chad Marshall, Jason Sturdevant, Chris McCoy, Luke Lin, Elaine James, Dan Pioske, Kara Lyons-Pardue, Brittany Wilson, Adam Stokes, and Matt Novenson. SueJeanne Koh, you have been an invaluable writing and dialogue partner with whom I shared my thoughts and work in their most inchoate stages. Esther Park, Hanah Kim, Michelle Kim, Alice Lee, Joanne Moon, Kate Kim, and Daniela Lee, I could not have done this without you. Much love and appreciation to my friends at Azusa Pacific University for being such wonderful and supportive colleagues; I look forward to forging many collaborations, projects, and friendships with my new colleagues at Fuller Seminary.

My work, personhood, and vocation have been nourished and enlivened by friends and mentors from PANAAWTM (Pacific, Asian, and North American Asian Women in Theology and Ministry), APARRI (Asian Pacific American Religions Research Initiative), ATSI (Asian Theological Summer Institute), and the Wabash Center for Teaching and Learning. These communities and organizations have been vital sources of solidarity, wisdom, and strength—and much-needed table fellowship! I am so grateful to Ekko Church for loving and embracing me as your pastor and sister. It is my hope that my scholarship strengthens you, just as our covenant life together strengthens me and grounds my scholarship. Special thanks to my dear friends and pastors, Bryan and Michelle Kim, for allowing me to partner with you in carrying out the work of the gospel. Much love to members of Calvary Korean Methodist Church and Graceway Church, where my family and I found our home during our eight years living in New Jersey.

I would not be standing here today without the prayers and unflagging support of my family. Boundless love and thanks to my parents Chung and Joseph Hur and to Dong and Kee Ok, Ben and Linnea Hur, and Jerry and Song Ok. Sharon Cho, you are an honorary member of our family, and I can never thank you enough for helping Ricky and me care for the kids during some of the most crucial stages in the writing of this book. Deepest gratitude and love to my husband and best friend, Ricky Ok, for your unflinching and wholehearted support and belief in me. To our three wonderful kids, Martin, Arielle, and Theodore, I love you so much! Thank you for preventing me from being a successful workaholic and for gracing my life with your playful presence and persistent love. You are my joy and my crown.

Finally, I must once again thank Scott Bartchy. You are the reason I became a biblical scholar. It was in your classes and during our conversations at UCLA that I discovered my love for the New Testament and its community-shaping, relationship-transforming, and behavior-altering ethic. Thank you for being a beloved and generous teacher, mentor, friend, and brother to me all these years. It is to you that I dedicate this book.

Abbreviations

All abbreviations of primary sources are taken from *The SBL Handbook of Style.* 2nd ed. Atlanta: SBL Press, 2014.

AB	Anchor Bible
BECNT	Baker Exegetical Commentary on the New Testament
BDAG	Bauer–Danker–Arndt–Gingrich
CBQ	*Catholic Biblical Quarterly*
ExAud	*Ex Auditu*
ESV	English Standard Version
ExpTim	*Expository Times*
HNT	Handbuch zum Neuen Testament
HTR	*Harvard Theological Review*
ICC	International Critical Commentary
JETS	*Journal of the Evangelical Theological Society*
JSNTSup	*Journal for the Study of the New Testament Supplement Series*
KEK	Kritisch-exegetischer Kommentar über das Neue Testament
L&N	Louw, Johannes P., and Eugene A. Nida, eds., *Greek-English Lexicon of the New Testament: Based on Semantic Domains,* 2nd ed., New York: United Bible Societies, 989
LCL	Loeb Classical Library
LNTS	Library of New Testament Studies
LXX	Septuagint
NAPBR	National Association of Baptist Professors of Religion
NASB	New American Standard Bible
Neot	*Neotestimentica*
NET	New English Translation
NICNT	New International Commentary on the New Testament

NovTSup	Novum Testamentum Supplement
NRSV	New Revised Standard Version
NT	New Testament
NTG	New Testament Guides
NTS	*New Testament Studies*
OT	Old Testament
PCPhS	Proceedings of the Cambridge Philological Society
PSTJ	*Perkins (School of Theology) Journal*
RSV	Revised Standard Version
S.J.	Society of Jesus
SNTSMS	Society for New Testament Studies Monograph Series
THNTC	The Two Horizons New Testament Commentary
WBC	Word Biblical Commentary
WTJ	*Westminster Theological Journal*
WUNT	Wissenschaftliche Untersuchungen zum Neuen Testament

1

Introduction: What Do Ethnicity and Identity Have to Do with 1 Peter?

How do new converts *become* Christian? In what ways does being "born anew" change the way Christians relate to the world, their families, and one another? How are believers to understand and live into their new identities and make sense of who they are no longer? The letter of 1 Peter offers insights into the process of Christian identity formation in its efforts to shape and sustain a cohesive, resilient, and countercultural group identity for its addressees. This monograph examines how and why the author of 1 Peter depicts Christian identity as an ethnic identity. Peter[1] employs various literary and rhetorical strategies—such as establishing a sense of shared history and ancestry, delineating boundaries, stereotyping and negatively characterizing "the other," emphasizing distinct conduct or a common culture, and applying ethnic categories to his addressees—to help construct his understanding of what it means to be a Christian relative to non-Christians. These strategies bear striking resemblances to what modern anthropologists and sociologists describe as the characteristics of ethnic groups.[2] What stands out among the various definitions of ethnic communities is the importance of shared myths, which include myths of origin (common descent) and election, and the orientation to the past or "ethno-history" (i.e., its origins, ancestors, and historical formation).[3]

---

[1] Throughout this study, I will use the traditional name when referring to the letter's author for the sake of convenience. While it is impossible to know with certainty who actually composed 1 Peter, I take the position that the letter was composed pseudonymously and addresses situations that reflect a date after Peter the apostle was already dead (around 70–95 CE). The letter itself gives us clues that the author possessed a certain level of Greek education, knowledge of the Septuagint, and addresses conflicts not between Jews and Gentiles but rather between Gentile converts and their non-Christian Gentile neighbors. For an argument against the traditional Petrine authorship of 1 Peter and for a dating of the letter sometime after 70 CE and before 120 CE, see Paul A. Holloway, *Coping with Prejudice: 1 Peter in Social-Psychological Perspective* (Tübingen: Mohr Siebeck, 2009), 15–17. For an argument for traditional Petrine authorship of 1 Peter, see Karen H. Jobes, *1 Peter* (BECNT; Grand Rapids: Baker Academic, 2005), 5–19. See David G. Horrell for a concise overview of both viewpoints and key reasons why traditional Petrine authorship has been questioned (*1 Peter* [NTG; London: T&T Clark, 2008], 20–3).

[2] See, e.g., Anthony D. Smith's description of the main features that *ethnies* typically exhibit in *The Ethnic Origins of Nations* (Oxford: Oxford University Press, 1986), 22–31; John Hutchinson and Anthony D. Smith, "Introduction," in *Ethnicity*, eds. John Hutchinson and Anthony D. Smith (Oxford: Oxford University Press, 1996), 6–7.

[3] Hutchinson and Smith, "Introduction," 7.

The reason why Peter characterizes Christian identity as a kind of ethnic identity is to engender a powerful sense of solidarity for his largely Gentile[4] addressees who, as addressed in Chapter 2, experienced social alienation and estrangement from the wider society *as a result* of their conversion.[5] His socially beleaguered addressees have a future destiny that is bound up in their unique, shared past as people chosen by God the Father and born anew to a living hope through the resurrection of Christ from the dead. The ransoming blood of Christ has disidentified them from their Gentile past (1.18-19) and has reidentified them as the people of God. Peter's appropriation of Israel's unique identity-forming language (γένος, ἱεράτευμα, ἔθνος, and λαός) inscribes them into the narrative of God's elect and holy people, Israel, and provides them with a more cohesive and resilient sense of collective identity as Christ followers. By depicting Christian identity as an ethnic identity akin to the unique religious-ethnic identity of the Jews, Peter seeks to foster internal cohesion among the community of believers, who are struggling to forge a distinctive and durable group identity and resist external pressures to conform to a way of life unbefitting the people of God.

Defining the Terms

Before going any further, I will define what I mean when I use the terms "identity" and, specifically, "ethnic identity." Beginning in the 1960s, scholars working in the vast array of disciplines in the social sciences and humanities have taken an intense interest in questions concerning identity.[6] In the field of New Testament studies, "identity" has become an increasingly popular term used to explore the social contexts and conflicts that give rise to biblical texts[7] and to understand the different processes by which early Christians came to understand themselves.[8] When writing about early Christian

---

[4] On the ethnic-religious makeup of the author of 1 Peter's audience, see pp. 10–11.
[5] I agree with John H. Elliott that the author of 1 Peter is addressing not only the spiritual alienation of his addressees but their social alienation (*A Home for the Homeless: A Sociological Exegesis of 1 Peter, Its Situation and Strategy* [Philadelphia: Fortress Press, 1981], 481). However, I fundamentally disagree with Elliott's view that their social alienation has to do with their socio-legal status *prior* to their conversion. See Horrell, "Aliens and Strangers? The Socio-Economic Location of the Addressees of 1 Peter," in *Becoming Christian: Essays on 1 Peter and the Making of Christian Identity* (LNTS 394; London: T&T Clark, 2013), 118.
[6] For a list of the pioneering social scientists who have written explicitly on "identity" and a summary of the heterogeneous ways many of them have used "identity" for social analysis, see Rogers Brubaker and Frederick Cooper, "Beyond 'Identity,'" *Theory and Society* 29, no. 1 (2000): 1–47, which has been republished in Rogers Brubaker, *Ethnicity without Groups* (Cambridge: Harvard University Press, 2006). See also Philip Gleason, "Identifying Identity: A Semantic History," *The Journal of American History* 69, no. 4 (1983): 910–31.
[7] See, e.g., Philip F. Esler, *Conflict and Identity in Roman: The Social Setting of Paul's Letter* (Minneapolis: Augsburg Fortress, 2003). For a voluminous example of how biblical scholars are applying social identity theory to their interpretation of NT texts, see J. Brian Tucker and A. Baker Coleman, eds., *T&T Clark Handbook to Social Identity in the New Testament* (London: Bloomsbury, 2014).
[8] See, e.g., Judith M. Lieu, *Christian Identity in the Jewish and Graeco-Roman World* (Oxford: Oxford University Press, 2004). Lieu addresses how early Christians sought to construct what it means to be Christian within the complex environment of the Hellenistic world and carefully demonstrates how Christian attempts at self-definition did not occur in isolation but alongside Jews, Greeks, and Romans, who also struggled to define themselves. See also Lieu, *Neither Jew nor Greek? Constructing*

identity on the basis of early Christian texts, there is a paradox: On the one hand, it is primarily through early Christian texts, such as 1 Peter, that we can come to understand early Christian identity formation. Texts themselves have an important role in shaping Christian identity, as is evident in the role Scripture plays for Peter in providing the language and imagery for his construction of what it means to be Christian. On the other hand, "the phenomenon of identity cannot be limited to the ideas and words that Christ-believers in these communities used to express their self-understanding."[9] For this reason, various interdisciplinary approaches have been applied to help shed light on the primary texts available to us. The use of social scientific perspectives and approaches has proven particularly helpful for illuminating some of the ways in which the letter of 1 Peter contributes to the making of Christian identity.[10]

Although the concept of identity has a prominent place in recent scholarly research and the term is used frequently in everyday discourse, its meaning is difficult to capture and is often taken for granted.[11] Identity, in its most basic sense, is "the human capacity to know 'who's who' (and hence 'what's what')."[12] It involves multidimensional mappings of how individuals and/or groups understand themselves, how others understand them, how they understand others, etc.[13] Rather than being a "thing" people possess, identification is a process that people do in order to sort out who they and who others are both at the individual and collective level.[14] This interplay

---

Early Christianity (2nd ed., London: T&T Clark, 2002); idem, "'Impregnable Ramparts and Walls of Iron': Boundary and Identity in Early 'Judaism' and 'Christianity,'" NTS 48 (2002): 297–313. For a collection of essays devoted to the analysis of NT texts and demonstrating how they reveal the processes of identity formation, see Bengt Holmberg and Mikael Winninge, eds., *Identity Formation in the New Testament* (WUNT 227; Tübingen: Mohr Siebeck, 2008).

[9] Holmberg and Winninge, *Identity Formation*, vii.

[10] For example, John H. Elliott pioneered the social-scientific criticism of New Testament texts, beginning with the publication, in 1981, of his groundbreaking monograph, which offered a full-scale study of 1 Peter using social scientific analysis, *A Home for the Homeless*. David L. Balch also applied social scientific methodology to the study of 1 Peter in *Let Wives Be Submissive: The Domestic Code in I Peter* (Chico, CA: Society of Biblical Literature, 1981). The contemporaneous publications of their works sparked a lively and generative debate concerning the nature of the social alienation faced by Peter's addressees and strategies offered by the author concerning how to engage the dominant culture. Paul A. Holloway has applied the findings from social psychology to his study of 1 Peter to demonstrate how Peter offers coping strategies to console his addressees, who are facing "anti-Christian prejudice" (*Coping with Prejudice*). These strategies of consolation resemble the strategies described by modern social psychologists studying targets of prejudice. As to the topic of the formation of Christian identity in 1 Peter, no scholar has contributed more than David Horrell. See, e.g., Horrell, *Becoming Christian*.

[11] For example, Charles Taylor describes the ineffable and multifaceted nature of identity when he writes, "But in fact our identity is deeper and more many-sided than any of our possible articulations of it" (*Sources of the Self: The Making of the Modern Identity* [Cambridge: Harvard University Press, 1989], 29). For a short list of brief but nevertheless quite confusing and opaque definitions of "identity" by social scientists, see James D. Fearon, "What Is Identity (As We Now Use the Word)?" (Unpublished manuscript, Stanford University, November 3, 1999).

[12] Richard Jenkins, *Social Identity* (4th ed.; London: Routledge, 2014), 6. It must be acknowledged that not all individuals possess the same capacity and resources to sort out who's who and what's what and make claims based on identity constructions from which they have drawn a stronger sense of who they are. See Sam Wong, *Exploring Unseen Social Capital in Community Participation* (Amsterdam: Amsterdam University Press, 2007).

[13] Jenkins, *Social Identity*, 6.

[14] Ibid., 6. 14. This sorting out or classifying of "who's who" is rarely disinterested, internally consistent, or congruous with how other groups perceive themselves (Jenkins, *Social Identity*, 6–8).

of individual and collective identity only makes sense within relationships, whether between individuals or groups.[15] Richard Jenkins suggests that how people categorize others is often much more consequential than how they identify themselves.[16] For example, if people of Asian descent identify as American while other ethnic groups and the dominant group (white Americans) perceive them as being less American and hence more foreign, Asian Americans often experience dissonance. This dissonance can result in the increased struggle to form a unified and integrated identity, which can lead to depressive symptoms and a lower level of civic participation relative to the white Americans.[17] However, I argue in Chapter 3 that the way in which Peter urges his addressees to self-identify as an elect, holy people of God, born anew to a living hope and as members of a spiritual household and spiritual patrilineage, has enormous consequence on how they respond to the external misperceptions of their identity and to subsequent persecution and offers theological resources to see their stigmatized identity as a distinct and honored identity.

Two common threads that can be traced among the many heterogeneous ways identity has been defined by social scientists and literary critics and used in everyday discourse are the two senses implied in the concept of identity—one that is "social" and the other that is "personal." James D. Fearon formulates a definition of identity that captures both of these senses:

> "Identity" means either (a) a social category, defined by membership rules and allegedly characteristic attributes of expected behaviors, or (b) a socially distinguishable feature that a person takes a special pride in or views as unchangeable but socially consequential (or, of course, both (a) and (b) at once).[18]

Identity as a social category refers to the social groupings (e.g., race, ethnicity, nation, political party) in which people place themselves and what they understand to be the implicit or explicit rules of membership for these social groupings.[19] Identity as something personal refers to the sources that give a person or group a sense of self-respect and dignity, not simply the categories to which people think they belong.[20] While there is no necessary linkage between the social and personal dimensions of identity, there is often much overlap, as in the case with ethnic identity. Ethnic identity can serve as both a social category in which people place themselves and as a source of pride. It is this double sense of identity—identity as social category and identity as the basis for self-respect and dignity—that I intend to convey when I use the term. Thus, "identity" in this study refers to the category that defines group membership for Peter's

---

[15] Ibid., 5, 7.
[16] Ibid., 16.
[17] See Janette H. Ok, "Always Ethnic, Never 'American': Reading 1 Peter through the Lens of the 'Perpetual Foreigner' Stereotype," in *T&T Clark Handbook to Asian and Asian American Biblical Hermeneutics*, eds. Seung Ai Yang and Uriah Y. Kim (New York: T&T Clark, 2019), 417–26.
[18] Fearon, "What Is Identity?" 36. Of course, the membership rules and the characteristics of social categories are often subject to dispute. Social scientists refer to the contestation over labels and their moral valence as "identity politics" (ibid., 14n19).
[19] Ibid., 14–15.
[20] Ibid., 25, 36–7.

audience and also to the sources of their collective sense of self-respect and dignity, which the author presents as essential aspects of who they are.

What then is *ethnic* identity? The adjective "ethnic" has its origins in the Greek word ἔθνος, which, in turn, derived from the word ἐθνικός. In Homer, ἔθνος identified a group or class of beings, such as warriors or young men, who shared a common identification.²¹ After Homer, it referred to "nation, people" or later to "foreign, barbarous nations" in contrast to the Greeks, or in the LXX to "non-Jews," or in the NT to "Gentiles" or "Gentile Christians."²² Herodotus' most famous and cited articulation of ἔθνος, which can be summed up as the idea of common blood (real or perceived), common language, shared religious practice, and shared customs that give rise to a sense of peoplehood, is itself one of his many uses of the term (8.144).

The "real or perceived" aspect of common blood described above is significant. It has become the consensus view among social scientists that ethnicity is socially constructed. The idea of shared descent, central to many ancient and modern conceptions of ethnic identity, is difficult, if not impossible, to ascertain. Nonetheless, its significance cannot be underestimated. Steve Fenton explains,

> The very idea that people (believe they) have some common identity—and more than that, a common interest and destiny—because of their (belief in a) shared past, including especially their (belief in) shared descent from the same set of ancestors, or at least roughly the same kind of ancestors, is clearly a powerful idea in human history.²³

"Belief in" does not mean that ethnicity is an illusory concept, for all people actually do have ancestors.²⁴ What is elusive about claims to shared ancestors, however, is when people choose to remember them, which ancestors they deem important, how much their idea of ancestry corresponds with the facts of ancestry, and what are the circumstances in which ethnic identity takes on greater or lesser importance.²⁵

According to the *Oxford Living Dictionary*, "ethnicity" refers to the "fact or state of belonging to a social group that has a common national or cultural tradition."²⁶

---

[21] *Iliad* 2.91; 3.32; 7.115; 11.72. Jonathan M. Hall, *Ethnic Identity in Greek Antiquity* (Cambridge: Cambridge University Press, 1997), 35.

[22] LSJ.

[23] Steve Fenton, "Debate Explaining Ethnicity," *Journal of Ethnic and Migration Studies* 30, no. 4 (2004): 831–5, 831–2.

[24] Ibid., 832.

[25] Ibid., 832, 834.

[26] *English Oxford Living Dictionary*, "Ethnicity," accessed October 26, 2017, https://en.oxforddictionaries.com/definition/ethnicity. The term "ethnicity" is relatively new. Nathan Glazer and Daniel Moynihan point to the fact that the term makes its earliest appearance in the *Oxford English Dictionary* in 1972 (Nathan Glazer and Daniel P. Moynihan, eds., *Ethnicity: Theory and Experience* [Cambridge: Harvard University Press, 1975], 1). The term "ethnic" is derived from the Greek *ethnos*, which derived from *ethnikos* (Thomas Hylland Eriksen, "Ethnicity, Race and Nation," in *The Ethnicity Reader: Nationalism, Multiculturalism, and Migration*, eds. Montserrat Guibernau and John Rex, 2nd ed. [Cambridge; Malden, MA: Polity, 2010], 46). While modern approaches to ethnicity differ in the way they define "ethnicity," the term refers to the sense of kinship, group solidarity, and common culture that has played a significant role in all societies in every period and continent (Hutchinson and Smith, "Introduction," 3).

This definition differs significantly from that of the *Compact Oxford English Dictionary* (1993), which defines "ethnic" as "pertaining to nations not Christian; pertaining to a race or nation; having common racial, cultural, religious or linguistic characteristics especially designating a racial or other group within a larger system."[27] The former definition says nothing about notions of shared ancestry, whereas the latter definition presents "race," "nation," and "ethnicity" as intertwined.

Social scientists have taken various approaches to defining the core similarities and divergences among these terms, particularly "race" and "ethnicity." The concept of an "ethnic group" is closely associated with the terms "race" and "nation," as all three convey a sense of peoplehood based on shared descent and culture and thus occupy the same linguistic territory without meaning exactly the same thing.[28] While the concepts of ethnicity race, and nation cannot be easily separated, they do have some divergences, even as they share the single core of referring to descent and culture communities. Fenton attempts to delineate the commonalities and differences among race, nation, and ethnic group in the following way:

Race refers to descent and culture communities with two specific additions:

1. the idea that "local" groups are instances of abstractly conceived divisions of humankind; and
2. the idea that race makes explicit reference to physical or "visible" difference as the primary marker of difference and inequality.

Nation refers to descent and culture communities with one specific addition: the assumption that nations are or should be associated with a state or state-like political form.

Ethnic group refers to descent and culture communities with three specific additions:

1. that the group is a kind of subset within a nation-state;
2. that the point of reference of difference is typically cultural difference and cultural markers of social boundaries rather than physical appearance; and
3. often, that the group referred to is "other" (foreign, exotic, minority) to some majority who are presumed not to be "ethnic."[29]

An ethnic group can thus be understood in relation to one's nation and ethnicity in relation to one's nationality. The creation of the nation-state around the late eighteenth and early nineteenth centuries involved the merging of ethnic boundaries with political ones, such that "old loyalties to the lord or monarch were replaced by loyalty to the nation" centered upon the ideology that its members shared a common culture and sense of belonging that could function as a new common ethnicity constructed in a symbolic manner.[30] Ethnic and national identities share are both

---

[27] Cited by Fenton, *Ethnicity*, 2nd ed. (Cambridge; Malden, MA: Polity, 2010), 12–13.
[28] Fenton, *Ethnicity*, 13.
[29] Ibid., 22.
[30] Montserrat Guibernau and John Rex, eds., "Introduction," in *The Ethnicity Reader: Nationalism, Multiculturalism, and Migration*, 2nd ed. (Cambridge; Malden, MA: Polity, 2010), 4.

"*about ancestry.*"³¹ Race can be understood as distinct from ethnicity in that it is a broader classification or division of humankind that is not necessarily a subset within a nation-state. This is evident in the way in which the United States Census Bureau describes classifications for "race."³²

In her influential and important book, *Why This New Race*, Denise Buell intentionally deploys the terms "race" and "ethnicity" interchangeably in her examination of Christian strategies of self-definition, as represented in her use of the phrase "ethnoracial."³³ One aim of her book is to vitiate the pervasive modern notion that early Christians sought to transcend the particularities of racial identities and that ancient notions of race can and must be clearly differentiated from modern notions of racialization and racism. As Buell explains,

> I am insisting that we need to bring together two kinds of discussions that have largely been kept distinct: discussions about the relationship between Jewishness and Christianness and discussions about the relationship between Christianity and race, which in America especially has been dominated by a black/white binary. In doing so, I question the value of distinguishing ethnicity from race and assess how the present informs historical analysis.³⁴

In both ancient and modern usage, γένος and ἔθνος are often used interchangeably, and discourses on ethnicity and race often overlap. I agree with Buell and others, such as Andreas Wimmer, that "there is no clear-cut line" between ethnicity, race, and, nationhood "that would justify establishing entirely separate objects of analysis to be addressed with different analytical language."³⁵ Race and ethnicity are both subjective, socially constructed, and often overlapping and interchangeable categories. And yet, while it is true that "race" and "ethnicity" share a lot in common both etymologically and historically, race and ethnicity are not one and the same thing. Buell herself notes that the modern term "race" is more useful than "ethnicity" when used in a universalizing way, since the latter connotes "only particularity."³⁶

---

[31] Fenton, "Debate Explaining Ethnicity," 831.

[32] White (a person having origins in any of the original peoples of Europe, the Middle East, or North Africa); Black or African American (a person having origins in any of the Black racial groups of Africa); American Indian or Alaska Native (a person having origins in any of the original peoples of North and South America [including Central America] and who maintains tribal affiliation or community attachment); Asian (a person having origins in any of the original peoples of the Far East, Southeast Asia, or the Indian subcontinent including, for example, Cambodia, China, India, Japan, Korea, Malaysia, Pakistan, the Philippine Islands, Thailand, and Vietnam); and Native Hawaiian or Other Pacific Islander (a person having origins in any of the original peoples of Hawaii, Guam, Samoa, or other Pacific Islands). The U.S. Census Bureau, October 16, 2020, accessed February 20, 2021, https://www.census.gov/topics/population/race/about.html.

[33] Denise Kimber Buell, *Why This New Race: Ethnic Reasoning in Early Christianity* (New York: Columbia University Press, 2005), 1–34.

[34] Ibid., xii.

[35] Andreas Wimmer, *Ethnic Boundary Making: Institutions, Power, Networks* (Oxford; New York: Oxford University Press, 2013), 7–8.

[36] Ibid., 3, n. 8. Buell, *Why This New Race*, 14, 16, 17.

It is precisely the particularity of ethnic identity that I seek to investigate.³⁷ Thus, in this study, "ethnic identity" refers to a way of being viewed by members of one's own group as belonging to one another on the basis of shared descent and culture, in contrast to other ethnic groups. While 1 Peter makes explicit use of both *genos* and *ethnos* (2.9) and I agree with Buell that distinctions made between race, ethnicity, and religion are untidy and overlapping, I do not use race and ethnicity interchangeably because I wish to avoid conflating notions of biological or physical differences associated with the term "race" with the cultural and social distinctiveness associated with "ethnicity." For Peter, the Christian community's "way of life" (ἀναστροφή), which can be understood in terms of a distinctive culture, is closely linked to their ancestry (1.14–15, 18).³⁸ Peter emphasizes the shared patrilineage, distinct conduct, and elect status of his readers in order to heighten their sense of in-group belonging and strengthen their sense of difference from non-believers, because they otherwise blend in all too well with their fellow Gentiles. Like the white Norwegian Christians living in Grønland, Oslo, Norway, whom I address in Chapter 4, Peter's addressees have the option to conceal their Christian identity in a way that Norwegian Muslims of Middle-Eastern descent cannot. By presenting Christians as belonging to an ethnic group based not on ostensible physical difference but on cultural difference and putative claims of shared blood, Peter seeks to build internal cohesion and self-understanding that prevents his readers from concealing, covering, or denying their association with Christ and other Christ followers.

As for the term "Christian identity," David Horrell has demonstrated that the label Χριστιανός (1 Pet 4.16) serves as the "earliest witness to the crucial process whereby the term was transformed from a hostile label applied by outsiders to a self-designation borne with honor."³⁹ Although Χριστιανός appears two times in Acts (11.26 and 26.28), Luke tells us little about the term's meaning or significance. First Peter, however, provides a window into the way in which Χριστιανός emerged out of the encounter between Christians and outsiders and the need for Christians to negotiate their

---

[37] In this study, "ethnicity" serves as an "etic" category through which I examine the ways in which identity formation takes shape in the letter. That is, I will refer to the systematic set of ethnic concepts that we find in both modern ethnicity studies and ancient Greek and Roman texts to understand Peter's "emic" perspective on and construction of identity. The terms *emic* and *etic* were coined by American linguist Kenneth L. Pike (*Language in Relation to a Unified Theory of the Structure of Human Behavior* [2nd ed.; Mouton: The Hague, 1967]). Pike specified that the "etic viewpoint studies behavior as from outside of a particular system," while the "emic viewpoint results from studying behavior as from inside the system" (ibid., 37). Etic categories, such as "Asian American high school students," are imposed externally in public discourse but may be irrelevant within that particular demographic. Emic categories, such as "Vietnamese" or "Korean" or aspects of external style, extracurricular activities, or socioeconomic status, may be very relevant for members who fall into the category "Asian American high school students" but less so to external observers. For a brief description of etic and emic distinctions, see Michol Hoffmann, "Sociolinguistic Interviews," in *Research Methods in Sociolinguistics: A Practical Guide*, eds. Janet Holmes and Kirk Hazen, 25–41 (Malden, MA: Wiley-Blackwell, 2014), 28.

[38] See David G. Horrell, "Ethnicisation, Marriage and Early Christian Identity: Critical Reflections on 1 Corinthians 7, 1 Peter 3 and Modern New Testament Scholarship," *NTS* 62 (2016): 439–60, 453.

[39] David G. Horrell, "The Label Χριστιανός (1 Peter 4.16): Suffering, Conflict, and the Making of Christian Identity," in *Becoming Christian*, 164–210, 165.

relationship to society, as they faced both formal and informal hostilities.[40] The fact that Peter attempts to reappropriate Χριστιανός so that it no longer functions as a source of stigma but rather serves as a badge of honor demonstrates, on the one hand, how fluid Christian identity was for the letter's addressees and, on the other hand, how the early Christians living in Anatolia lived distinctly enough to be slandered as "Christians." Peter thus shapes and defines what it means to be Christian using ethnic reasoning in order to help his addressees make Christian identity primary, all-encompassing, superordinate to all other identities.

Buell defines "ethnic reasoning" as "the modes of persuasion" that often included the language of peoplehood and human difference and that move between poles of "fixity and fluidity."[41] She challenges the common notion that early Christians sought to transcend ethnicity in order to make universalizing claims that anyone can become a Christian. She argues that early Christians conceived of their identity in racial or ethnic terms because doing so enabled them to define Christianness as both a distinct category in contrast to other people and an inclusive category made up of individuals from a range of different races and ethnicities.[42] Buell calls attention to the dynamic character of ethnicity. The fluid and fixed nature of ethnicity made it possible for early Christians to capitalize on ethnicity as a way to understand themselves as having an "essence" while simultaneously undergoing continuous transformation.

In this study, "ethnic reasoning" refers specifically to the way in which Peter makes metaphorical use of the vocabulary of peoplehood as a rhetorical strategy to help his addressees conceive of their communal identity as grounded in their common essence as people who share common ancestry through the blood of Christ and a (new) birth story. In other words, it refers to the way in which the language and concepts of shared blood, peoplehood, human difference, etc., serve as an important point of entry for defining what it means to be Christian and as a means for helping his addressees to define themselves in contrast to the "other," so that they can disidentify from their former way of life. Ethnicity is a fluid, subjective concept that is often understood as being permanent and objective. Peter constructs Christian identity as an ethnic identity because doing so has the potential to create a stronger, more tangible, and fixed sense of social cohesion among people who may not otherwise see themselves as belonging to one another.

It must be acknowledged that Peter was not preoccupied with the concept of "identity" or "ethnic identity" as defined above. However, in an attempt to establish what it means to be Christian and forge a cohesive, Christ-imitating community of believers, Peter makes use of rhetorical strategies that bear close resemblance to the processes of identity formation as described by theorists Fredrik Barth and Erving Goffman, both of whom I address in Chapter 4.[43] Peter employs such rhetorical

---

[40] Ibid., 176, 209–10.
[41] Buell, *Why This New Race*, 2, 3, 9, 40.
[42] Ibid., 3, 13, 45, 56, 128, 138–9, 166.
[43] See Fredrik Barth, ed., *Ethnic Groups and Boundaries: The Social Organization of Culture Difference* (Bergen, Oslo: Universitetsforlaget, 1969); Erving Goffman, *The Presentation of Self in Everyday Life* (New York: Anchor, 1959); Erving Goffman, *Stigma: Notes on the Management of Spoiled Identity* (Englewood Cliffs, NJ: Prentice-Hall, 1963).

strategies to help his addressees better withstand the alienating and disorienting forces of being maligned and slandered as "evildoers" (1 Pet 2.12; 4.4) and "suffering for doing right" and "good" (3.14, 17) and as "Christians" (4.16). This study thus assumes that the modern concepts of *identity* and, more specifically, *ethnic identity* are "transhistorically and transculturally"[44] applicable to the Anatolian audience of 1 Peter. The language of identity and ethnicity functions as heuristic devices that help to illuminate the strategy employed by the author to construct what it means to be Christian.

Ethnic-Religious Composition

In determining the ethnic/religious composition of the author of 1 Peter's intended audience, scholarly consensus has ranged from describing the letter as addressed exclusively to Jewish converts to describing it as being comprised of exclusively Gentile converts.[45] The consensus today views the audience addressed in 1 Peter as mixed, with the majority being Gentile.[46] With a significant number of Jews in Asia Minor, the presence of Jewish converts in these Christian communities is possible.[47] The fact that the letter itself makes significant references to his addressees' former way of life (1.14; 1.18; 2.10) and to the Gentile-like conduct in which they no longer participate to the surprise of their neighbors (4.3–4) makes it highly plausible that the author of 1 Peter writes with a primarily Gentile audience in mind. Thus, while it is impossible to know the precise ethnic-religious makeup of Peter's actual audience, the author gives us clues

---

[44] See Fearon, "What Is Identity?," 10.

[45] For a list of scholarly positions on the issue prior to 1832, see Wilhelm Steiger, *Exposition of the First Epistle of Peter*, trans. Patrick Fairbairn (Edinburg: T&T Clark, 1836 [1832]), 19–20; cited by Troy W. Martin, *Metaphor and Composition in 1 Peter*, SBLDS 131 (Atlanta: Scholars Press, 1992), 45.

[46] For example, Elliott, *A Home for the Homeless*, 38; Steven Bechtler, *Following in His Steps: Suffering, Community, and Christology in 1 Peter*, SBLDS 162 (Atlanta: Scholars Press, 1998), 61, 63, 45–6, 65–7; Leonhard Goppelt, *A Commentary on I Peter*, ed. Ferdinand Hahn, trans. John E. Alsup (Grand Rapids: Eerdmans, 1993), 6; Reinhard Feldmeier, *Der Erste Brief Des Petrus*, THNT 15, no. 1 (Leipzig: Evangelische Verlagsanstalt, 2005), 29; Horrell, *1 Peter*, 48.

[47] Josephus (*Ant.* 12.147–53) and Philo (*Leg. Gai.* 33 §245) attest to a significant number of Jews living in Asia Minor. See Emil Schürer, *The History of the Jewish People in the Age of Jesus Christ (175 B.C. –A.D. 135)* (rev. ed. Geza Vermes, Fergus Millar, Matthew Black, and Martin Goodman; vol. 3:1; Edinburgh: T&T Clark, 1986); Paul R. Trebilco, *Jewish Communities in Asia Minor* (SNTSMS 69; Cambridge: Cambridge University Press, 1991). For examples of scholars who hold the view that the letter's author imagines a primarily Jewish audience, see Russell G. Moy, "Resident Aliens of the Diaspora: 1 Peter and Chinese Protestants in San Francisco," *Semeia* 90, no. 91 (2002): 51–67. Moy sees a strong parallel between the first-century Jewish resident aliens addressed in 1 Peter and the nineteenth-century Chinese Protestants living in San Francisco. Both diaspora ethnic minority groups were marginalized and ostracized for their foreignness. See also Jennifer T. Kaalund, *Reading Hebrews and 1 Peter with the African American Great Migration: Diaspora, Place, and Identity* (London: LNTS; T&T Clark, 2019), 112–13. Kaalund understands that audience of 1 Peter as being primarily Jewish based on the language of diaspora and exile and other characteristics of the text (e.g., "you and your former ignorance" [1 Pet 1.14-16]) that could be attributed to thoroughly Hellenized Jews just as easily as to Gentiles. Ben Witherington III (*Letters and Homilies for Hellenized Christians Volume II: A Social-Rhetorical Commentary on 1-2 Peter* [Downers Grove, IL: Intervarsity Press, 2007], 24) identifies 1 Peter's audience as Hellenized Jewish Christians.

to his imagined audience and writes to them as if they are Gentiles.[48] The rhetorical strategy of Peter sheds light on the ethnic-religious identity of the letter's recipients, as Stephen Bechtler explains:

> This is not to say that 1 Peter's orientation to gentiles represents a rhetorical strategy designed to exclude Jewish Christians from the letter's readership but only that 1 Peter depicts that origin of the problem addressed as an *intragentile* conflict: It is nonbelieving gentiles who are reviling believing gentiles because the latter have adopted a strange, new religion along with its antisocial lifestyle.[49]

The major antithesis operating in Peter's construction of ethnicity is that between the people of God and the people *not* of God. Rather than make a Jew/Gentile dichotomy, Peter broadens the identification of Israel as a γένος ἐκλεκτόν, βασίλειον ἱεράτευμα, ἔθνος ἅγιον, λαὸς εἰς περιποίησιν (2.9–10) to include his addressees and contrasts this exceptional and holy people with those to whom he refers in one sweeping opposing category, the "Gentiles" (τὰ ἔθνη, 2.9, 12; 4.3).[50]

Conclusion

This study examines how the author of 1 Peter creates an ethnic identity for his beleaguered addressees facing anti-Christian hostility and subsequent persecution in order to strengthen their sense of Christian identity. In the second chapter, I survey how Greek ethnicity was constructed and deployed by various ancient authors. What makes ancient Greek ethnic identity uniquely different from other collective identities is how it arises from the idea of common descent and becomes more communally cohesive when Greeks come into conflict with and under the subjugation of the "other." The third chapter demonstrates how Peter constructs Christian identity as an ethnic identity. By constructing Christian identity through the use of "ethnic reasoning," Peter seeks to prevent his addressees from reverting to their former way of life and to help them live faithfully among Gentiles as an elect and holy people of God born anew to a living hope. In Chapter 4, I consider how Fredrik Barth's concept of "ethnic boundaries" and Erving Goffman's study on stigma management can be critically and fruitfully applied to 1 Peter. Peter constructs Christian identity along explicitly ethnic lines as a strategy to disidentify believers from previous "Gentile" ways of life and contest and reappropriate the stigma associated with being "Christian" to reduce the temptation for Christians to revert to their former identity. Chapter 5 concludes by explaining how in 1 Peter, Christian distinctiveness is reinforced through bonds of blood. I also offer further implications of my study in the areas of Asian American and Canonical Studies.

---

[48] Holloway, *Coping with Prejudice*, 19; Horrell, "Aliens and Strangers?" 121.
[49] Bechtler, *Following in His Steps*, 63.
[50] I capitalize "Gentiles" throughout this study to emphasize the oppositional categories I see Peter constructing between those who are the people of God (*qua* the Jews) and the rest who are not (Gentiles).

In 1 Peter 4.16, "Christian" functions as a social identity ascribed to the letter's addressees that is meant to deride, shame, and stigmatize them. However, I argue that Peter reappropriates this social stigma as a badge of honor by imbuing it with ethnic reasoning because he understands that notions of peoplehood and shared ancestry along the lines of the sort of group identity shared by the Jews provide explanatory force and community-forming potential and make it difficult for them to revert to their former way of life. Thus, by describing Christian identity as an ethnic identity, Peter provides a point of entry for their group-understanding based not on the precarious nature of their relationship with non-Christians but according to their predestined and permanent status as "a chosen race, a royal priesthood, a holy nation, God's own people" called out of darkness and into his marvelous light to proclaim God's mighty acts (2.9–10).

2

Defining and Defying Ethnicity in the Ancient World

Introduction

In his famous introductory statement, Herodotus explains his purpose for writing *Histories*:

> This is the presentation of the inquiry of Herodotus of Halicarnassus, in order that the events that have occurred through human agency shall not become extinct because of the course of time and that the great and marvelous deeds demonstrated by both the Greeks and the barbarians shall not lose their fame—and that goes both for their older actions and achievements and for the reason why they began to be at war with one another.[1] (1.1.1)

Implicit in this bold assertion is the idea that the history and identity of the Greeks cannot be understood apart from their contact and conflict with non-Greeks or "barbarians" (τὰ βαρβάροισι). Herodotus also states here as a matter of course that recording the past for posterity requires that he preserve the "astonishing achievements" of both Greeks and non-Greeks (ἔργα μεγάλα τε καὶ θωμαστά).[2] The encounters and enmity between Greeks and Persians, in particular, preoccupy Herodotus' "inquiry." Herodotus' detailed ἱστορία demonstrate that Greek relations with and perceptions of barbarians were neither inevitably hostile nor entirely negative. His work also reveals the fluidity of Greek self-definition while asserting the criteria for what it means to be Greek.

Herodotus' elastic understanding of ἔθνος can be summed up as the idea of common blood (real or perceived), common language, shared religious practice, and shared customs that give rise to a sense of peoplehood (8.144).[3] These four markers of

---

[1] Trans. Lisa Irene Lau, *Moral History from Herodotus to Diodorus Siculus* (Edinburgh: Edinburgh University Press, 2016), 172.
[2] Benjamin Isaac, *The Invention of Racism in Classical Antiquity* (Princeton: Princeton University Press, 2004), 262.
[3] Jeremy McInerney, "Ethnos and Ethnicity in Early Greece," in *Ancient Perceptions of Greek Ethnicity* (Center for Hellenic Studies Colloquia 5; Cambridge: Harvard University Press, 2001), 51.

Greek ethnicity (blood, language, religion, and customs), however, were neither static nor permanent.[4] The famous passage in Herodotus (8.144) serves as the *locus classicus* for the ideal of Panhellenism and also for its weakness.[5] For, despite this confident assertion of a united Panhellenic Greek identity, the context out of which this statement arises—with the Lacedaemonians sending Spartan envoys to seek reassurance from the Athenian envoys that Athens would not Medize—sheds light on the reality that among the Greeks, "Medism was common, and interstate *stasis* even commoner."[6] In other words, the Greeks experienced inter-*polis* conflict and colluded with the Persians more often than they embodied the ideal of "We the Greeks."

Herodotus' formulation of a unified Panhellenic identity can be seen as the result or culmination of the slow development of Greek ethnic consciousness precipitated by the upheaval of the Persian Wars[7] and the development of Panhellenic institutions, such as the Olympic Games.[8] The rise of the Persians bears considerable responsibility for the final shaping of the Greek/barbarian dichotomy and the final casting of the Persians as the barbarian *par excellence*.[9] There were, in fact, many factors in addition to the Greek–Persian conflicts that contributed to the fertile conditions out of which a Greek ethnic self-consciousness and interest in other ethnic groups gave rise: the growth of Athenian democracy and hegemony, the Peloponnesian War, and the rising interest in ethnography, historiography, medicine, and philosophy.[10] Scholarly consensus, however, views the Persian Wars as the critical turning point in Hellenic history and in the conception of what it means to be Greek.[11]

This chapter examines how Greek ethnicity was constructed and deployed by various authors toward the end of the fifth century BCE and then during the first two centuries of the Roman empire. It begins the Persian Wars as represented first by Aeschylus and then by Herodotus as the starting point for my study because this

---

[4] Katerina Zacharia, "Herodotus' Four Markers of Greek Identity," in *Hellenisms: Culture, Identity, and Ethnicity from Antiquity to Modernity*, ed. Katerina Zacharia (Burlington, VT: Ashgate, 2008), 27. In order to compete in the Olympic Games, athletes had to prove that they were Greek.

[5] Peter Green, *From Ikaria to the Stars: Classical Mythification, Ancient and Modern* (Austin: University of Texas Press, 2004), 107.

[6] Ibid., 107.

[7] See Edith Hall, *Inventing the Barbarian: Greek Self-Definition through Tragedy* (Oxford: Clarendon Press, 1989), 9.

[8] Katerina Zacharia, "Introduction," in *Hellenisms*, 4.

[9] Green, *From Ikaria to the Stars*, 112.

[10] Efi Papadodima, "Ethnicity and the Stage," in *A Companion to Ethnicity in the Ancient Mediterranean*, ed. Jeremy McInerney (Malden, MA: Wiley-Blackwell, 2014), 256.

[11] See, e.g., Arnaldo D. Momigliano, *Alien Wisdom: The Limits of Hellenization* (Cambridge: Cambridge University Press, 1975); David Konstan, "To Hellēnikon Ethnos: Ethnicity and the Construction of Ancient Greek Identity," in *Ancient Perceptions*, 29–50; Rosalind Thomas, "Ethnicity, Genealogy, and Hellenism in Herodotus," in *Ancient Perceptions*, 213–33; Suzanne Saïd, "The Discourse of Identity in Greek Rhetoric from Isocrates to Aristides," in *Ancient Perceptions*, 275–99. Erich S. Gruen challenges the scholarly status quo by arguing that while the Persian Wars represent a watershed moment in Greek history, the sources do not offer black-and-white images of Greek–Persian relations. Rather, Herodotus, in particular, presents nuanced, fluid, ambiguous depictions of non-Greek cultural identities ("Herodotus and Persia," in *Cultural Identity in the Ancient Mediterranean* [Los Angeles: Getty Research Institute, 2011], 67–85).

period in Hellenic history represents a significant shift in the Greek attitude toward the "other" as a result of contact and conflict with the Persians. It demonstrates how a strong sense of shared Greek identity or a growing sense of Greek ethnic consciousness emerged as "a reactive phenomenon"[12] to the Persian Wars. Even as Greek ethnic identity shifted and adapted according to varying socio-political factors, the enduring characteristic that made Greeks Greek was a sense of common blood. Under the first two centuries of Roman rule, the Greeks' sense of collective ethnic identity remained much intact, not only because the Romans gave Greeks special freedoms, but also because the more the Romans pushed up against the Greeks, the more the Greeks felt united as a people. Thus, my examination of ancient Greek identity discourse reveals that what sets ancient ethnic identity apart from other collective identities is how it arises from the idea of shared blood or comment descent, and that Greek ethnic identity becomes more socially significant and communally cohesive when Greek people come into conflict with and under the subjugation of "others."

Framing the Study of Greek Ethnic Identity

The concept "other" is one that Jeremy McInerney describes as a "clumsy, inchoate phenomenon" that historians, ethnographers, and anthropologists have tried for centuries to depict in satisfying, comprehensible, and coherent ways.[13] Ancient Greek portrayals of non-Greeks served to provide a sense of peoplehood or common identity that emerged in contact with those perceived as ostensibly different from Greeks themselves. In the preface to her influential book, *Inventing the Barbarian*, Edith Hall writes, "ethnic stereotypes, ancient and modern, though revealing almost nothing about the groups they are intended to define, say a great deal about the community which produces them."[14] When the Greeks write about the barbarians, Hall argues that they usually do so as a means to describe themselves.[15] Prior to the fifth century BCE, language more than anything set Greeks apart from non-Greeks; hence, the idea of the barbarian emerged originally as a way to distinguish between those who spoke Greek and those who did not.[16] It was not until the fifth century during the Persian Wars that the Greeks invented a political notion of the barbarian "as the universal anti-Greek against whom Hellenic—especially Athenian—culture was defined."[17] A Panhellenic sense of collective identity thus emerged through the polarization Greek and barbarian.[18]

---

[12] Konstan, "To Hellênikon Ethnos," 30.
[13] Jeremy McInerney, "Ethnicity: An Introduction," in *A Companion to Ethnicity*, 2.
[14] Hall, *Inventing the Barbarian*, ix.
[15] Ibid., 1. In a similar fashion, Simon Hornblower asserts, "Persia gave the Greeks their identity, or the means for recognizing it" (*The Greek World 479–323 BC*, 2nd ed. [London: Routledge, 1991], 11, as cited in Jonathan M. Hall, *Ethnic Identity in Greek Antiquity* [Cambridge, UK: Cambridge University Press, 1997], 44).
[16] Hall, *Inventing the Barbarian*, 5. In antiquity, the grammarians and Strabo used the term Ἑλληνισμός (Hellenism) to denote "correct Greek" (Zacharia, "Introduction," 1).
[17] Hall, *Inventing the Barbarian*, 5.
[18] Ibid., 6.

Both Edith Hall's *Inventing the Barbarian* and François Hartog's *The Mirror of Herodotus*[19] are influenced by a Foucauldian discourse of otherness[20] and call attention to the ways in which the Greeks formed and articulated their collective identity based on their imaginary portrait of the *barbaroi* through the use of oppositional "us-them" binaries.[21] Furthermore, both scholars base their studies on the anthropological methodologies that have formed their respective intellectual paradigms.[22] Hartog's work emerges from the French structuralist school of Claude Lévy-Strauss and concentrates on Herodotus' portrayal of Scythian barbarians north of the Black Sea.[23] He argues that the Scythian narrative is an imaginary construct that illuminates or helps shape Hellenic identity (specifically Athenian national characteristics) more than it explains Scythia. Hall analyzes Greek ethnocentrism and portrayal of the "other" in Athenian tragedy, especially Aeschylus' *Persians*. Her study bears the influence of functionalist anthropology, especially the work of Mary Douglas, in the way she presupposes that a strong connection exists between Greek intellectual thought and social reality.[24] Seeing the Persian Wars as the pivotal turning point in Greek ethnic consciousness, Hall argues that Aeschylus' fifth-century tragedy *Persians* marks the transition from a vague notion of "other" based primarily on differences in language to the formation of a "homogenous category 'non-Greek.'"[25]

In his watershed book, *Ethnic Identity in Greek Antiquity*, Jonathan Hall rigorously contextualizes theoretical approaches to ethnicity within the study of Hellenic identity construction.[26] Hall's methodology was influenced by the work of sociologist Anthony D. Smith, who argues in his classic *The Ethnic Origins of Nations* that nationalism has pre-modern origins in ethnic groups, which Smith terms *ethnie*.[27] *Ethnie*, or pre-national ethnic groups, features basic elements, such as common language, the myth of common descent, a shared history, distinct cultural traits, and a specific territory. Applying Smith's categories to his study of Greek ethnic identities, Hall specifies the "core elements" that differentiate ethnic identity from all other group identities: "a putative subscription to a myth of common descent and kinship, an association

---

[19] François Hartog, *The Mirror of Herodotus: The Representation of the Other in the Writing of History*, trans. Janet Loyd (Berkley: University of California Press, 1988; originally published as *Le Miroir d' Hérodote: Essai sur la représentation* de l'autre, Paris: Bibliothèque des Histoires, 1980).

[20] Nino Luraghi, "The Study of Greek Ethnic Identities," in *A Companion to Ethnicity*, 214.

[21] See Chapter 3 ("Alien Wisdom: Greeks v. Barbarians") of Paul Cartledge, *The Greeks: A Portrait of Self and Others* (Oxford: Oxford University Press, 1993), in which Cartledge provides a portrait of how the Greeks imagined and invented the barbarian, drawing on the contributions made by E. Hall and Hartog.

[22] Luraghi, "The Study," 215.

[23] Ibid.

[24] Ibid.

[25] Hall, *Inventing the Barbarian*, 12.

[26] Jonathan M. Hall, *Ethnic Identity in Greek Antiquity* (Cambridge; New York: Cambridge University Press, 1997).

[27] Anthony D. Smith, *The Ethnic Origins of Nations* (Oxford: Oxford University Press, 1986). Contra Ernest Gellner, *Nations and Nationalism* (Oxford: Blackwell, 1983); Benedict Anderson, *Imagined Communities: Reflections on the Origin and Spread of Nationalism* (London: Verso, 1983); and E. J. Hobsbawm, *Nations and Nationalism since 1780* (Cambridge: Cambridge University Press, 1990), who see nationalism as a relatively recent phenomenon.

with a specific territory, and a sense of shared history."[28] It is a myth, specifically the myth of descent and kinship, which serves as the basis for ethnic identity.[29] Thus, Hall agrees with the current consensus among anthropologists that "ethnic identity is *socially constructed and subjectively perceived.*"[30] This emphasis on the common myth of descent maintained by ethnic groups, rather than on the *content* of an ethnic group, is influenced by the work of Barth.[31] Barth's research marks the shift in anthropological approaches to ethnicity from the focus on an ethnic group's common characteristics or "core personality" to its maintenance of "ascriptive" boundaries.[32]

The approaches of E. Hall, Hartog, and J. Hall rest on the assumption that one learns about Greek self-definition through the ways in which Greeks imagine or depict the barbarian and that the binary between Greeks and barbarians arose during and after the Persian Wars. More recently, Erich Gruen has sought to cast doubt on the prevailing scholarly consensus that the Persian Wars intensified Greek images of the "other" and molded Greek identity in contrast with the "barbarian."[33] Gruen persuasively argues that Greeks, Romans, and Jews had far more "mixed, nuanced and complex" opinions of barbarians than previously acknowledged.[34] Ironically, however, in his attempt to close the ethnic chasms between the Greeks and the Persians based on the argument that they belong to the same lineage, Gruen reasserts J. Hall's insistence that common descent more than any other factor is an indispensable feature of ethnic group identity.

The Emergence of Panhellenism and the Concept of the Barbarian

The rise of a Greek ethnic consciousness must be understood with the concomitant evolution of the pejorative notion of the non-Greek barbarian and the Greek ideal of Panhellenism. As early as Homer, we find the term ἔθνος ἑταίρων used broadly to denote groups of people living together or bands of men (*Il.* 7.115). The word Πανέλληνες likely goes back to Homer (*Il.* 2.530), although Homer does not provide a consistent or developed concept of Panhellenism, nor does he suffuse the term with the idea of a unified Greek identity. However difficult it is to pin down a definition of the term, it is generally agreed among classists that large-scale Panhellenism emerged by the beginning of the Classical period (the period between the Persian Wars in the fifth

---

[28] Jonathan M. Hall, *Hellenicity: Between Ethnicity and Culture* (Chicago: University of Chicago Press, 2002), 9.
[29] Hall, *Ethnic Identity*, 41.
[30] Ibid., 19. Original emphasis. J. Hall underestimates the lack of interest among contemporary classicists on issues of identity and ethnicity, given the impact of works published prior, such as Hartog's *The Mirror of Herodotus*, Hall's *Inventing the Barbarian*; Cartledge, *The Greeks*; Martin Bernal, *Black Athena: Afroasiatic Roots of Classical Civilization*, vols. 1–2, 3 vols. (New Brunswick, NJ: Rutgers University Press, 1987).
[31] In Chapter 4, I return to Barth and how his work illuminates the rhetorical strategy of Peter.
[32] Barth, *Ethnic Groups*, 14; Hall, *Ethnic Identity*, 24.
[33] Erich S. Gruen, *Rethinking the Other in Antiquity*, Martin Classical Lectures (Princeton: Princeton University Press, 2011).
[34] Ibid., 3.

century BCE and the death of Alexander the Great in 323 BCE).³⁵ However, some have argued for the appearance of a nascent form of Panhellenism prior to this period.³⁶

A. M. Snodgrass, for example, sees archeological and historical evidence for Panhellenism as early as in the eighth century in the institutions of the Olympic games, the Oracle at Delphi, and Homer's poetry.³⁷ Shawn Ross argues that "an undeveloped and unstable proto-Hellenism" can be seen in the *Iliad* (eighth century BCE).³⁸ In Book 4, for example, Homer describes how linguistic diversity is found only among the Trojan forces defending Troy, not among the Achaean forces besieging the city. Homer recognizes the difference between the linguistic cacophony of the Trojans and the linguistic homogeneity of the Achaeans.³⁹ Although linguistic diversity is only occasionally emphasized by Homer in the *Iliad* (see also *Il.* 2.802–6 and 2.867–69), the distinction Homer makes between the Trojans and the Achaeans possibly indicates the nascent semblance of a non-oppositional but shared Greek identity among the Achaeans with language serving as its basic criterion.⁴⁰

Gregory Nagy, building upon Snodgrass' definition of Panhellenism, also sees Panhellenism in the eighth century as "the pattern of intensified intercommunication between the city-states of Hellas," rather than conceiving it in oppositional terms.⁴¹ This view enables Nagy to present Panhellenic poetry as an evolutionary synthesis of local traditions that are most common to all.⁴² Panhellenism can thus be understood as the fluid diffusion and synthesis of local Greek particularities that reached the widest audience but that did not necessarily manifest in a strongly unified Greek ethnic

---

³⁵ See, e.g., Hall, *Inventing the Barbarian*, 4–5, 76–9, 117–21, 177–9; Hartog, *The Mirror of Herodotus*, 10–11, 193–9, 206; Cartledge, *The Greeks*, 12–13. See also Konstan, "To Hellênikon Ethnos," 31–2, who argues that in Books 9–12 of the *Odyssey*, Homer does not conceive of the contrasts he makes between the civilized and uncivilized worlds as a contrast between Greeks and non-Greeks.

³⁶ For example, A. M. Snodgrass, *The Dark Age of Greece: An Archaeological Survey of the Eleventh to the Eighth Centuries BC* (Edinburgh: Edinburgh University Press, 1971), 55–7, 419–21, 434–6.

³⁷ Ibid., 421, 435.

³⁸ Shawn A. Ross, "Barbarophonos: Language and Panhellenism in the *Iliad*," *Classical Philology*, 100, no. 4 (2005): 299–316, 299. Hall argues for the sixth century BCE as the critical point for the development of "aggregative" proto-Hellenism, which is just prior to the Persian Wars, but later than the date posited by Snodgrass and Ross (*Ethnic Identity*, 47–51). See also Hall, *Hellenicity*, 130–4. Dating for the *Iliad* and the *Odyssey* is a matter of debate. Dates from the Late Bronze Age through the seventh century have been proposed for the socio-historical context reflected in the poems. Dates from the eighth century to the sixth century have been proposed for the composition or completion of the poems. See Ross' discussion on the dating of the *Iliad* and *Odyssey* in "Barbarophonos," 299–300 n. 1.

³⁹ Ross, "Barbarophonos," 299. Ross cites *Il.* 4.333–8, where Homer likens clamor of the Trojan forces to "myriads of ewes" that "bleat incessantly," for "there was no speech shared by all of them, nor one voice,/instead their tongue was mingled, as they were men summoned from many lands" (Trans. Ross [ibid., 305]).

⁴⁰ Ross, "Barbarophonos," 299, 313–14. Cf. Hilary Mackie, *Talking Trojan: Speech and Community in the* Iliad (Lanhan, MD: Rowman & Littlefield, 1996), who does not interpret linguistic differences between the Trojans and Achaeans as a reflection of real differences between Greek and non-Greeks but rather views them as a reflection of the social and political tensions internal to eighth-century society.

⁴¹ See Snodgrass, *Dark Age*, 421–35; Gregory Nagy, *Pindar's Homer: The Lyric Possession of an Epic Past* (Baltimore: Johns Hopkins University Press, 1990), 52.

⁴² Nagy, *Pindar's Homer*, 53–4.

identity. Nagy's understanding of Panhellenism thus makes it possible to avoid making the choice between Greek cultural unity presumed by Herodotus and social diversity documented by others (e.g., Aristotle *Politics* 7.1327b). It also makes it possible to avoid linking Panhellenism inextricably to the rise of an ethnic consciousness.

However, even if the origins of Panhellenism are not necessarily found in the construction of the monolithic barbarian "other," Panhellenic identity required the "psychological and cultural upheaval" of the Persian Wars to come to fruition.[43] That is, although Panhellenism did not germinate from an inherently oppositional idea or interaction, the united front of "we the Greeks" manifested itself in the context of Persian opposition. Ethnic self-consciousness, while not equivalent to Panhellenic consciousness, finds sharper relief when contrasted with those whom the Greeks consider "other."

Prior to the Persian Wars, "barbarians" referred generally to non-Greek speakers. Homer uses the term when speaking of the Carians, who "speak in foreign tongue" or are "barbarian speaking" (βαρβαρόφωνοι) (*Il.* 2.867), but he does so only in this one instance and not in a pejorative or political sense.[44] When narrating the events of the Trojan War in both the *Iliad* and the *Odyssey*, Homer resists directing the audience to take sides and make ethnic distinctions between the Trojans and the Achaeans (Greeks).[45] However, if Homer does demonstrate a bias in his depictions of both groups, Hall argues that he does so in favor of the Trojans by providing nuance and intimate details about them in their peacetime communal, personal, and civic lives, which are meant to heighten the *pathos* of their upcoming destruction.[46] The savage behavior of the Greek hero, Achilles, puts his heroism at odds with both Hellenic and Trojan values. It is Hector who suggests that both he and Achilles pledge to uphold the right of the other to a decent funeral and Achilles who denies his enemy the right to proper burial when he desecrates Hector's corpse (*Il.* 22.256–9).[47] When recounting the Trojan War, Homer treats the Trojans and the Greeks on an equal basis and as ethnically indistinguishable.

The polis serves as the central institution in Homeric verse. Homer's poetry presents an artistic and idealized portrayal of the "imagined social relations of the heroic age" that does not correspond exactly to ways in which monarchs ruled over their own districts and households during the Mycenaean period or the rise of the Ionian city-states of the eighth and seventh centuries.[48] However, the social patterns described in Homeric poetry provide insight into the ways Greeks as well as non-Greeks organized power relations.[49] Homer divides humanity between rulers (aristocrats) and subjects (the common people) but not between Greek and barbarian.[50] Nor does he provide a

---

[43] Ross, "Barbarophonos," 314.
[44] A. T. Murray translates βαρβαρόφωνοι as "uncouth speech," which is more condescending but not pejorative (*Iliad*, vol. 1, 2 vols. [Cambridge: Harvard University Press], 1924).
[45] Hall, *Inventing the Barbarian*, 23–32.
[46] Ibid., 30–1.
[47] Ibid., 26–7.
[48] Ibid., 14.
[49] Ibid.
[50] Ibid., 14, 16.

Hellene/barbarian antithesis in terms of language, ethnography, or rhetoric.⁵¹ Thus, even though the term "barbarian-speaking" appears as early as Homer, the political and more pejorative divide between Greeks and βαρβαρόφωνοι did not take its cues from him.⁵²

Imagining Persia and Constructing Greekness

It was not until Aeschylus' *Persians* (472 BCE)⁵³ that the term βάρβαρος took on a more political and pejorative meaning.⁵⁴ Athenian tragedians of the fifth century made subtle comparisons between Greeks and barbarians, such as those found in *Persians*, which later developed into full-scale rhetoric that emphasized the differences in political ideals between Greeks and non-Greeks.⁵⁵ In order for the *Persians* to be understood and appreciated fully, as Hall explains, readers must interpret the play not as a source for historical facts but rather as "a document of the Athenian collective *imagination*" and as "a truthful record of the ways in which the Athenians *liked to think about* their enemy."⁵⁶ Aeschylus treats the Persians at times with surprising nuance and sympathy when depicting their psychological dimensions—feelings of longing, hatred, and terror, while suffusing his play "with the glow of the great Greek victory over the barbarian."⁵⁷

Set entirely in Susa, the imperial capital of the Persian Empire, *Persians* dramatizes a fictional scene in which the royal court of Persia receives word that the Greeks have defeated the Persians at Salamis from the presumed perspective of the Persians without ever presenting a Greek character on stage—the play's entire cast of characters are

---

⁵¹ Ibid., 32.
⁵² In the same way, the use of the parallel term ἀλλόθροος (e.g., *Od.* 1.183, 3.302, 15.453) does not have culturally pejorative connotations.
⁵³ Aeschylus' *Persians* is the only complete text about the Persian Wars to survive that was written by an author with personal experience of the Greco-Persian conflicts (Edith Hall, *Greek Tragedy: Suffering under the Sun* [Oxford: Oxford University Press, 2010], 202). Aeschylus produced *Persians* in 472 BCE, only seven years after the war it dramatized (Rebecca F. Kennedy, C. Sydnor Roy, and Max L. Goldman, eds., *Race and Ethnicity in the Classical World: An Anthology of Primary Sources in Translation* [Indianapolis: Hackett, 2013], 203).
⁵⁴ Hall, *Inventing the Barbarian*, 16; Green, *From Ikaria to the Stars*, 112, 115. By the sixth century, the seldom use of the term βάρβαρος took on a slightly more contemptuous tone, while still emphasizing linguistic difference, as evident when Anacreon's (fr. S313 Page SLG) says, "[I fear] you may use barbarian terms" (μή πως βάρβαρα βάξῃς), as cited and translated by idem, 112. Contra Simon Hornblower, who sees early evidence in the *Iliad* (2.867; 21.130–2; 24.722) that the concept of the barbarian was invented prior to the Persian Wars, although he agrees that "barbarian" acquired the disparaging sense "brutal, rude" thereafter ("Greek Identity in the Archaic and Classical Periods," in *Hellenisms*, 38–9).
⁵⁵ Hall, *Inventing the Barbarian*, 16. Aeschylus' predecessor and rival dramatist, Phrynichus, had already staged a play devoted in part to the Persian Wars seen from the perspective of the devastated Persians. See Alan H. Sommerstein, ed., *Aeschylus I. Persians, Seven against Thebes, Suppliants, Prometheus Bound*, trans. Sommerstein, Alan H., LCL 145 (Cambridge: Harvard University Press, 2008), 2–3.
⁵⁶ Hall, *Greek Tragedy*, 202.
⁵⁷ Sommerstein, *Aeschylus I*, 6.

Persian.⁵⁸ The play opens with the chorus of elders expressing their troubled hearts concerning the homecoming of their lord, King Xerxes, and his "many-manned army" (1–19). They describe Xerxes as "savage in war, ruling over many-peopled Asia, he drives his extraordinary flock across the whole earth in two ways, entrusting them to his stout, reliable commanders by both land and sea—a godlike mortal of the golden race" (70–80).⁵⁹ Such a description starkly contrasts the appearance of a tattered, battered, and defeated Xerxes who appears at the end of the play. According to Hall, Aeschylus in *Persians* dramatizes the emotions of the Persians in such a way that enables the Greeks to relive their own emotions of longing, hatred, and terror they experienced when they witnessed Xerxes sack Athens before defeating him later at the battle of Salamis and Plataea: through "covert exorcism of their own psychological pain, the Greeks could maintain their comfortable, masculine, and ethnically superior identity of unemotional Greeks."⁶⁰ The tragedian's empathetic presentation of the Persians provides the Greeks with a cathartic release of their own pain, grief, and loss suffered during the wars.

In contrast, Gruen argues that Aeschylus does not promote the inherent superiority of the Greeks over and against the barbarians.⁶¹ Rather than blame the Persians for their downfall, Aeschylus places the onus on divine intervention for the outcome of events that favored the Greeks but did not result from Greek valor.⁶² Furthermore, Aeschylus presents Persians and Greeks as belonging to the same genealogical root, which resonates with the legend that the Greek demigod Perseus fathered the ancestor of the Persians.⁶³ Gruen points to the vivid dream of the Persian queen prior to the battle of Salamis in which she dreamed she saw two extraordinarily beautiful sisters who were both well-dressed, one in lovely Persian garb and the other in Dorian (Greek).⁶⁴ Although these women are of the "same race," one sister dwelt in her fatherland, Greece, while the other resided in "a barbarian land." When a conflict arises between the sisters, Xerxes, the queen's son, tries to control and quiet them by yoking both women under his chariot and tying leather straps under their throats. One sister (representing the Persians) offers no resistance to Xerxes and proudly stands in the harness. The other sister (representing the Greeks), however, puts up a fight and manages to rip off the harness and smash the yoke down the middle, causing Xerxes to fall. Thus, despite some of the unflattering depictions or descriptions of the Persians

---

⁵⁸ Gruen emphasizes this point in *Rethinking the Other in Antiquity*, 10.
⁵⁹ Trans. Sommerstein, *Aeschylus I*.
⁶⁰ Hall, *Greek Tragedy*, 203–4; see also 56–69. Others who hold the view that the *Persians* expresses Greek superiority over the Persians: e.g., Pericles Georges, *Barbarian Asia and the Greek Experience* (Baltimore: Johns Hopkins University Press, 1994); and Hall, *Hellenicity*, 176–7.
⁶¹ Gruen, *Rethinking the Other in Antiquity*, 11: "Persians may enjoy wealth and splendor, but Aeschylus nowhere suggests Greek austerity or self-denial as national traits. The idea of luxury and extravagance as signaling Persian decadence, the intimations of Persian effeminacy as against Hellenic manliness, the 'Orientalizing,' in short, of the barbarian is hard to discern in the *Persae*."
⁶² Ibid., 16–19. See, e.g., Aesch. *Pers.* 93–114; 441–4; 723–5.
⁶³ Ibid., 20. See also Lynette G. Mitchell, "Greeks, Barbarians and Aeschylus' 'Suppliants,'" *Greece Rome* 53, no. 2 (2006): 205.
⁶⁴ Aesch. *Pers.* 176–99.

found in the play, Gruen contends that *Persians* functions as genuine tragedy that describes the tragic and divinely engendered fate of Greece's enemy without castigating the Persians as the political, cultural, religious, and ethnic barbarian "other" or posing an essentialist divide between Persian despotism and the ideals of Greek democracy.[65] The will of the Gods determines the inexorable fate of both peoples, not the differences between them.[66]

Gruen's overstated assertion that "there is no hint of an ethnic chasm between Greek and Persian" in *Persians*[67] is based on the fact that Aeschylus presents both people groups as belonging to the same lineage. Kinship relationships can be tense and fraught with comparisons, especially when they intersect with the Greek/barbarian polarity.[68] Furthermore, the fact that the kinship was "dreamed" in the play does not help bridge the cultural distance between the Greeks and Persians. The way Aeschylus chooses to establish kinship between two warring peoples may provide a basis for justifying the superiority of one family member over another rather than for establishing common ground and minimizing difference. In seeking to reconstruct Aeschylus' intentions, however, Gruen rightly contends the playwright does not seek to present a derogatory or disparaging image of the Persians.[69]

By the time Aeschylus writes *Persians* seven years after the Persian War, however, the polarization between the Hellene and barbarian had been codified in Greek thought.[70] In fifth-century literature, especially in Athens, themes of Greek superiority and Persian decadence became clichés.[71] When Herodotus recounts Xerxes commanding his men to lay 300 lashes on the Hellespont (7.35.1), he writes, "he told those who laid on the lashes to say these words, of violence arrogance, worthy of a barbarian: 'You bitter water, our master lays this punishment upon you because you have wronged him, though he never did you any wrong'" (7.35.2).[72] Herodotus' use of barbarian here is undoubtedly derogatory, since he implies that Xerxes' violent, furious retaliation against the Hellespont corresponds to the irrational and cruel nature of barbarians.

By emphasizing the difference between the Greeks and Persians, Herodotus does more than critique Persian practices. He constructs Greek ethnicity: "The only way in which cultural heterogeneity could appear more uniform was by contrasting it with practices that were even more heterogeneous, and this is precisely what Herodotus achieved through the barbarian excurses."[73] When, for example, Herodotus describes

---

[65] Gruen, *Rethinking the Other in Antiquity*, 21.
[66] Ibid., 16.
[67] Ibid., 20.
[68] See Mitchell ("Greeks, Barbarians," esp. 205–6), who reads Aeschylus' *Suppliants* as a revision of *Persians* that reflects not only Aeschylus' more complex understanding of the Greek relationship to the barbarian world, but also the ways in which attitudes toward barbarians were being "confronted, contested, and changed" in the mid-fifth century.
[69] Gruen, *Rethinking the Other in Antiquity*, 19.
[70] Hall, *Inventing the Barbarian*, 57.
[71] Thomas, "Ethnicity, Genealogy," 228.
[72] Herodotus, *Herodotus: The History*, trans. David Grene (Chicago: University of Chicago Press, 1988), 482.
[73] Hall, *Ethnic Identity*, 45. So also Zacharia, "Herodotus' Four Markers," 27.

the "customs" (νόμος) of Persian worship practices, he writes, "it is not their custom to make and set up statues and temples and altars, but those who do such things they think foolish, because, I suppose, they have never believed the gods to be like men, as the Greeks do" (1.131.1).[74] In 8.144.2, the Athenian representatives provide the Spartan envoys with the list of reasons why Athens refuses to make a pact with the Persians and enslave Hellas, beginning with the need to avenge the destruction of the "statues and temples of our gods." The religious cults of the Greeks were certainly not uniform.[75] However, when compared to the religious practices of the Persians and in the face of Persian political and military threat, the heterogeneous and often contentious and polis-identifying Greeks could create a united front against a common enemy now defined as the barbarian par excellence. Athenian intellectuals thus promoted their own version of Panhellenism in the attempt to create a collective identity among the quarreling Greeks by pitting them against the Achaemenid Empire of Persia, which they presented as their "true, natural, and historical foe."[76]

It was not long after the Greeks defeated the Persians in a united effort that they began to compete among themselves for power and income.[77] The rivalry between Athens and Sparta, who fought as allies eighteen years prior in the Persian Wars (499–449 BCE), led to the catastrophic intra-Greek power struggle known as the Peloponnesian War (431–404 BCE), which Thucydides so carefully chronicles. Such rapid dissolution of the Panhellenistic ideal, which arose during the Persian Wars, reveals just how temporary and fragile the idea of Hellenic solidarity and how deeply rooted the reality of Hellenic fragmentation really was.[78] It also points to the power of external threat or conflict in creating social cohesion however short lived. The invention of the barbarian with its many shades of meaning thus occurred throughout the period during and after the Persian Wars among the Athenian elite, who began to see the foreignness of barbarians as the source of their inferiority and the justification for their subjectivity.[79]

The Proof Is in the Stock: Defining Greek Ethnicity

While it was easy for the Greeks to differentiate themselves from the Persians as a monolithic "other," it proved more difficult for them to delineate what exactly qualified as Greekness. By and large, the Greeks did not often attempt to formulate definitions of Greekness, and Herodotus' formulation in 8.144 serves more as the exception than

---

[74] Herodotus, *Herodotus*, trans. A. D. Godley (London; New York: W. Heinemann; G.P. Putnam's Sons), 1921.
[75] See, e.g., Walter Burkert, *Greek Religion: Archaic and Classical*, trans. John Raffan (Oxford: Blackwell, 1985).
[76] Green, *From Ikaria to the Stars*, 110.
[77] Hall, *Greek Tragedy*, 105.
[78] Papadodima, "Companion to Ethnicity," 256.
[79] For example, Herodotus warns through the words of Cyrus, "From soft countries come soft men. It is not possible that from the same land stems a growth of wondrous fruit and men who are good soldiers" (9.122; trans. Grene).

the rule. Herodotus' strong assertion of Greekness figured prominently at times of crisis, such as the Persian threat, but was not permanently upheld. Colonial evidence finds significant religious and linguistic differences between certain Greek city-states, such as the closely neighboring Athens and Thebes.[80] However, while "the idea of a single Greek identity is a chimera," it would be equally wrong to imagine that each of the hundreds of Greek city-states fiercely possessed and affirmed a separate ethnicity.[81]

Greeks were fond of binaries and used them to define themselves not only against barbarians but also against Greeks.[82] For example, Greeks categorized themselves along a Dorian/Ionian divide. In his account of the Ionians, Herodotus reports that the Ionians claim to have founded just twelve Ionian cities, because prior to their expulsion by the Achaeans, they were among them only twelve divisions of Ionians who lived in the Ionian Peloponnese; thus, these twelve cities represented those of nobler Ionian blood (1.145–6). Herodotus, however, challenges such putative claims, noting that so much non-Ionian blood has intermingled with Ionian blood that even Athenian elites from the heart of Athens "who think of themselves as the bluest of blood of the Ionians" took Carian, not Ionian, wives (1.146). In emphasizing the fictive quality of Ionic ethnic identity, Herodotus reveals how the Ionians conceived of themselves as belonging to a primordial group based on claims of shared ancestry (1.146–7).[83]

In order to participate in the Olympic Games, which only Greeks could do, Alexander of Macedonia (Alexander I) sets out to prove his family's Hellenic heritage before the official committee in charge of the games (*Hist.* 5.22.1–2):

> But the descendants of Perdiccas are, in fact, Greeks (as they themselves say) I happen to know; and I will, moreover, prove that they are Greeks in the latter part of my history. Besides, those marshals of the games, who arrange the Olympics, have given the same in judgment. For when Alexander chose to compete and entered the arena for the purpose, certain of the Greeks who were his competitors would have debarred him, on the grounds that this was no contest for foreign contestants but for Greeks only. Alexander then proved that he was an Argive and was therefore adjudged to be a Greek and took his part in the footrace, where he ran a dead heat with the winner.[84]

Herodotus does not explain here exactly how Alexander persuades the committee that he was Greek (Argive) by descent,[85] but he does make known his personal conviction that Macedonian kings are in fact Greek (5.22.1).[86] It is interesting to note how the official

---

[80] Zacharia, "Herodotus' Four Markers," 27.
[81] Ibid.
[82] On the subgroups by which Greeks asserted themselves, such as colonial milieu and polis membership and citizenship, see Hornblower, "Greek Identity," 44–54.
[83] McInerney, "Ethnos and Ethnicity in Early Greece," 58–9.
[84] Herodotus, *Herodotus*, 364. Trans. Grene.
[85] On Alexander's alleged Hellenic credentials and on the Macedonians, see Hall, "Contested Ethnicities: Perceptions of Macedonia within Evolving Definitions of Greek Identity," in *Ancient Perceptions*, 168.
[86] See Rosaria Vignolo Munson, "Herodotus and Ethnicity." In the fourth century, Demosthenes (*Philippics* 3.31) staunchly declares the exact opposite conviction that the Macedonian kings

verdict on Alexander's ethnicity differs from that of the Greek athletes, who see him as a barbarian. This difference in perception appears again, for example, when Spartan envoys, in their attempt to persuade Athens against making special terms with Xerxes, argue that Persians cannot be trusted because "in barbarians there is neither faith nor truth" (8.142.5)[87] or when the Athenian representatives refer to Alexander as a "barbarian" in order to reassure Spartan envoys of their loyalty to Greece (8.144.1). Herodotus returns to the question of Alexander's lineage (8.137-9), but he does not attempt to provide any proof or further argument for his prior assertion that Alexander is of Greek stock (5.22.1).[88] It appears that proving one's stock matters less to Herodotus than asserting one's stock.

The term ὅμαιμον ("of the same blood"), which begins Herodotus' famous formulation of Greek ethnic identity (8.144.2), appears twice earlier in the *Histories*. It first occurs in 1.151.2 when Herodotus describes the people of Arisba as being "enslaved by their kinsmen of Methymna" (ἠνδραπόδισαν Μηθυμναῖοι ἐόντας ὁμαίμους). It is heard a second time in 5.49.3 on the lips of Aristagoras the Milesian when he entreats the Spartans, famous for their powerful, well-trained army, "to save your Ionian kinsmen" from slavery (Ἴωνας ... ἄνδρας ὁμαίμονας). Being of the same blood for Herodotus provides just enough commonality to bind the Greeks in the midst of their differences while leaving definitions of Greek ethnic identity open to interpretation and to the inclusion or exclusion of cultural dimensions.[89]

What makes Herodotus' formulation in 8.144.2 so innovative, according to Hall, is the juxtaposition of being of the same blood with being of the same religion and customs.[90] The physical traits, language, religion, and/or cultural orientations appended to the idea of common blood do not change the basic criterion for ethnicity.[91] Rather, Herodotus broadens the definition of what it means to be Greek to include more aspects, such as religious and cultural habits.[92] Thus, Hall asserts that the "myth of shared descent" ranks above all other features as the most important criterion that sets ethnic group identity apart from other social groups.[93] His constructivist view of

---

are indeed not of Greek ancestry. These disagreements tell us that the Hellenism of Alexander I was disputed by the Greeks and that Herodotus' four criteria did not easily apply to Macedon (Hornblower, "Greek Identity," 55).

[87] Trans. Godley, LCL.
[88] Munson, "Companion to Ethnicity," 343.
[89] Herodotus' open-ended definition, for example, leaves unanswered just how far in the past bloodlines must go, what it means to share in biological and social kinship, and to what degree the idea of common territory factors into the idea of ethnicity (S. Rebecca Martin, "Ethnicity and Representation," in *A Companion to Ethnicity*, 357).
[90] Hall, *Ethnic Identity*, 44-5; Hall, *Hellenicity*, 190-1.
[91] Hall, *Hellenicity*, 191.
[92] Ibid., 191-3.
[93] Hall, *Ethnic Identity*, 25. Contra Rosalind Thomas, who argues that the ethnic character of both the Greeks and Persians largely depends on the customs of their laws (νόμοι), but that laws could change to the extent that even the Persians were capable of democracy, should they so choose (*Herodotus in Context: Ethnography, Science and the Art of Persuasion* [Cambridge: Cambridge University Press, 2000], 226). See Hdt. 1.210.2, where Herodotus seems to suggest that Persia could accept democracy in their own state or permit democracies elsewhere to persist. Thomas notes that the dominant cliché among fifth-century Greeks was that the Persians were ruled by tyranny, whereas the Greeks were ruled by liberty, a stereotype that Herodotus both accepts and challenges (ibid., 116).

ethnicity presents it as an imagined, rather than a verifiable, objective reality.[94] Hall thus calls shared descent a "myth" because biological or genetic evidence for such an assertion has no relevance. What makes shared descent "true" is the recognition and consensual agreement of *putative* shared ancestry.[95] Therefore, the proof of a group's ethnicity is not in the pudding, so to speak, but in the group's supposed stock.

Both *polis* and ethnic identity proved to be unstable[96] and yet fluid concepts, as evident in the rather confusing way Herodotus speaks of the Athenians in 1.57. Herodotus suggests here that the Athenian race (τὸ Ἀττικὸν ἔθνος) was Pelasgian in origins. Because Pelasgians originally spoke a non-Greek language (βάρβαρον γλῶσσαν), Herodotus assumes "the Attic race ... must have changed their language when it became one with the Greeks [Hellenes]."[97] This is ironic if not disturbing when considering that Herodotus later articulates from the mouths of Athenians the criteria for Greekness, which they prided themselves in possessing.[98] The very people who Herodotus suggests are not originally of Greek descent and language later determine who among other Greek city-states qualifies as Greek.

Writing after Herodotus, Isocrates warns fellow Greeks that the title "'Hellenes' suggests no longer a race (τό γένος) but an intelligence ... applied rather to those who share our culture than to those who share a common blood (φύσις)" (*Panegyricus* 50).[99] His point is that Greeks cannot take their ethnic identity for granted; descent cannot be relied upon at the expense of political and educational aspects of Greekness.[100] Isocrates' concern reflects the continued significance of the criteria of blood and descent for Greek self-definition after the Persian Wars. It also signals the increasing importance that will be given to education and culture for the self-understanding of Hellenes living in the Greek world left by Alexander the Great.[101]

Greek Ethnicity under Roman Rule

The conflict between Persia and the Greek city-states gave rise to Herodotus' sense of a unified Greek ethnic identity. This cohesive Greek ethnic sense of solidarity and collective ethnic identity based on common blood, common language, common cult foundations and sacrifices, and similar customs coalesced around a common, powerful, and barbarian foe. It manifested itself, however, in different ways when the Greeks

---

[94] Two books that have had great impact on the study of ethnic groups are Eric Hobsbawm and Terence Ranger, eds., *The Invention of Tradition* (Cambridge: Cambridge University Press, 1983); Benedict Anderson, *Imagined Communities*. Such works have warned against the dangers of over-concretizing "descent and culture communities" while at the same time starting a trend within ethnicity studies to understand ethnic labels as mere constructions, imaginings, or inventions (Fenton, *Ethnicity*, 4).
[95] Hall, *Ethnic Identity*, 25.
[96] See Thomas, *Herodotus in Context*, 121.
[97] Trans. Grene.
[98] Hornblower, "Greek Identity," 41.
[99] Trans. George Norlin, LCL.
[100] Saïd, "Discourse of Identity," 285.
[101] For an exploration of Greek identity in the Hellenistic Period, see Burstein, "Greek Identity in the Hellenistic Period," in *Hellenisms*, 59–77.

found themselves forcefully conquered by the Romans, who were neither Greeks nor barbarians. Romans had different criteria for self-definition than Greeks.[102] Romans also perceived and governed Greeks differently from their other subjects. These unique factors created a dynamic tension that made it possible for Greeks to become Roman while remaining Greek[103] and for Romans to take what they wanted from Greek culture and even insert themselves into the Hellenic tradition without becoming Greek.[104]

The first two centuries of Roman rule gradually fused the reciprocal movement that had been taking place between Greek and Roman cultures for centuries.[105] The process of Hellenization (the bringing of Greek culture to Rome) and of Romanization[106] involved bilateral give-and-take. In their encounter with Rome, the Greeks lost their political independence but maintained their linguistic and cultural autonomy.[107] Roman imperial power forced the Greeks to redefine their notions of their identity, just as the Persians had done in the past and the Ottomans would do in the future.[108]

Rome's Civilizing Mission

The Romans understood their imperial mission as a civilizing mission. Cicero (106–43 BCE), for example, writes in a famous letter to his brother, Quintus, who was governing Asia:

---

[102] Richard Duncan-Jones, *The Economy of the Roman Empire: Qualitative Studies* (Cambridge: Cambridge University Press, 1982), 1. It must be noted that, in antiquity, ethnic identity was primarily an elite concern. The vast majority of people in the empire lived in rural areas and were engaged in agriculture. They placed greater importance on family, clan, and town for self-definition than on ethnicity, and some among them even encountered those who spoke different languages, worshipped different gods, and practiced different customs. However, we are left with little to no written record of how most ancients weighed the many different components of their personal identity. Even among the elites, ethnicity was a fluid concept: "One man feels an Athenian in Alexandria, but a Greek in Rome; another is a Pharisee in Jerusalem but a Jew in Antioch" (Ronald Mellor, "Graecia Capta: The Confrontation between Greek and Roman Identity," in *Hellenisms*, 79).

[103] Greg Woolf, "Becoming Roman, Staying Greek: Culture, Identity and the Civilizing Process in the Roman East," PCPhS 40 (1994): 116–43.

[104] Mellor, "*Graecia Capta*," 85.

[105] Ibid., 81.

[106] *Romanization* is a contested term, often understood as either the process of cultural or political assimilation. Ramsey MacMullen defines Romanization as the spread of a way of life created in Italy to the provinces that did not result in cultural uniformity (Ramsay MacMullen, *Romanization in the Time of Augustus* [New Haven: Yale University Press, 2000], xi). Greg Woolf defines Romanization as "a convenient shorthand for the series of cultural change that created an imperial civilization, within which both differences and similarities came to form a coherent pattern" (*Becoming Roman: The Origin of Provincial Civilization in Gaul* [Cambridge: Cambridge University Press, 1998], 7). The process of becoming a Roman was a slow one, according to Woolf, and involved far more complex changes than simply rejection of one cultural system for another (ibid., 10). Ronald Mellor, emphasizing how Romanization was a multi-dimensional and multi-directional synthesis between Greek and Roman cultures, describes Romanization as the process through which "Greco-Roman civilization spread throughout the Mediterranean world and to Northern Europe" ("*Graecia Capta*," 81).

[107] Mellor, "*Graecia Capta*," 82.

[108] Ibid., 120.

> What if the casting of lots has allocated you Africans or Spaniards or Gauls to rule over?—wild and barbarous peoples, even then you would owe it to your own *humanitas* to take into account what suited them and to concern yourself with their well-being and safety. But seeing as how we rule that very race of men in which not only is true *humanitas* found but from whom it is believed to spread to others, we are at the very least obligated to give them what they have given us.[109]

Here Cicero expresses the idea that all "wild and barbarous peoples" (*immanisbus ac barbaris nationibus*) benefit from the civilizing mission of Rome.[110] However, it also demonstrates how Cicero understands Rome's mission to civilize barbarians differently from its obligation to "that very race of men," i.e., the Greeks, whom he credits for introducing *humanitas* to the Romans. The Romans, in turn, bear the responsibility of spreading *humanitas* throughout the world. Such imperializing logic made it possible for Romans to justify subjugating Greeks, while also acknowledging their indebtedness to them as the inventors of *humanitas*. Rome thus understood its mission to Greeks as different from but complimentary to their civilizing mission to barbarians.[111] The Romans saw themselves as borrowing freely from Greek civilization while civilizing Greeks through Roman morality and government.[112]

Pliny the Elder's (23–79 CE) statement in *Natural History* 3.39 is well-known for being one of the few surviving passages that resembles something like a mission statement of the Roman empire, which is, as he explains,

> to make even the sky clearer, to gather the scattered powers and pacify the customs and bring together the discordant and wild idioms of so many peoples by the shared use of a language of communication, and to give civilization to mankind (*humanitatem homini*), and in short, to bring about a single nation from all the peoples in the whole world.[113]

According to Pliny, Rome's mission is to gift humankind with *humanitas* and create a single *patria* from "all the peoples in the world." He relates Rome's cultural and moral vocation of civilizing humankind with the mission of establishing the Roman empire as the *patria* of all those it has gathered from "scattered powers." Rome could unite "discordant and wild tongues," not necessarily by spreading the singular use of Latin throughout the empire but by implementing a common morality or an enduring set of values upon its citizens without imposing rigidly defined policies that diminished the civic and cultural diversity and particularity among its provinces.[114] As for the Greek

---

[109] *Ad Quintum fratrem* 1.1.27; trans. Woolf, "Becoming Roman," 119.
[110] Barbarians could be civilized by Rome and hence Romanized without ever experiencing the privileges and protections of the law granted to Roman citizens alone.
[111] Woolf, "Becoming Roman," 118.
[112] Mellor, "*Graecia Capta*," 105.
[113] Trans. James Clackson and Geoffrey Horrocks, *The Blackwell History of the Latin Language* (Malden, MA: Wiley-Blackwell, 2010), 229.
[114] Woolf, "Becoming Roman," 124–5.

cities of the east, the Romans sought to oversee them in their efforts to self-govern and intervene only when necessary.[115]

In *Epistles* 8.24, Pliny the Younger urges his friend Maximus to treat Greeks in province of Achaia with deference for their great past:

> Respect the gods their founders and the names they bear, respect their ancient glory and their very age, which in man commands our veneration, in cities our reverence. Pay regard to their antiquity, their heroic deeds, and the legends of their past .... always bear in mind that this is the land which provided us with justice and gave us laws, not after conquering us but at our request; that is Athens you go to and Sparta you rule, and to rob them of the name and shadow of freedom, which is all that now remains to them, would be an act of cruelty, ignorance and barbarism.[116]

Pliny's advice subtly shifts in tone, as he expresses the view that while the Romans received justice and law from the Greeks, they did so out of choice, not force. The fact that he finds it necessary to remind Maximus not to look down upon the free Greek cities reveals how Romans distinguished vastly between the Greeks of the past, who invented civilization, and Greeks of the present, who were no longer what they once were.[117]

Admiration for Greek civilization had its limits.[118] The Greek preoccupation with the past (during the imperial period) only reinforced the Roman view that present-day Greeks were overindulgent.[119] After having pardoned the Athenians for their support of Pompey, Julius Caesar asks them with frustration and incredulity, "How often will the glory of your ancestors save you from your self-destruction?" (Appian, *Bell. civ.* 2.88).[120] Tacitus criticizes the Greeks for their arbitrary embellishment of their past (*Hist.* 2.4.1). But Greeks had other flaws. Cicero describes them as lazy (*Sest.* 110). Seneca criticizes them for busying themselves with trifling activities and wasting their time speculating about trivial matters (*Vit. beat.* 13.2).[121] Juvenal derides

---

[115] Ibid., 124. In *Epistles* 10.79 and 80, Pliny the Younger provides evidence that emperors very rarely imposed new constitutions on the Greek cities of Bithynia-Pontus, preferring, instead, to adjust and modify existing local civic policies in a piecemeal fashion. In 5.20, Pliny complains about the Bithynians whom he oversees, in part, because of their Greekness and stubbornness. The Romans, however, found it necessary to intervene on multiple occasions. Pliny's correspondence with Trajan (*Ep.* 10) reveals that Bithynia-Pontus has turned out to be a relatively high-maintenance province with numerous deficiencies, such as the growth of Christian superstition, the decrease in traditional temple worship, and the plummeting sale of animals for sacrifice.

[116] Trans. Betty Radice, LCL.

[117] *Recordare quid quaeque civitas fuerit, non ut despicias quod esse desierit* (Pliny, *Ep.* 8.24).

[118] Mellor, "*Graecia Capta*," 104.

[119] Woolf, "Becoming Roman," 132.

[120] Trans. Horace White, LCL.

[121] Older Romans, such as Cicero and Virgil, attributed Rome's success to *gravitas*, in contrast to the Greek *levitas*. However, the high moral standards of service to the state and restraint from excessive luxury and ostentation that characterized the Roman *mos maiorum* had nearly disappeared by the second century BCE, as Senators competed in "cultural of one-upmanship" over who could build the most Greek-style homes, host the most sumptuous banquets, and be surrounded by the largest entourage of Greek poets and intellectuals (Mellor, "*Graecia Capta*," 93).

and distrusts Greeks because they are too loquacious, smooth talking, flattering, disingenuous, and promiscuous (*Sat.* 3.85–110).[122]

Although Rome granted Greeks entitlements that distinguished them from barbarians, their decadence made them over-civilized and placed them on the other side of the spectrum of the under-civilized barbarism, such as the Gauls, Spaniards, and Africans. The Romans, in contrast, posited themselves as the geographical, temporal, and moral median "situated between a barbarous past and a potentially decadent future."[123] When explaining to Pliny his moral responsibilities as governor over Bithynia-Pontus, Trajan writes, "I chose you for your practical wisdom (*prudentia*) so that you would preside over the moulding [*sic*] of the behavior of your province (*formandis istius prouinciae moribus*), and establish the norms which would be good for the enduring peacefulness of the province" (*Ep.* 10.117).[124] Trajan's expectations for Pliny reveal the patronizing idea that Greek behavior or morals (*mos*) could and should be tempered and restrained. The Greeks, although significant for their past, were now in decline and in need of reforming.

Remaining Greek while Becoming Roman

The process of Romanization for Greeks involved assimilation and resistance and occurred concomitantly with Hellenization, such that "Hellenization and Romanization were each a process of selection."[125] Greek elites benefited from Roman rule, which both protected and enriched them. The most prominent among them acquired Roman citizenship, which they proudly displayed, before receiving positions in the equestrian order and the senate.[126] They identified with Roman power but not with Roman history or culture, whereas Roman elites identified with Greek literary and artistic culture (and even tried to live like the Greeks) without desiring to become

---

[122] Strabo describes his fellow Greeks as "the most talkative of men" (3.4.19).

[123] Woolf, "Becoming Roman," 121.

[124] Pliny the Younger, *Pliny the Younger Complete Letters*, trans. P. G. Walsh (Oxford: Oxford University Press, 2006).

[125] Mellor, "*Graecia Capta*," 86.

[126] Woolf, "Becoming Roman," 125. To become Roman, however, was not the same as attaining Roman citizenship. As A. N. Sherwin-White explains, self-Romanization in the provinces was no sure indication of imperial activity, and loyalty to Rome emerged quite separately from the desire for Roman citizenship (*The Roman Citizenship*, 2nd ed. [Oxford: Clarendon, 1973], 222–3). Under the principate, Roman citizenship extended beyond its initial connection with Italian birth or origin and, later, connection with Latin culture, as it became a "passive citizenship ... sought no longer for its political significance but as an honour or out of sentiment" (ibid., 222). Roman citizenship thus became less a symbol of the old privileges and duties of the *Cives Romani* and more a sign of Rome's ability to unite the Empire within one system of law (A. N. Sherwin-White, *The Roman Citizenship*, 2nd ed. [Oxford: Clarendon, 1973], 222). The first large-scale extension of Roman citizenship in provincial areas took place under Julius Caesar and Augustus, but it was limited to those who could prove their genuine Italian immigration (ibid., 225). Rome more commonly granted Latin rights (*ius Latii*), rather than full citizenship, within its provinces, though the granting of Latin rights to purely native communities was rare (ibid., 225).

Greek.¹²⁷ Writers of the Second Sophistic exaggerated the glories of the Greek past and emphasized the uniqueness of their culture quite possibly as a way to cope with their own feelings of alienation and hostility.¹²⁸ However, even they had close political and economic ties with the empire and helped encourage the importation of new styles into Greek cities.¹²⁹

Greek identity continued to be celebrated and rehearsed among a much wider audience through festivals, cults, and assemblies.¹³⁰ While descent and language figured prominently in Greek self-definition of identity, material culture did not. This is not, however, because Greek culture did not manifest itself materially, because it did, as is evident in the way Romans adopted Greek institutions and practices, such as the gymnasium, symposium, *paedeia*, homosexuality, and the Second Sophistic.¹³¹ However, Greeks did not define themselves in terms of a particular Greek style. Rather, they continued to define themselves according to Herodotus' four criteria for Greek ethnic identity: as people who possessed a common descent, spoke a common language, worshipped the same gods, and shared certain customs. This is evident in the way ancient scholars preoccupied themselves with finding out the origins of various Greek and non-Greek peoples and the ritual celebration of the heroic founders of Greek city-states.¹³² While Greeks traced these markers back to mythical times, they did not associate them with material culture.¹³³ Greeks did not see architectural style as a major signifier of cultural affiliation. Romans, however, saw architecture as a sign of civilization or as a sign of dangerously un-Roman activity.

In sharp contrast, Romans placed very little stock in common descent for defining what it meant to be Roman. Rather than see *humanitas* as the property of a particular people (as the Greeks did), the Romans defined it primarily in terms of *mores* (customs, morality, way of life): living in cities, living from agriculture, living at peace, living according to laws and to the common aspiration to a set of intellectual and ethical ideas exemplified by the aristocracy in Rome.¹³⁴ Romans conceived of identity based on membership in a political and religious community with common values and *mores*. Although Romans had no single model in mind for the way they intervened in the life

---

[127] Mellor, "*Graecia Capta*," 117. Plutarch (*Praecepta gerendae reipublicae*) recognized that, under Imperial Rome, Greece enjoyed prosperity and peace (cf. Simon Swain, *Hellenism and Empire: Language, Classicism, and Power in the Greek World, A.D. 50–250* [Oxford: Clarendon, 1996], 158–83). Christopher P. Jones refers to Plutarch as one of the first Greek intellectuals to view the Roman empire as an insider (*Plutarch and Rome* [Oxford: Clarendon, 1971], 124). By the second century CE, Greek was the language of power, even as Rome's legal and governmental system was constructed in Latin. This is evident in the fact that the Roman elite was almost completely bilingual. Romans spoke Greek, but Greeks strongly resisted speaking Latin (Mellor, "*Graecia Capta*," 117). See also Woolf, "Becoming Roman," 129.
[128] On the Second Sophistic, see Simon Swain, *Hellenism and Empire* and Maud W. Gleason, *Making Men: Sophists and Self-Presentation in Ancient Rome* (Princeton: Princeton University Press, 1995).
[129] Woolf, "Becoming Roman," 128.
[130] Woolf, "Becoming Roman," 128.
[131] Woolf, "Becoming Roman," 130.
[132] Ibid., 129.
[133] Ibid., 140 n. 51.
[134] Ibid., 120.

of Greek cities, we can see that Romans saw their efforts as going beyond pragmatic needs. They consistently saw their changes as a means of cultivating civilization and of imposing *mores* throughout the world.

Tacitus' description of Agricola's governorship over Roman Britain demonstrates how Romans defined themselves by Rome's civilization mission and material culture:

> In order that a population scattered and uncivilised, and proportionately ready for war might be habituated by comfort to peace and quiet, he would exhort individuals, assist communities, to erect temples, market-places, houses: he praised the energetic, rebuked the indolent, and the rivalry for his compliments took the place of coercion .... As a result, the nation which used to reject the Latin language began to aspire to rhetoric: further, the wearing of our dress became a distinction, and the toga came into fashion,[135] and little by little, the Britons went astray into alluring vices: to the promenade, the bath, the well-appointed dinner table. The simple natives gave the name of "culture" to this factor of their slavery.[136]

Tacitus' description of Agricola's Romanizing activities in Britain echoes the mission statement of Rome expressed by the Elder Pliny's to "give civilization to mankind" (*Hist. Nat.* 3.39). Agricola carries out Rome's mission to civilize and hence Romanize barbarians not only by erecting temples and other forms of Roman architecture but also by giving the "sons of chieftains" (*principum filios*) what amounted to a Roman education. Tacitus does not object to his father-in-law's Romanizing measures. However, he does fault the Britons for succumbing to the vices of Roman decadence: porticoes, baths, and sumptuous meals, which are the same three excesses satirized by Juvenal: *balnea ... porticus ... cenatio* (7.278–85) and now no longer in fashion in the capital.

Roman identity was not an ethnic identity as it was for the Greeks. Rather, Romans understood "being Roman" as a cultural identity that was fluid and often contested. As Woolf explains, Roman culture involved

> the range of objects, beliefs and practices that were characteristic of people who considered themselves to be, and were widely acknowledged as, Roman .... Often the acceptance as 'Roman' (or at least as not 'un-Roman') of some new style or practice—marble statues, silk clothes, homosexuality—entailed debate and

---

[135] According to Suetonius (*Claud.* 15), the wearing of a toga was restricted to Roman citizens. The fact that Britons are mentioned by Tacitus as wearing togas reflects the significant expansion of citizenship during the Flavian period (Sherwin-White, *The Roman Citizenship*, 258). In *Annals* 3.40, Tacitus expresses his mild disgust for the transformation of citizenship in his own day, whereas Pliny's (*Pan.* 37.2–5) lack of personal comment when mentioning the matter reveals how commonplace the extension of citizenship had become (ibid.).

[136] Tacitus, *Agr.* 21 (Hutton and Peterson, LCL). Contrary to Tacitus' depiction of Romanization in Britain, even as local elites adopted many aspects of Roman culture, native customs were not completely done away with but rather existed alongside or in combination with Roman customs (Carl Mazurek, "*Agricola* 21 and the Flavian Romanization of Britain," *Hirundo* VI [2007]: 45).

conflict. Becoming Roman was not a matter of acquiring a ready-made cultural package, then, so much as joining the insiders' debate about what that package did or ought to consist of at that particular time.[137]

In the West, provincial elites were encouraged to emulate Roman style as a way to demonstrate their adherence to the values of *humanitas* and reject their savage past.[138] In the East, however, Roman elites emulated rather than rejected the Greek past.[139] Sherwin-White describes Romanization as a process in which subjects demonstrate their loyalty to Rome. In the West, such loyalty took on a material form, whereas in the East, loyalty manifested in its devotion to the emperors.[140]

Conclusion

At the time when Herodotus offers four indications of Greekness (blood, language, religion, and customs), Greek dialects varied significantly, and local religious rites figured more importantly than shared Panhellenic festivals. These disparities between fact and fiction or between precise and loose self-definition mattered less when Greeks chose to define themselves against or in contrast to the barbarian. However, this antithesis between Greek and barbarian that arose sharply after the Persian Wars had to be reimagined and reconfigured during the Hellenistic Period and Roman Period (this chapter focusing on the first two centuries) when Greeks confronted different circumstances and different others. While Greek self-definition was fluid, the importance of common blood remained fixed throughout the centuries. Culture did not determine whether a person was a Greek, as is evident in the way Greeks, especially in the East, could adopt Roman material culture without losing a strong sense of Greekness. They could remain Greek while becoming Roman because Greeks did not define themselves according to material culture, and Romans did not require Greeks to give up their Greekness so long as they were willing to adopt aspects of Romanness.

Because Greek ethnic identity was based on fluid and fixed notions of shared descent, Dionysius of Halicarnassus (ca. 20 BCE) could cope with Greek subjugation to the Romans by reconfiguring the past in order to prove that Rome was originally a "Greek city" (*Antiq. Rom.* 1.89.1) made up the Greeks of the highest pedigree:

---

[137] Woolf, *Becoming Roman*, 11.
[138] Woolf, "Becoming Roman," 128. On the Romanization of Gaul, see Woolf, *Becoming Roman*. On the Batavians in the early Roman empire, see Nico Roymans, *Ethnic Identity and Imperial Power: The Batavians in the Early Roman Empire* (Amsterdam: Amsterdam University Press, 2004).
[139] Woolf, "Becoming Roman," 128.
[140] Sherwin-White, *The Roman Citizenship*, 222. For a classic study on the Greek cults of the Roman emperor in Asia minor and why Greeks in the east treated him like a god, see S. R. F. Price, *Rituals and Power: The Roman Imperial Cult in Asia Minor*, rev. ed. (Cambridge: Cambridge University Press, 1985). See Stephen Mitchell, *Anatolia: Land, Men, and Gods in Asia Minor, Vol I: The Celts and the Impact of Roman Rule* (Oxford: Clarendon, 1993).

> For one will find no nation that is more ancient or more Greek than these. But the admixture of the barbarians with the Romans, by which the city forgot many of its ancient institutions, happened at a later time .... For many others by living among barbarians have in a short time forgotten all their Greek heritage (τὸ Ἑλληνικὸν ἀπέμαθον), so that they neither speak the Greek language nor observe the customs of the Greeks nor acknowledge the same gods nor have the same equitable laws.[141]

One could still be Greek through blood ties, while being deprived of other Greek identity markers, namely Greek language, religion, and customs. The antithetical Greek vs. "other" way of constructing Greek ethnic identity, first expressed by Herodotus as a result of the Greek–Persian conflict, did not manifest itself in a third category for the Romans, who did not fit as easily under the category of "barbarian." Thus, Greeks such as Dionysius incorporated the Romans into their Greek past as a way to cope with their subjugation to the seemingly impregnable military power of Rome. He also did this to deal with ironic tension that Roman society was based on both Greek and Roman elements.[142] In lamenting how those of pristine Greek origin could in a short time forget their illustrious heritage and behave as "the most savage of all barbarians" (89.4), Dionysius reiterates just how important origins mattered for Greek self-understanding, regardless of whether a Greek acted less like a Greek and more like the barbarians who surrounded them.

The way in which Greeks understood and maintained a resilient sense of Greekness over the centuries was by dividing the world between Greek and barbarian, orienting themselves to their illustrious past in order to cope with their present state of affairs, and appealing to the myth of common descent. As we shall see in the next chapter, Peter also employs the similar strategy of appealing to the past (election and birth story) and to common descent (shared patrilineage and blood ties) to define and shape for his addressees what it means to be Christian in a society hostile to this identity. Peter, however, insists on the importance of living according to a distinct way of life patterned after the example of Christ and characterized by a culture of holiness and obedience. Their past election and future inheritance must have present ramifications for the way they are to live among Gentiles and as people born anew to a living hope through the resurrection of Christ from the dead.

---

[141] Dionysius of Halicarnassus. *Antiq. rom.* 1.89.3–4 (Cary, LCL).
[142] See Emilio Gabba, *Dionysius and the History of Archaic Rome* (Sather Classical Lectures; vol. 56; Berkeley: University of California Press, 1991).

3

Common Blood: Establishing a New Patrilineage through the Blood of Christ

Introduction

This chapter examines the ways in which Peter creates, in effect, a shared ethnicity as he seeks to forge a distinct, cohesive, and positive group identity for his beleaguered addressees who must endure anti-Christian hostility and subsequent persecution.[1] I argue that he constructs Christian identity as an ethnic identity by using ethnic language and an early form of ethnic reasoning.[2] That is, Peter employs the vocabulary of shared blood, peoplehood (e.g., *ethnos*, *laos*, *genos*), and human difference as an important point of entry for defining what it means to be Christian and as a means for his addressees to define themselves in contrast to "outsiders" (i.e., the "Gentiles"). By ethnic identity, I mean the sense of peoplehood that arises from putative claims of shared blood, common language, shared religious practice, and shared customs based on Herodotus' elastic understanding of ethnicity (*Histories* 8.144). By ethnic identity, I am also referring to the definition given by modern sociologists. In general, "ethnic" can be described as being about descent and culture and "ethnic groups" as descent and culture communities.[3] More specifically,

---

[1] There is evidence throughout the letter of hostility, persecution, and suffering in the form of slander, ridicule, false accusation, stigmatization, and even possibly formal charges made against them (1.6, 2.12, 2.19, 2.21–5, 3.9, 14–16, 17; 4.1, 13–16; 5.8–10; note especially 4.12: Ἀγαπητοί, μὴ ξενίζεσθε τῇ ἐν ὑμῖν πυρώσει πρὸς πειρασμὸν ὑμῖν γινομένῃ ὡς ξένου ὑμῖν συμβαίνοντος), which Paul Holloway refers to as "social prejudice" (*Coping with Prejudice*, 40–66). I agree with David Horrell that it is unnecessary to exclude the possibility that the letter's addressees experienced suffering in the form of legal trials and executions even while holding the majority view that the hostility and suffering in the letter were primarily social or popular in nature, as the situation depicted and reflected in the Pliny–Trajan correspondence bears some resemblance to the situation portrayed in 1 Peter. See Horrell, "The Label Χριστιανός." See also Holloway, *Coping with Prejudice*, 18. Contra Elliott, *1 Peter: A New Translation with Introduction and Commentary* (AB 37B; New York: Doubleday, 2000), 792–4. The focus of this study, however, is not on *why* the letter's recipients are suffering, but on *how* Peter seeks to help them to cope with and respond to suffering. I date the letter of 1 Peter somewhere around 70–95 CE. For an overview of the combination of relevant factors in favor of this broad dating, see Horrell, *1 Peter*, NTG (London: T&T Clark, 2008), 20–3.

[2] See pp. 7–9 for how I apply Buell's definition of "ethnic reasoning" to my study of 1 Peter.

[3] Fenton, *Ethnicity*, 3.

Anthony D. Smith argues that *ethnies* (ethnic groups) "habitually exhibit," although in varying degrees, the following characteristics:

1. a common *proper name*, to identity and express the "essence" of the community;
2. a myth of *common ancestry*, a myth rather than a fact, a myth that includes the idea of a common origin in time and place and that gives an *ethnie* a sense of fictive kinship …;
3. shared *historical memories*, or even better, shared memories of a common past or pasts, including heroes, events, and their commemoration;
4. one or more *elements of common culture*, which need not be specified but normally include religion, customs, and language;
5. a *link* with a *homeland*, not necessarily its physical occupation by the *ethnie*, only its symbolic attachment to the ancestral land, as with diaspora peoples;
6. a *sense of solidarity* on the part of at least some sections of the *ethnie's* population.[4]

It is striking how Herodotus' four markers of Greekness parallel Smith's definition, particularly the myth of a common ancestry, elements of common culture, and a sense of solidarity. It is also remarkable how the letter of 1 Peter "includes all aspects in some form or other" of the features of *ethnie* described by Smith.[5]

Peter constructs an ethnicity for his predominantly Gentile audience[6] in the following ways: (1) by establishing their relationship to God and to one another, not along shared biological bloodlines or territorial attachments but through election, new birth, and the ransoming blood of Christ; (2) by instructing them to live according to a new culture characterized by obedience and holiness; (3) by linking them with a heavenly homeland and as members of an eschatological household of God and by depicting them as a diaspora people who are dislocated from mainstream society; (4) by drawing on Israel's identity-defining designations to describe his addressees as a rhetorical strategy to construct Christian identity as an ethnoreligious identity—i.e., as a divinely engendered people characterized by religio-cultural practices patterned after the example of Christ; and (5) by strengthening their sense of communal identity as Χριστιανοί, so that when they suffer as a result of this identity, they do so for the right reasons and in the right ways. Peter constructs Christian identity as an ethnic identity because he seeks to prevent his addressees from reverting back to

---

[4] Hutchinson and Smith, "Introduction," 6–7. For a fuller discussion of Smith's definition, see Anthony D. Smith, *The Ethnic Origins of Nations* (Oxford: Oxford University Press, 1986), 22–31. Love L. Sechrest (*A Former Jew: Paul and the Dialectics of Race* [LNTS 410; London: T&T Clark, 2009], 48–50) and David G. Horrell ("'Race', 'Nation', 'People': Ethnoracial Identity Construction in 1 Pet. 2.9," in *Becoming Christian*, 133–63, 159) also draw on Smith's work and present his definition of an ethnic community.

[5] Horrell, "'Race', Nation', 'People': Ethnoracial Identity Construction in 1 Pet. 2.9," in *Becoming Christian: Essays on 1 Peter and the Making of Christian Identity* (LNTS 394; London: Bloomsbury T&T Clark, 2013), 33–63, 159.

[6] See pp. 10–11 for the ethnic-religious composition of 1 Peter's intended audience.

their former way of life and help them live faithfully among Gentiles as an elect and holy people of God born anew to a living hope.

Establishing God as Father

Jonathan Hall asserts, "Above all else, though, it must be the myth of shared descent which ranks paramount among the features that distinguish ethnic from other social groups, and more often than not, it is proof of descent that will act as a defining criterion of ethnicity."[7] What makes shared descent "true" is the recognition and consensual agreement of *putative* shared ancestry.[8] In that same vein, the blood that runs through and unites the Christian communities scattered throughout Asia Minor is not biological but spiritual. Peter constructs what Hall would call a myth of origins for his addressees. Christ's blood has ransomed them from the meaningless conduct passed down from their forefathers and enables them to be included in Israel's vocation as the people of God (1.18; 2.9–10). What makes Christians members of the same "spiritual house" (οἶκος πνευματικός) (2.5; cf. 4.17) is not that they share the same ancestors but that they share the same heavenly Father. This relationship with the Father and then with each other as his children is made possible as a result of the person, body, and blood of Jesus Christ, who died and rose again for them (1.3, 18, 2.22–4).

In 1 Peter, the idea of shared descent arises as Peter establishes his addressees' elect status. In the letter's prescript, Peter begins to delineate a spiritual genealogy for his predominantly Gentile audience based on the fact that Christians are "chosen (ἐκλεκτός) … according to the foreknowledge of God the Father" (1.1–2) and "born anew to a living hope through the resurrection of Jesus Christ from the dead" (1.3b). Such descriptors serve as basis for their identity as "people of God" (2.10). Rather than use the language and logic of adoption (υἱοθεσία) by the Spirit to explain how Gentiles are also sons and heirs of God as Paul does,[9] Peter links the idea of election to that of spiritual regeneration (ἀναγεννάω) to explain how his addressees can invoke God as Father and understand themselves as God's children (1.3, 14, 17, 23).[10]

According to Peter, God the Father elects believers "as the result[11] of his foreknowledge" (κατὰ πρόγνωσιν θεοῦ πατρός) in 1.2a. "Foreknowledge"

---

[7] Hall, *Ethnic Identity*, 25.
[8] Ibid.
[9] Rom 8.15–17, 23; Gal 4.1–7; cf. Eph 1.3–6. Caroline Johnson Hodge addresses how Paul uses the metaphor of adoption by the Spirit to reconstruct the origins of Gentiles in *If Sons, Then Heirs: A Study of Kinship and Ethnicity in the Letters of Paul* (Oxford: Oxford University Press, 2007), 67–77. For a thorough investigation of how Paul uses υἱοθεσία in his letters, see James M. Scott, *Adoption as Sons of God: An Exegetical Investigation into the Background of ΥΙΟΘΕΣΙΑ in the Pauline Corpus* (WUNT 2, vol. 48; Tübingen: J. C. B. Mohr [Paul Siebeck], 1992).
[10] The meaning of ἀναγεννάω conveyed in 1 Pet 1.3 appears by implication in John 3.3–8 when Jesus tells Nicodemus that "no one can see the kingdom of God without being born from above" (ἐὰν μή τις γεννηθῇ ἄνωθεν, οὐ δύναται ἰδεῖν τὴν βασιλείαν τοῦ θεοῦ).
[11] So, e.g., J. Kelly, *A Commentary on the Epistles of Peter and of Jude* (New York: Harper & Row, 1969), 42; Goppelt, *Der Erste Petrusbrief*, ed. Ferdinand Hahn, KEK 12/1 (Göttingen: Vandenhoeck & Ruprecht, 1978), 92. So also, Lauri Thurén, *Argument and Theology in 1 Peter: The Origins of Christian Paraenesis* (JSNTSup 114; Sheffield: Sheffield Academic Press, 1995), 92.

(πρόγνωσις) expresses the loving intentionality of God the Father to choose Christians to become his children (1.14), household (2.5; 4.17), and people (1.9-10).[12] The use of "foreknowledge" in 1.2a parallels God's primordial "choosing" (προεγνωσμένου)[13] of Christ in 1.20, which Peter also depicts, along with Christ's "appearing" (φανερωθέντος), as a loving act of God the Father done "for the sake of" the letter's addressees (δι' ὑμᾶς). The emphatic position of δι' ὑμᾶς in 1.20 reinforces the point Peter seeks to make in 1.10-12, namely, that the prophets, in "prophesying about the grace which God would give to you," understood that "their service was not rendered for their own benefit, but for yours."[14] The repeated use of the second person plural in 1.10 (εἰς ὑμᾶς), 1.12 (ὑμῖν), and 1.20 (δι' ὑμᾶς) serves to reinforce the point Peter has already made by emphasizing God's foreknowledge in 1.2 and 1.20. Namely, God's election of Christ and election of Christians was not a divine afterthought or an arbitrary decision but a carefully planned and much-anticipated choice[15] of a loving, caring, and gracious father *on behalf* of the estranged and persecuted Christians addressed in the letter.[16] What God has done in eternity past in choosing or calling Christians "finds historical expression in the social experience of the individuals and a community."[17]

God's eternal decision to preordain the Christians addressed in the letter is made effective through the "Spirit's sanctifying activity" (ἐν ἁγιασμῷ πνεύματος) (1.2b).[18]

---

[12] Cf. Jdt 9.6; 11.19; Acts 2.23. With J. Ramsey Michaels (*1 Peter* [WBC 49; Waco, TX: Word, 1988]. 10-11) and Goppelt (*A Commentary on I Peter*, 72-3). Goppelt understands πρόγνωσις as divine predetermination that is "as effective as election" (ibid., 73). Michaels sees πρόγνωσις as "synonymous with what Peter five times refers to as being 'called'" (1.15; 2.9, 21; 3.9; 5.10)" (*1 Peter*, 10).

[13] Cf. Rom 8.29; 11.2.

[14] For an in-depth treatment of 1 Pet 1.10-12, see Benjamin Sargent, *Written to Serve: The Use of Scripture in 1 Peter* (LNTS 547; London: Bloomsbury T&T Clark, 2015). Sargent sees in 1 Peter a "primitive apocalyptic approach" to scriptural interpretation (in contrast to a typological approach) that views the past as less important than the present. The letter, Sargent argues, does not present a theological narrative of continuity with Israel of the past and Christian communities of the present. Rather it offers a paraenetic or ecclesiological hermeneutic that views the prophets as serving the eschatological communities to whom the author writes (ibid., 18-49).

[15] Kelly notes that "foreknowledge" in 1.2 (cf. 1.20) refers less to God knowing what will happen in the future and more to "His effective choice" to call Christians "His own" and members of "the redeemed community" (*A Commentary on the Epistles of Peter and of Jude*, 42-3). Contra Paul A. Himes, *Foreknowledge and Social Identity in 1 Peter* (Eugene, OR: Pickwick, 2014). Himes argues that foreknowledge in 1 Peter is not as closely tied to God's salvific work as most scholars presume but that it should be taken in a "prescient" or "mantic" sense to mean God's knowledge of the future rather than God's foreordination (ibid., 181, 183).

[16] A similar concept of divine foreknowledge can be found in Jer 1.5, although the prophet Jeremiah does not employ the language of πρόγνωσις or προγινώσκω as we find in 1 Pet 1.2, 20: "Before I formed you in the womb, I knew you [ἐπίσταμαι], and before you came out of the womb, I sanctified you [ἁγιάζω] you; I appointed you to be a prophet to the nations." Cf. Francis Wright Beare, *The First Epistle of Peter: The Greek Text with Introduction and Notes*, 3rd ed. (Oxford: Blackwell, 1970), 76. Even prior to conception and birth, God conceived of, sanctified, and ordained the prophet Jeremiah. In the same way, Peter claims that God knew the letter's recipients before they were born anew (1.3; 1.23).

[17] Michaels, *1 Peter*, 10.

[18] Cf. 2 Thess 2.13, which employs the same phrase (ἐν ἁγιασμῷ πνεύματος) in order to convey a very similar thought: "God chose you as the first fruits for the purpose of salvation *by means of the Spirit's sanctifying activity* and belief in the truth" (italics mine). See Kelly, *Epistles of Peter*, 43.

When the phrase ἐν ἁγιασμῷ is read instrumentally,[19] followed by the subjective genitive πνεύματος,[20] it places the emphasis on the activity of the Spirit by indicating the means by which God's electing activity is accomplished. The Spirit's sanctifying activity involves setting apart for God those whom God has chosen (cf. 2.9).[21] By means of the Spirit, God makes holy those he has predestined to be holy.[22] Believers are thus redefined by their election as people who have been made holy by the Spirit.[23]

Holiness and obedience are related concepts in 1.2 (cf. 1.15, 22). In the difficult phrase εἰς ὑπακοὴν καὶ ῥαντισμὸν αἵματος Ἰησοῦ Χριστοῦ in 1.2b, the preposition εἰς and its meaning have been a source of disagreement among interpreters. The prevailing view sees εἰς as being telic in force, pointing to the goal or, more specifically, to the purpose of God's election: "for the purpose of obedience and the sprinkling of blood."[24] Francis H. Agnew proposes a convincing alternative understanding by arguing for a causal rendering of εἰς, such that Ἰησοῦ Χριστοῦ functions as a subjective genitive for both ὑπακοή and ῥαντισμὸν αἵματος and εἰς refers to the means through which God elects his people: "*because of* the obedience and sprinkling of the blood of Jesus Christ"

---

[19] So, e.g., ibid.; Beare, *The First Epistle of Peter*, 76; Ernest Best, *1 Peter, New Century Bible* (London: Oliphants, 1971), 71; Paul J. Achtemeier, *1 Peter: A Commentary on First Peter*, Hermeneia (Minneapolis: Augsburg Fortress, 1996), 86. Contra Joel B. Green, who presses for a locative reading of ἐν ("in the sanctification of the Spirit"), so that it answers the question of where those who are "not at home" might find their home: "Peter's audience has been relocated in a new space: 'in the realm of holiness engendered by the Holy Spirit'" (*1 Peter*, THNTC [Grand Rapids: Eerdmans, 2007], 19–20). See also Edward Gordon Selwyn, who renders ἐν in the locative sense to mean "in the sphere of" (*The First Epistle of St. Peter: The Greek Text with Introduction, Notes and Essays* [London: Macmillan, 1958], 119).

[20] So, e.g., Fenton John Anthony Hort, *The First Epistle of St. Peter: I.1-II.17: The Greek Text with Introductory Lecture, Commentary, and Additional Notes* (London: Macmillan, 1898), 21; Selwyn, *The First Epistle of St. Peter*, 119, 249; Michaels, *1 Peter*, 86. Contra Green who takes πνεύματος as a genitive of production. See also Victor Paul Furnish ("Elect Sojourners in Christ: An Approach to the Theology of 1 Peter," *PSTJ* 28, no. 3 [1975]: 1–11, 5), who points to the possibility of understanding the spirit as "the sphere within which."

[21] Achtemeier, *1 Peter*, 87; Charles A. Bigg, *Critical and Exegetical Commentary on the Epistles of St. Peter and St. Jude*, ICC (New York: Scribner's Sons, 1901), 92.

[22] Best: "What God had destined [Christians] to be, he now makes them to be, viz., holy" (*1 Peter*, 71). The theme of holiness is found elsewhere in the letter (1.15, 16, 19, 22; 2.5, 9; 3.15).

[23] God's elect are thus not relocated into a new space of holiness, but they have been brought into a new state of holiness.

[24] Achtemeier, *1 Peter*, 87. So, e.g., Beare, *The First Epistle of Peter*, 76; Goppelt, *A Commentary on I Peter*, 74. It is an attractive translation, since in the verses that follow (1.3–5), εἰς points to the purpose and/or result of new birth, which itself is the result of God's electing activity. Following Hans Windisch (*Die Katholischen Briefe* [3rd ed., HNT 15; Tübingen: Mohr, 1951]), many English translations gave Ἰησοῦ Χριστοῦ the dual functions as the objective genitive of ὑπακοήν and the possessive genitive of ῥαντισμὸν αἵματος, so that the phrase is rendered as "for obedience to Jesus Christ and for sprinkling of his blood" (RSV). See also, e.g., NRSV, ESV, and NASB. Selwyn describes this understanding of the genitive Ἰησοῦ Χριστοῦ to be functioning in two different ways as grammatically "not necessary" (*The First Epistle of St. Peter*, 120), while Achtemeier goes further to call it "something of a grammatical monstrosity and surely confusing to the reader/listener" (*1 Peter*, 87).

(1.1–2).²⁵ Agnew's reading puts the emphasis on God's salvific activity through Christ that parallels Peter's use of διά in 1.3c to describe how new birth is made possible "through the resurrection of Jesus Christ from the dead."

Exodus 24.3–8 provides the likely backdrop to the phrase ῥαντισμὸν αἵματος Ἰησοῦ Χριστοῦ, since the ceremony establishing the covenant between God and Israel involves the people pledging their obedience to the Lord (24.3, 7) and Moses sprinkling the blood of bull-calves on the people (LXX Exod 24.8).²⁶ The order of events in Exodus 24.3–8 account matches that of 1 Peter 1.2. That is, the emphasis on the obedience (ἀκούω) of the people in Ex 24.7 is followed in v. 8 by the sprinkling (κατασκεδάννυμι) of blood.²⁷ The possessive genitive Ἰησοῦ Χριστοῦ in 1 Peter 1.2b specifies that it is Jesus Christ's blood that consecrates this covenant between God and his elect. While the idea of atonement or of vicarious suffering is not present in the Exodus 24, the "sprinkling of the blood of Jesus Christ" in 1.2c refers to his sacrificial death, not only in the sense of blood sacrifice, "which binds the worshipper and his God together in vital communion, establishing between them a current of life in which both alike participate,"²⁸ but also in the sense that Christ's blood is liberating (λυτρόομαι) (1.18–19; cf. Heb 9.15).

Peter praises God first and foremost as ὁ θεὸς καὶ πατὴρ τοῦ κυρίου ἡμῶν Ἰησοῦ Χριστοῦ (1.3; cf. 2 Cor 1.3; Eph 1.3).²⁹ His doxological language presents God's

---

[25] Francis H. Agnew, "1 Peter 1.2—An Alternative Translation," *CBQ* 45 (1983): 68–73. For a closer analysis of the difficulties of Agnew's proposal, see Sydney H. T. Page, "Obedience and Blood-Sprinkling in 1 Peter 1.2," *WTJ* 72, no. 2 (2010): 291–8. Agnew's reading has been adopted by John H. Elliott, *1 Peter: A New Translation with Introduction and Commentary*, AB 37B (New York: Anchor Bible, 2001), 319; Earl J. Richard, *Reading 1 Peter, Jude, and 2 Peter: A Literary and Theological Commentary* (Macon, GA: Smyth & Helwys, 2000), 32; and Green, *1 Peter*, 20.

[26] So also, e.g., Francis Wright Beare, *The First Epistle of Peter: The Greek Text with Introduction and Notes* (3rd ed.; Oxford: Blackwell, 1970), 77; Best, *1 Peter*, 71–2; Selwyn, *The First Epistle of St. Peter*, 120; Kelly, *Epistles of Peter*, 44; Achtemeier, *1 Peter*, 88. Goppelt, in contrast, asserts that the formula of obedience and the sprinkling of blood "undoubtedly points to baptism," evoking early Christian tradition of baptism (cf. Heb 10.22) (*A Commentary on I Peter*, 71–2). More specifically, Goppelt suggests that the formula in 1.2b derives from a Palestinian-Syrian baptismal catechesis (cf. *Did.* 7.1), prompted by the Essenes (cf. 1 QS 3.6–8) (ibid.). Andrew Mūtūa Mbuvi suggests Num 19 (cf. Lev 16.11–19) as the more probable backdrop to 1.2b, arguing that the sprinkling of Jesus Christ's blood must be understood within the context of atonement (contra covenant) and in reference to the tabernacle, rather than the people, in order to consecrate it as the sanctuary of God (*Temple, Exile, and Identity in 1 Peter* [LNTS 345; London: T&T Clark, 2007], 33–4). Mbuvi, however, takes no account of the role of obedience in 1.2b. That said, the sprinkling of Jesus' Christ's blood could also be a possible allusion to the consecration of priests (cf. 2.9) via the sprinkling with blood, as performed by the priest Eleazar in Num 19.4.

[27] Kelly, *Epistles of Peter*, 72.

[28] Beare, *First Epistle of Peter*, 77. The possessive pronoun ἡμῶν indicates that those who confess Christ as Lord are those whom God has brought forth as a new people, linking the idea of election and confession.

[29] The fatherhood of God can be traced to passages in the Law and the Prophets, such as Ex 4.22–3, where God refers to Israel as his "firstborn son," and Hos 11.1, where God's love for Israel is likened to that of a father for his son. See Deut 32.6; 2 Sm 7.14; 1 Chr 17.13; 22.10; 28.6; Ps 68.5; 89.26; Isa 63.16; 64.8; Jer 3.4, 19; 31.9; Mal 1.6; 2.10. Other OT texts, e.g., Hos 11.1–8, speak of Israel as God's child, even though God is not mentioned explicitly as Father. The theme of God as Father has significance in other Jewish texts, e.g., Wis 2.16 and 3 Macc 5.7. God's fatherhood and Israel's election have a close connection, since being children of God means that Israel possesses a special status, favor, and intimacy with God that the other nations do not (e.g., Deut 32.4, 7–14, 36–43).

fatherhood in relation to Jesus rather than in relation to Israel.[30] Peter describes God as the father of Jesus Christ not to "supplant" God as the "God of Israel"[31] but in order to identify God's relationship to his chosen addressees "no longer only through Israel's election but conclusively through the sending of his Son."[32] The relationship between God and those whom God "begets anew" (ἀναγεννάω) (1.3, 23) is made possible through God's Son, Jesus Christ (δι' ... Ἰησοῦ Χριστοῦ), whom God resurrected from the dead. Thus, apart from God's relationship with Jesus Christ, Gentile Christians would have no relationship with God as πατήρ and no status as God's people (2.9b–10). Christ thus plays an essential role in the begetting anew of Gentile believers. However, the central agent of new birth is God the Father, whose merciful activity has created a new reality for those chosen by God (1.1–3).

The verb ἀναγεννάω appears only twice in the NT and both times in 1 Peter (1.3; 23). In the LXX, we find a few instances where God "begets" (γεννάω) Israel (Deut 32.18), David as his adopted son (Ps 2.7), and Wisdom (Prov 8.25); however, in these examples, God does not beget anew.[33] Josephus makes use of the word but in a very different sense, referring to the ashes of Sodom's fiery destruction "arising afresh" (ἀναγεννωμένη) in the fruit of what remains of the land.[34] Philodemus and Diodorus Siculus (both 1 BCE) give similar accounts of how Dionysus returned back to life after his death. According to Philodemus (*De pietate*), Dionysus is said to have had been born three times: once from his mother, another from the thigh of Zeus, and a third time, after being dismembered by the Titans. He "came back to life" (ἀναβιόω) when Rhea reassembled his limbs.[35] Diodorus similarly explains that Dionysus "experienced new birth as if for the first time" (ἐξ ἀρχῆς νέον γεννηθῆναι) when Demeter had brought his parts back together again.[36] However, in these examples, Dionysus was physically, but not spiritually, reborn or reconstituted.

The meaning of ἀναγεννάω as conveyed in 1 Peter 1.3 and 1.23 appears by implication in John 3.3–8 when Jesus tells Nicodemus that "no one can see the kingdom of God without being born from above" (ἐὰν μή τις γεννηθῇ ἄνωθεν, οὐ

God's election of Israel as his children also means that Israel is expected to honor God as their father and behave in ways that set them apart from other nations (e.g., Deut 32.5–6, 14–35; Mal 1.6). God's fatherhood is also associated with God's special covenant with David and his descendants (2 Sam 7.14), redemptive activity (Isa 63.16), compassion (Ps 103.13–14), protection and justice (Ps 68.5), and restoration of Israel back to proper relationship with God the Father (Jer 3.4, 19). See Willem A. VanGemeren, "'Abba' in the Old Testament," *JETS* 31.4 (1988): 392–3.

[30] Cf. the "Blessed be the Lord the God of Israel" doxologies found in, e.g., 1 Sam 25.32; 1 Kgs 1.48; 1 Chr 29.10; and 2 Chr 6.4.
[31] As Achtemeier suggests (*1 Peter*, 94, n. 16).
[32] Goppelt, *A Commentary on I Peter*, 80; Achtemeier, *1 Peter*, 94, n. 16.
[33] David A. deSilva, *Honor, Patronage, Kinship & Purity: Unlocking New Testament Culture* (Downers Grove, IL: InterVarsity, 2000), 43–50, 158.
[34] *J.W.* 4.484.
[35] Philodemus, *Piet.* (Henrichs, *Cron.* Erc. 5, 1975.35)(*OF* 59 I-11). In Philodemus, *On Anger* (*P.Herc.* 182, frag 17, col 2, line 19), Philodemus uses the phrase ἀναγεν[ν]ᾶ[ν πάλι]ν.
[36] Diodorus Siculus, *Bib. hist.* 3.62.6 (*OF* 59 III). Trans. Paola Corrente, "The Gods Who Die and Come Back to Life: The Orphic Dionysus and His Parallels in the Near-East (*OF* 59 I–III and 327 II)" in Miguel Herrero de Jáuregui et al., eds., *Tracing Orpheus: Studies of Orphic Fragments* (Berlin: Walter de Gruyter, 2011), 71.

δύναται ἰδεῖν τὴν βασιλείαν τοῦ θεοῦ).[37] The preposition ἄνωθεν has both spatial and temporal ambiguities, which is why Nicodemus in 3.4 understands Jesus as meaning "born again" in a temporal sense, which is a possible but limited interpretation.[38] John, however, leads his audience to take Jesus to mean the spatial "born from above" (3.31; 19.11; cf. 8.23).[39] Such a spatial interpretation accords with John's vertical dualism, which contrasts God's heavenly realm with the earthly realm.[40] Thus, being "born from above" means being born from God (3.3). Likewise being "born of water and Spirit" (3.5) refers to being spiritually reborn.[41] Understandably, Nicodemus finds it unthinkable that God would require Jews to undergo a second birth through supernatural means, since Jews were born into the covenant by natural birth.[42] According to John, one can only grasp the meaning of being "born from above" through divine revelation and can only experience such rebirth through divine intervention. While the theme of divine revelation undergirds the conversation about rebirth between Jesus and Nicodemus in John 3, the theme of divine election undergirds the concept of new birth in 1 Peter 1. That is, in 1 Peter, election (1.1-2) precedes the new birth of the letter's recipients (1.3), such that they have been chosen and foreordained by God (1.10-12, 20) to be his people (2.9-10) even *prior* to their conversion.

In 1 Peter 1.3, Peter refers to the spiritual rebirth in a believer's life that is made possible because of God's merciful initiative to raise his Son, Jesus Christ, from the dead. J. Ramsey Michaels likens the aorist active participle ἀναγεννήσας to a virtual title, "the Begetter" or "the Progenitor," which conveys that a divine and paternal act of bringing into being a new existence has taken place.[43] While believers are certainly the ones being re-begotten, God is the active agent of re-begetting. God the Father of Jesus Christ has brought forth a new people in accordance with his great mercy and by means of the resurrection of Christ from the dead. Christians can now claim God as their progenitor and can look forward to a glorious future (1.3-4) that remains secure even as life in spiritual exile is fraught with suffering, slander, hostility, hardship, and persecution (e.g., 1.5-9; 1.17; 5.4, 6, 10).

For Peter, new birth is a metaphor for the "radical transformation from a dead-ended existence to new life" (cf. 2.1, 5, 9-10, 24bc) as Peter traces believers' movement from "darkness to light" (2.9) and the subsequent transition from a former to a present existence (2.10, 25; 4.2-4; cf. 1.18-19).[44] What grows out of new birth is what Joel Green calls the "conversion of the imagination"—that is, a dramatically different way

---

[37] See also Titus 3.5-7, which connects the idea of mercy, rebirth (παλιγγενεσία), and future hope.
[38] Raymond E. Brown, *The Gospel According to John* (AB; vol. 29-29A; Garden City, NY: Doubleday, 1966), 130-1.
[39] Craig S. Keener, *The Gospel of John: A Commentary* (Peabody, MA: Hendrickson, 2003), 538.
[40] Ibid., 538-9. Both the Greeks and Jews could conceive of the gods or God "from above." See Keener, 538 n. 45 and 539 n. 46, for a list of Greek and Jewish texts that associate God with heaven.
[41] Ibid., 539. See Keener for an overview of Hellenistic rebirth and Jewish contexts for rebirth (ibid., 539-44). Keener understands the idea of re-creation found in John 3.3, 5-8 as having no direct parallel in Greek or Jewish understanding of rebirth (541, 544).
[42] Ibid., 544.
[43] Michaels, *1 Peter*, 18. Michaels suggests τόν γεννήσαντα, "the parent," as a possible NT equivalent (1 Jn 5.1; cf. LXX Deut 32.18).
[44] Elliott, *1 Peter*, 332.

of seeing, thinking, and behaving.[45] Logically then, such a decisive transformation is enacted in baptism (3.21) and can be equated with baptismal conversion.[46] However, new birth encompasses more than baptismal conversion.[47] Through the metaphor of divine re-begetting, Peter connects God's purposes with Christ's actions in order to redefine the identity of God's elect.[48]

"As Obedient Children"

The idea that believers are "chosen ... according to the foreknowledge of God the Father by means of the Spirit's sanctifying activity because of the obedience and sprinkling of the blood of Jesus Christ" (1.1–2), has consequences for those born anew to a living hope (1.3). The radical transformation of divine new birth manifests in a posture and way of conduct that appropriately reflects their relationship to God the Father. For Peter, the obedience on the part of God's children manifests in their nonconformity to the desires (ταῖς πρότερον ... ἐπιθυμίαις) which characterized their former non-Christian way of life: "As obedient children, you must no longer be shaped by the evil desires that characterized your former time of ignorance" (1.14b). While the term ἐπιθυμία could occasionally be morally neutral or even positive,[49] among Greco-Roman moral philosophers and in Israelite and Christian circles, it had generally negative connotations with overlapping shades of meanings: "insatiable craving, selfish yearning, sexual lust, uncontrolled passion (in contrast to reason), coveting, compulsive ambition, self-indulgence."[50] Peter imbues the term with pejorative meaning. By attaching to ἐπιθυμία the qualifying words σαρκικῶν (2.11) and ἀνθρώπων (4.2), Peter emphasizes the self-seeking, self-indulging, insatiable, uncontrolled, lustful nature of the moral condition

---

[45] Green, *1 Peter*, 25–6.
[46] So Elliott, *1 Peter*, 331–2. On the role of conversion in 1 Peter, see Beverly Roberts Gaventa, who sees new birth as a metaphor for baptismal conversion (*From Darkness to Light: Aspects of Conversion in the New Testament* [Philadelphia: Fortress, 1986], 130–45). Kelly states beyond a doubt: "After the address, the letter proper starts by offering praise and thanks to God for the wonderful inheritance upon which the recipients have entered through their baptism ... the baptismal note of i. 3–5 (cf. the reference to rebirth) is unmistakable" (*Epistles of Peter*, 46).
[47] So Achtemeier (*1 Peter*, 94), who sees Peter's use of ἀναγεννάω in 1.3 as having a broader meaning than baptism, while not excluding the idea of baptism as being an aspect of new birth. Achtemeier is more emphatic on the non-baptismal nature of new birth in "Newborn Babes and Living Stones: Literal and Figurative in 1 Peter," in *To Touch the Text: Biblical and Related Studies in Honor of Joseph Fitzmyer, S.J.*, eds. Maurya P. Horgan and Paul J. Kobelski (New York: Crossroad, 1989), 207–36. Here he argues that baptism is not a reference to new birth but an illustration of salvation (ibid., 224).
[48] Steven J. Kraftchick, "Reborn to a Living Hope: A Christology of 1 Peter," in *Reading 1–2 Peter and Jude: A Resource for Students* (Resources for Biblical Study 77; Atlanta: Society of Biblical Literature, 2014), 83. The letter overall is highly Christological while also being thoroughly theocentric and ecclesiastically oriented (ibid.). So Achtemeier, who regards 1 Peter as "one of the most thoroughly christological writings in the New Testament" ("Suffering Servant and Suffering Christ in 1 Peter," in *The Future of Christology: Essays in Honor of Leander E. Keck*, eds. Abraham J. Malherbe and Wayne A. Meeks [New York: Crossroad, 1993], 176).
[49] For example, Luke 22.15; Phil 1.23.
[50] Elliott, *1 Peter*, 358. For example, Seneca *Ep.* 124.3; Dio Chrysostom, *Lib. myth* 5.16; Wis 4.12; Macc 1.22; Rom 1.24; Jas 1.14–15.

characteristic of his addressees prior to conversion.⁵¹ "Desires," for Peter, also refer to the evil cravings characteristic of the surrounding Gentile culture (2.11; 4.2-4) or what Paul calls "the world" (Rom 12.2).⁵² What makes God's children obedient is that they are no longer passively "shaped" by or "conformed" (συσχηματίζομαι)⁵³ to the desires that formerly patterned their behaviors (1.14). Rather, as indicated by the adversative conjunction, ἀλλά, they must actively pattern their behavior after "the holy one who called you" (τὸν καλέσαντα ὑμᾶς ἅγιον, 1.15). As Green vividly expresses, "For Peter, 'desire' and 'holiness' appear as opposing forces each capable of drawing persons into its orbit, conforming human character and actions to its ways and so sculpting human life."⁵⁴

Peter's emphasis in 1.13-21 on disidentifying with their past underscores how Peter perceives his audience as being made up of Gentile converts. Peter does not tell his addressees to keep the commands of God. Rather, he commands them to resist the fleshly cravings and futile way of life from which Christ has liberated them (1.18-19), because they now have no place in their present and future life as elect and obedient children of God. Thus, in 1.14-17, Peter reiterates the loving nature of God the Father and presents the exhortations to not conform to the passions of their former ignorance and to be holy within a theological and relational framework: they are obedient children of a benevolent and holy Father (1.15-16; cf. 1.1-5) whose Fatherhood includes his role as judge and redeemer (1.17).⁵⁵ Just as God's identity as Father cannot be separated from his role as judge and redeemer, so also the identity of the children of God cannot be separated from their call to be obedient and holy. The importance of obedience as characterizing the children of God is reiterated in 4.17 when Peter asserts that God's judgment begins with the household of God and will end with those who do not obey the gospel of God. By contrasting those who belong to the "household of God" with those who disobey the "gospel of God," Peter wants his readers to understand in black and white terms that obedience characterizes the children of God and disobedience characterizes those who are not God's children and hence do not belong in the household of God. In 2.7-8, Peter explains that the unbelieving disobey the word because "for this purpose they were destined." Just as those chosen by God have been chosen for the purpose of obedience (1.1, 14), so also those who are by implication *not* chosen are consequently destined for disobedience. Despite these contrasts between those who believe and obey and those who do not believe and disobey, Peter maintains that God will judge both those within and outside of his household.⁵⁶

---

⁵¹ Elliott, *1 Peter*, 358-9.
⁵² So also Peter H. Davids, *The First Epistle of Peter*, NICNT (Grand Rapids: Eerdmans, 1990), 67.
⁵³ The only other place in the NT where this verb appears is in Rom 12.2.
⁵⁴ Green, *1 Peter*, 38.
⁵⁵ Best, *1 Peter*, 87.
⁵⁶ Cf. Matt 3.9; Luke 3.8, where John the Baptist warns Sadducees and Pharisees that they should not take for granted their privileged status as Abraham's children. In the case of 1 Pet 1.17 and 4.17, Peter both assures believers of their belongingness to God their Father and exhorts them to maintain a healthy or godly fear of the One who judges all people according to their actions. In light of the fact that the Lord is near (1.7, 13; 4.7) and out of reverent fear of their holy Father and Judge, Peter exhorts Christians to "be sober minded" (νήφοντες) (4.13; 4.7; 5.8) and to live according to their identity as God's children—an identity that is secure (e.g., 1.1-5; 3.14-16; 4.19; 5.7, 10) but subject to testing and judgment based on their obedient and holy conduct (1.6-7, 1.17; 4.17-18).

The idea of God as the one who calls believers recurs in 1 Peter. In 2.9 and 5.10, καλέω affirms their special elect status before God, and in 1.15; 2.21; and 3.9, καλέω provides a reason for how they should behave.[57] Being called by God is to have a special relationship with God and to live a life set apart for God, who will judge them impartially according to their "deeds" (τὸ ἔργον).[58] Their elect status and holy way of life inevitably put Christians at odds with their former values and lifestyle and to the prevailing values of the dominant culture (e.g., 2.11). Thus, Peter describes the present time in which Christian converts live (χρόνος)[59] as an alien or exilic existence (1.17; cf. 1.20).[60] Calling also reflects the intimacy between God the Father and his children. The holy one who calls believers (τὸν καλέσαντα ὑμᾶς ἅγιον) in 1.15 is the same God whom believers can call Father in 1.17.[61]

Thus, to be children of God is to be obedient *to* God. The phrase τέκνα ὑπακοῆς describes obedience as a fundamental aspect of his addressees' identity as God's children and thus as a central cultural value as God's people. They are children of God because God the Father has re-begotten them through the raising of his Son (1.3). They are obedient children of God because they have been "ransomed" from the profitless way of life passed down by their fathers with the precious blood of Christ (1.18–19). Once their status as obedient children is embraced, they can behave as the "chosen race, royal priesthood, holy nation, and people for [God's] possession" that God has called them to be in 2.9.

Connecting New Birth with Christ's Ransoming Blood

Although Peter makes no explicit mention of "blood" (αἷμα) in relation to God's "begetting anew" of his elect in 1.3, he clearly states that it is through "the resurrection of Jesus Christ from the dead" that this new existence is made possible.[62] The fact that Christ is raised from the dead (δι' ἀναστάσεως Ἰησοῦ Χριστοῦ ἐκ νεκρῶν) in 1.3 is significant and must not be overlooked. The phrase ἐκ νεκρῶν links God's begetting anew of believers to the sprinkling of the blood of Jesus Christ in 1.2 to the ransoming of believers by means of the costly blood of Christ in 1.18–19.

In 1.18–19, Peter blends the language of ransoming with sacrificial and paschal terminology: "Know that you were ransomed (ἐλυτρώθητε) from the futile way of life inherited from your ancestors, not with perishable things such as silver or gold, but with the precious blood (τιμίῳ αἵματι) of Christ, like that of a blameless and spotless lamb" (1.18–19). In classical usage, λυτρόω, though uncommon, meant to "release

---

[57] Elliott, *1 Peter*, 360.
[58] Calling in 1 Peter seems to be used synonymously with Israel's election and privileged status (ibid.). (see Isa 41.8–9; 42.6; 43.1; 45.3; 46.11; 48.12, 15).
[59] In contrast to their ταῖς πρότερον ἐν τῇ ἀγνοίᾳ in 1.14.
[60] For a temporal map of 1.13–21 and a helpful treatment on the significance of time in 1 Peter, see Green, *1 Peter*, 36–47.
[61] Cf. Isa 8.4; Jer 3.4, 19, where calling God Father is a privilege of God's children, whom God expects to act in faithful obedience.
[62] Cf. Acts 26.23; Rom 1.4; 6.5; 1 Cor 15.12, 21; Phil 3.10.

upon payment of the ransom" and in the middle to "redeem" or "ransom."[63] By the first century, λύτρον became a technical term for the money paid over to free a slave or buy a prisoner of war.[64] The verb λυτρόω occurs over nearly 100 times in the LXX (e.g., Exod 6.6; Lev 25.33; 2 Sam 7.23; 1 Macc 4.11; Ps 71.14), frequently in reference to God's "redeeming," "rescuing," or "ransoming" of Israel from slavery in Egypt (e.g., Exod 6.6; Deut 7.8; 9.26; 15.15; 21.18; 24.18) and from Babylonian exile (e.g., Isa 45.13; 52.3). In the NT, λυτρόω occurs only here and two other places and always in the middle or passive voice (Luke 24.21 and Titus 2.14). In 1 Peter 1.18–19, God serves as the active agent who ransoms believers through the blood of Christ, making it possible for them to live in reverent fear as obedient and holy children and not according to the impulses or desires of their former ignorance (1.14–17). The Petrine use of λυτρόομαι appears to be inspired in part by the concept of God's divine deliverance of Israel from slavery and exile,[65] as Peter conveys the idea that God ransomed Gentile believers from their "Egypt-like bondage"[66] to the way of life (1.15, 17) handed down to them from the fathers (πατροπαράδοτος). To Peter's Gentile readers, ἐλυτρώθητε would have likely brought to mind the Roman custom of sacral manumission, a process by which a slave (or his benefactor) put money into a god's temple treasury so as to be "ransomed" or "purchased" by that god, becoming the deity's property but a free person in society.[67] Peter's injunction in 2.16 to live as "free people" (ἐλεύθεροι) suggests that he thought of his readers in this way.[68] However, the fact that Peter cites the "blood of Christ" in 1.19 as the means through which believers are redeemed suggests that Peter drew from the early Christian tradition that reflected on the redemptive significance of Christ's death.[69]

Through his mention of corruptible "silver or gold" (cf. 1.7), Peter alludes to Isaiah 52.3, which refers to ransom without price ("you were sold for nothing and not with silver will you be ransomed") and extends it with Christ's blood. Christ's blood is the price paid for God's ransoming of believers, and his blood is τίμιος, not only because it is priceless but also because it is "precious" in the sight of God (2.4, 6).[70] The sacrificial nature of Christ's blood is made clearer when Peter likens it to that of a perfect lamb

---

[63] Beare, *First Epistle of Peter*, 103.
[64] Kelly, *Epistles of Peter*, 73.
[65] So also Richard, *Reading 1 Peter, Jude, and 2 Peter*, 64; Achtemeier, *1 Peter*, 127; Elliott, *1 Peter*, 369.
[66] Kelly, *Epistles of Peter*, 64; Richard, *Reading 1 Peter, Jude, and 2 Peter*, 74.
[67] Michaels, *1 Peter*, 64; Richard, *Reading 1 Peter, Jude, and 2 Peter*, 64. On sacral manumission, see Adolf Deissmann, *Light from the Ancient East: The New Testament Illustrated by Recently Discovered Texts of the Graeco-Roman World*, trans. Lionel R. M. Strachan (London: Hodder and Stoughton, 1911), 319–28.
[68] Michaels, *1 Peter*, 64.
[69] Mark 10.45; Matt 20.28. See also, e.g., Rom 3.24–5; Eph 1.7; 1 Tim 2.6; Heb 9.12, 15. Elliott, *1 Peter*, 370; Achtemeier, *1 Peter*, 127; Michaels, *1 Peter*, 63. Elliott argues for the influence of "a specifically Christian tradition in which the thought of Jesus as vicarious ransom for all (Mark 10.45) was developed through the use of Isa 53" (*1 Peter*, 370). While Peter may be alluding to Isa 53 in 1.18–19, he makes the parallel between God's suffering servant and Christ much more explicit in 2.21–25. See Michaels, *1 Peter*, 63–4.
[70] LXX Ps 115.6.

(ὡς ἀμνοῦ ἀμώμου καὶ ἀσπίλου).[71] As described in the Hebrew Scripture,[72] Christ fulfills the requirements for being a cultically "unblemished" (ἄμωμος) victim but is also morally "blameless," never having committed sin or spoken deceitfully (2.22). And while there are many places from the Hebrew Scriptures from where Peter may have drawn his language comparing Jesus as "a lamb without blemish or spot," it is "especially the image of the lamb[73] ... that brings home to Christian readers the christological, cruciform character of their new life. Christ is God's means for their release from slavery and will be presented as their model for conduct in the midst of suffering" (see 2.21–2; 4.13).[74]

Peter presumes in 1.18–19 that Christ's blood has redemptive power to liberate Christians from their past, so that they can live a radically transformed existence. This transformation had already been inaugurated when God caused them to be born anew through the resurrection of Jesus Christ from the dead (1.3). However, the focus of redemption is not sin and its consequences but "the futile way of life inherited from your ancestors."[75] The ransoming blood of Christ enables Christians to live into their entirely new identity and situation as children of God because it liberates them from having to live according to the profitless ways inherited from their ancestors, thereby disinheriting them from the dead-end ways of their former lineage (see 4.3–4). The price for this freedom was the "precious" or "costly blood of Christ" (1.19). Because of Christ's death and resurrection, those born anew can live "for a living hope" (1.3c), "for a heavenly inheritance that does not diminish, degrade, or depreciate in value" (1.4a), and "for a salvation ready to be revealed" (1.5b).[76] New birth is linked with Christ's blood because God's regenerative and redemptive activity is enacted by the death and resurrection of Christ.

The relationship between Christ's bloodshed and new birth is made clearer in 3.18–22 (cf. 2.24–5). Christ was "put to death (θανατόω) in the flesh but was made alive in the spirit" (v. 18). In this flesh-spirit contrast,[77] "put to death" refers to Christ's crucifixion, and "made alive" is another way of saying "raised from the dead."[78] When Christ died, Peter Davids explains, "he died as a whole person, not simply as a body (another meaning of 'flesh'). Christ was made alive (and note the *made* alive, for here, as usual, the action of the Father in raising him from the dead is assumed) because of his relationship to God."[79] In 3.21, Peter explicitly links baptism to salvation

---

[71] See Acts 20.28 and Heb 9.11–14.
[72] See, e.g., Exod 29.39; Lev 1.10; 3.6; Num 6.14; also Heb 9.14. Richard, *Reading 1 Peter, Jude, and 2 Peter*, 65.
[73] The image of the lamb is employed in the sacrificial system (Num 28–9; cf. Heb 9.11f), the Passover tradition (Exod 12.5—1 Cor 5.7 and John 19.36; cf. Exod 12.46) and the tradition of the Suffering Servant (Isa 53—John 1.29, 36; Acts 8.32). See ibid.
[74] Ibid.
[75] Green, *1 Peter*, 42.
[76] In the phrase εἰς ἐλπίδα ζῶσαν is the first three successive preposition εἰς phrases that identify the results of new birth.
[77] See Matt 26.41; John 6.63; Gal 5.16–25; Rom 8.1–17.
[78] Cf. John 5.32; Rom 4.17; 8.11; 1 Cor 15.22, 36, 45. Davids, *First Epistle of Peter*, 136.
[79] Ibid., 137.

δι' ἀναστάσεως Ἰησοῦ Χριστοῦ, which is the same phrase used in 1.3 to explain the means through which believers are born anew. Although Peter does not include ἐκ νεκρῶν in 3.18, Christ's death is undoubtedly implied. Although Peter does not include αἷμα in 1.3, his atoning bloodshed that leads to his death is assumed (1.2b). God has ransomed believers from their former existence through Christ's costly blood as of a spotless lamb 1.18-19. Thus, what links all the merciful acts of God the Father—election, new birth, and ransoming—is the blood of Christ (1.19).[80]

Employing the Logic of Patrilineal Descent

Through God's election of believers, the Spirit's sanctifying activity, the sprinkling of the blood of Jesus Christ, and Christ's resurrection from the dead, Peter constructs a new logic of kinship that in turn enables his Gentile readers to disidentify with the way of life passed on to them from their ancestors, so that God the Father is their progenitor and they can trace a new line of patrilineal descent to Jesus Christ, God's Son. Caroline Johnson Hodge describes the ideology of patrilineal descent as one that is based on the perception of "natural" kinship.[81] By "natural," Hodge means a logic of kinship that has authority because it is based on ideas of shared "blood," "flesh," and "seed"[82] and organic, biological processes on the one hand; and on the other hand, it appears removed from human agency and beyond human understanding and control.[83] This natural logic thus lends itself to "an aura of permanence and infallibility" while it also organizes and legitimates social relationships and identities in ways that are fluid and malleable.[84] This paradoxical dynamic found in the logic of kinship, in which blood ties are believed to be natural and immutable and yet can be manipulated and adjusted, also occurs with ethnic identities, which explains why ancient sources often blur the distinction between claims of kinship and ethnicity.[85]

Peter constructs a genealogy of his addressees in a manner that bears some resemblance to the way in which Julius Caesar constructs his own genealogy. In a eulogy to his aunt, Caesar claims, "My aunt Julia derived her descent, by the mother, from a race of kings, and by her father, from the Immortal Gods."[86] By "a race of kings" (*genus ab regibus*), Caesar means that her mother's family, Marcii Reges, can trace their stock from Ancus Marcius. By "the immortal gods" (*diis immortalibus*), he means that

---

[80] On the transition between the letter's prescript (1.1-2) and blessing section (beginning in 1.3), Philip Tite explains that the community's reception of grace and peace ("May grace and peace be yours in full measure," NET) at the end of 1.2 correlates to the praise of God the ("Blessed be") in 1.3 ("The Compositional Function of the Petrine Prescript: A Look at 1 Pet 1.1-3," *JETS* 39.1 [1996]: 47-56, 52). God bestows his gracious gifts of election, new birth, and living hope on account of his great mercy (Norman Hillyer, *1 and 2 Peter, Jude* [Peabody, MA: Hendrickson, 1992], 31).

[81] Hodge, *If Sons, Then Heirs*, 20.

[82] Terms that are all found in 1 Peter (αἷμα in 1.2; 19; σπορά in 1.23; σάρξ in 1.23; 3.18, 21; 4.1-2, 6).

[83] Hodge, *If Sons, Then Heirs*, 20.

[84] Ibid., 20-1.

[85] Ibid., 21.

[86] Suetonius, *Divus Julius* 6 (trans. Thomson).

her father's family can trace their stock as stemming from a branch of Aeneas, who belongs to the family tree of Venus. Caesar underscores his relationship to his aunt because he assumes that the pedigree of noble ancestors can serve to legitimate his own right to rule over and be most honored among mortals: "Our stock therefore has at once the sanctity of kings, whose power is supreme among mortal men, and the claim to reverence which attaches to the Gods, who hold sway over kings themselves."[87]

Julius Caesar claimed not only to possess Venus' patronage, but also and more importantly to descend from Venus' lineage.[88] He does so by tracing his aunt's bloodlines back to Venus. Peter claims that his addressees descend from God's lineage. He does so by tracing their relationship to God back to their election (1.1–2), new birth (1.3; 23), status as "obedient children" (1.14), and liberation from the "profitless conduct" handed down to them by their ancestors (1.18). However, unlike Caesar, Peter does not claim his addressees have biological ties to Christ. Rather, he asserts that their relation to God has no natural explanation, but only a supernatural justification with life-altering ramifications.

The assumption behind the ideology of patrilineal descent in the Greco-Roman world was that lineage could be traced through a line of male descendants, such that sons inherited the property of their fathers and incorporated their wives into their own line.[89] Philo, for example, explains how the nation (ὁ ἔθνος) of Israelites was divided into twelve tribes, each led by an appointed patriarch. They remained, however, united by their common decent from the same father, grandfather, and great-grandfather who were "the original founders of the whole nation" (γεγόνασιν ἀρκηγέται τοῦ ἔθνους):

> When the nation was originally divided into twelve tribes, there were at once appointed patriarchs equal in number to the tribes, being not merely of one house or family, but connected by a still more genuine relationship: for they were all brothers having one and the same father; and the father and grandfather of these men were, with their father, the original founders of the whole nation.[90]

Philo reflects the prevailing normative assumptions about descent and peoplehood in the ancient Mediterranean,[91] as each tribe professed a relationship to Abraham by virtue of Isaac and Jacob, which legitimated their worthiness to exist as a nation. What makes the twelve tribes' relationship "more genuine" (γνησιωτέρας) than even coming from the same house or family is that they belong to the most worthy and, hence, truest lineage.

---

[87] Suetonius, *Divus Julius* 6, (trans. J. C. Rolfe).
[88] Pompey also claimed Venus as his divine patroness, but it was Caesar who had already laid claim to her as his divine ancestress. According to Plutarch, Caesar's rival, Pompey, "feared lest the race of Caesar, which went back to Venus, was to receive glory and splendour through him" (*Pompey*, 68.2 [Perrin]).
[89] Hodge, *If Sons, Then Heirs*, 22. In reality, exceptions to and variations on this rule were common both out of necessity and strategy.
[90] Philo, *Rewards*, 57 (trans. C. D. Yonge).
[91] Hodge, *If Sons, Then Heirs*, 23.

In reality, exceptions to and variations on the ideology of patrilineal descent were common both out of necessity and strategy.[92] Julius Caesar, as mentioned above, calls attention to his aunt's maternal ancestry in order to prove her worth and increase his own. Hodge lists three related assumptions held by families or ethnic groups organized around patrilineal ideology: "(1) members descend from a common male ancestor; (2) they have inherited the characteristics of that ancestor; (3) they understand themselves as a corporate group linked by some organic connection."[93] While not all patrilineal groups assert these three assumptions simultaneously or hold to these assumptions exclusively, they do accept the idea that shared blood is a "natural" or inherent bond and that "blood relations" are authoritative in determining one's worth.[94]

Hodge asserts that in the ancient Mediterranean world, "you are your ancestors."[95] This explains precisely why Julius Caesar draws attention to his own remarkable ancestral ties and why the Apostle Paul goes to such great lengths to incorporate Gentiles into the lineage of Abraham. David deSilva also proposes that for people in the ancient world, "their merits begin with the merits (or debits) of their lineage."[96] Thus, those who choose to follow Christ inevitably change the way in which they relate to others. Rather than ascribe honor or status based on "the reputation of one's ancestral house,"[97] Christians belong to a new household (2.4; 4.17) with new sibling relationships (1.22), and they have a new Father in God (1.2, 3, 14, 17). At the same time, they are not to repudiate their family ties (2.18, 3.1-7), even if their families may repudiate or reject them (see 1.6-9; 3.9-14; 4.12-16).[98] According to the logic expressed in 1 Peter 2.19-20, followers of Christ must seek God's approval, even if it means losing the approval of others and suffering for the sake of Christ and their new identity in Christ (e.g., 3.14-17; 4.14-17). That said, Peter exhorts Christian slaves (2.18-25), wives (3.1-6), and husbands (3.7) to maintain peaceful relationships with their masters, husbands, and wives, respectively.

It is because Christians were "ransomed with the precious blood of Christ, as a lamb without blemish or spot" that they are now free to live according to new values and not those handed down to them by their ancestors (1.18-19).[99] Christ's sacrificial

---

[92] Ibid., 22.
[93] Ibid., 23.
[94] Ibid.
[95] Ibid., 19.
[96] deSilva, *Honor, Patronage, Kinship & Purity*, 158.
[97] Ibid.
[98] From the perspective of Roman elites and probably other Romans, too, Christian converts were the ones who repudiated their family ties, not the other way around. See, e.g., *Contra Celsum* 3.58. Peter, in contrast, sees Christ's ransoming blood as liberating Gentile converts from the worst of their inherited values, so that they can live as a new people living according to new values.
[99] In the LXX, the word ματαία, meaning "futile," "foolish," or "vain," describes Gentile idols (e.g., Lev 17.7; Jer 8.19; 10.15; cf. Acts 14.15). In 1 Peter, it refers to the behavior (ἀναστροφή) handed down from their ancestors (πατροπαράδοτος). Implicit in but not exclusive to one's inherited "profitless behavior" (ματαίας ... ἀναστροφῆς) is the worship of traditional gods. According to Selwyn, the term more broadly describes the ways of those who do not worship the true God, either because of their ignorance of God or apostasy from God. Selwyn, *The First Epistle of St. Peter*, 145. Because the word is used with πατροπαράδοτος in 1 Pet 1.18, Selwyn deems it likely that it refers to Gentile paganism (ibid.). Cf. Eph 4.17: ἐν ματαιότητι τοῦ νοὸς αὐτῶν (of the Gentiles).

and ransoming act on their behalf enables them to disidentify with their past and reidentify with their new existence: "[Christ] himself bore our sins in his body on the tree, so that we might die to sin and live to righteousness" (2.24). Furthermore, the Exodus imagery possibly serves to legitimize the addressees' identity as God's people, since they are God's people because God redeemed them from slavery, just as God redeemed Israel from Egypt and adopted them as sons.[100] Like Caesar, who sees his relationship to his aunt and, by association, to Venus as legitimating his right to rule, Peter wants believers to see their relationship to Christ and, by his ransoming act, to God the Father as legitimating their existence as an elect and holy community who belong to God (2.5, 9–10), are shaped by his word (1.23–5; 2.1–3), and characterized by obedience (e.g., 1.2, 14; 3.6) and honorable conduct (e.g., 2.11–12).

As mentioned above, Peter does not describe his addressees as "sons" nor make any connection between them and a legitimating ancestor, such as Abraham, as a way to inscribe them into the patrilineal logic espoused by Paul in Galatians and Romans.[101] Instead, he addresses the assumption "you are your ancestors" by turning the logic of patrilineal descent on its head. That is, Peter makes use of the prevailing idea that a person's lineage legitimates his or her identity by describing the conduct inherited from their ancestors as not only "profitless" (μάταιος), but as something from which believers needed to "be ransomed" (λυτρόομαι), thus severing them from the way of life inherited from their ancestors (1.18).

The constructivist view of ethnicity espoused by Hall explains how Peter can forge identity using ethnic reasoning and language. Ethnicity is a constructed and fluid idea yet is accepted as truth: groups who ascribe to their ethnic identity must believe it to be primordial and permanent, even as it is malleable.[102] In 1 Peter, the primordial understanding of Christian identity is based on Christ, who was "destined before the foundation of the world" (προεγνωσμένου μὲν πρὸ καταβολῆς κόσμου) (1.20) and whose blood ransoms them from having to adhere to or find security in their hereditary traits (1.18). The fact that Peter begins his exhortation in 1.13–21 with what Green refers to as "the end of the story" enables him to posit that the present circumstances can be evaluated according to the pattern of history that has been revealed and the nature of the end that is known.[103] By introducing this particular construal of "the times" (past, present, and future), Peter "orients his audience toward the future consummation of God's plan at the same time that he grounds their identity in a divine strategy that predates creation itself."[104] Thus, while their election is a reality that does not change, it is a reality that changes other realities. The fact that Christians are chosen, born anew, and ransomed means that all other factors formerly used by them to define their identity have lost their power. As Denise Buell aptly puts it, "ideas

---

[100] I am grateful to J. Ross Wagner for this insight.

[101] See Galatians 3–4 and Romans 4 and 11.

[102] For a study on the malleability or flexibility of race and ethnicity in Acts 16, see Eric D. Barreto, *Ethnic Negotiations: The Function of Race and Ethnicity in Acts 16* (WUNT 294; Tübingen: Mohr Siebeck, 2010).

[103] Green, *1 Peter*, 46. The end of the story refers to the final revelation of Jesus Christ (ἀποκαλύψει Ἰησοῦ Χριστοῦ; 1:13b).

[104] Ibid.

about race and ethnicity gain persuasive power by being subject to revision while purporting to speak about fundamental essences."[105]

Not Sons, but Children of God

Peter does not use son language in reference to his addressees. This absence seems striking, especially because he speaks of their heavenly inheritance (κληρονομία) bestowed upon them by God the Father in 1.4–5. In the OT, it is the rule, not the exception, that κληρονομία is passed down to sons.[106] Furthermore, Peter in 1.16 quotes from Lev 19.2, where God instructs Moses, "Speak to the congregation of the sons of Israel (τῶν υἱῶν Ισραηλ), and you shall say to them: You shall be holy, for I am holy, the Lord your God" (NETS). Peter may avoid using "sons" to refer to his addressees in order to apply ethnic reasoning and language to Christians without equating Gentile Christians with Jews. Israel's unique relationship with God can be traced along putative patrilineal bloodlines of their great patriarchs. Gentile Christians, however, cannot claim to share the same ancestors or belong to the same people group. Thus, Peter constructs for his addressees a new lineage and common descent through the blood of Christ in order to help them understand themselves as the children, people, and household of God.

By using the phrase τέκνα ὑπακοῆς, Peter establishes a special relationship of endearment, affection, and association between God the Father and his letter's addressees without confusing them as being one and the same as τῶν υἱῶν Ισραηλ.[107] As noted earlier, Peter in 1.3 blesses God as the Father of our Lord Jesus Christ, not of Israel, in order to include Gentile Christians in the patrilineage of God the Father through Christ. Thus, when Peter speaks of Christians along ethnic lines in 2.9–10, he does so in order to articulate their vocation and self-understanding as God's people in terms that belong to an actual community of Jews who understand themselves as belonging to one another and to God (e.g., Philo, *Spec* 1.52) without explicitly replacing Jews with Christians as the people of God.

Τέκνον shares the same root (τεκ) as the verb τίκτω, which means "to bring into the world"; of a father "to beget"; and of plants "to bear, produce."[108] Τίκτω, like γεννάω,

---

[105] Buell, *Why This New Race*, 7. See also Irad Malkin, ed., *Ancient Perceptions of Greek Ethnicity*, Center for Hellenic Studies Colloquia 5 (Cambridge: Harvard University Press, 2001), 6, 15–16; Gerd Baumann, *The Multicultural Riddle: Rethinking National, Ethnic and Religious Identities* (New York: Routledge, 1999), 90; Ann Laura Stoler, "Racial Histories and Their Regimes of Truth," *Polit. Power Soc. Theory* 11 (1997): 198–200.

[106] For example, LXX Num 27.7–11; 32.18; Josh 13.14; 13.28; 15.20; 16.5; 18.20, 28; 19.1, 8–9, 16, 23, 31, 39, 47; Ezra 9.12; Prov 13.22.

[107] Because Peter never speaks of Israel at all and uses the word "son" only once (5.13, "Mark, my son"), it is impossible to know that he would have distinguished between "sons of Israel, "sons of God," and "children of God." That said, Peter never speaks ill of Israel. Israel, however, serves as the backdrop or template for Peter's understanding of what it means to be a people of God for those who cannot claim to belong to Israel by natural blood ties but can claim to be part of God's people through supernatural means.

[108] Robert Scott, *An Intermediate Greek-English Lexicon: Founded upon the Seventh Edition of Liddell and Scott's Greek–English Lexicon*, ed. H. G. Liddell (Oxford, England: Benediction Classics, 2010).

when understood figuratively, refers to a rebirth or radical change in state.[109] Thus, by calling his audience τέκνα, Peter continues the theme of new birth (ἀναγεννάω), which he announced in 1.3 and reiterates in 1.23. Christians are spiritually reborn such that they have a completely transformed identity. They are children of God, not by physical birth, but by spiritual birth that occurs through Christ's resurrection from the dead as a result of God's election, forknowledge, and mercy and the Spirit's sanctifying power (1.1–3). The fact that their spiritual regeneration does not occur from the womb of a woman or the act of procreation is reiterated in 1.23: "having been born anew not from perishable but imperishable seed through the living and enduring word of God."

In the letter's section known as the *Haustafel* (2.18–3.7), Peter addresses appropriate relationships between slaves and masters, wives and husbands, and husbands and wives, but makes no mention of the relationship between children and fathers. The absence of any parent–child exhortation contrasts with the *Haustafeln* found in Col 3.18–4.1 and Eph 5.21–6.9.[110] In 1 Peter, the code has to do with relationships *within* domestic sphere where those in social and domestic positions of authority over Christians are unbelievers.[111] Even though Christians have a new identity and belong to a new family, they are still to remain in their former households and submit to pagan authority figures who do not submit to Christ. It is the fatherhood of God that redefines earthly relationships.[112]

It appears that Peter avoids using "son" language to describe Gentile Christians in order to emphasize that their relationship to God the Father as his heirs (1.4–5), children (1.14), and people (2.9–10) is not based on biological blood ties but on new birth (1.3, 23) that results from their election (1.1–2) and manifests in their obedience and holiness (1.14–17). In a similar way, it is possible that he avoids "father–children" language in the *Haustafel* in order to underemphasize the role and authority of one's earthly father and thereby emphasize God's role and authority as the Father of believers. The only place where the word "fathers" occurs in reference to human beings is in 1.18, when Peter asserts that believers have been ransomed from the "profitless way of life inherited from the fathers" (πατροπαράδοτος).

The adjective πατροπαράδοτος, which appears neither in the LXX nor elsewhere in the NT, occurs in Hellenistic literature with positive connotations.[113] According to Michaels, Peter's usage of πατροπαράδοτος in 1.18 appears to be "the earliest example

---

[109] L&N 23.52; 13.56.
[110] What is often referred to as the "domestic code" in Titus 2.1–10 also makes no mention of father–child relationship. Titus' primary focus—with the exception of slave and master (2.9)—centers on the relationships between older and younger members of the church. Peter also offers advice as to how elders and younger members of the church should conduct themselves (5.1–5) but in a section separate from his domestic code in 2.18–3.7.
[111] With the exception of the author's singular address to believing husbands in 3.7 and in contrast to the parallel NT household codes that address both husbands and wives as though they are in Christian marriages (Col 3.18–19; Eph 5.21–33; cf. 2.3–5).
[112] On the significance of 1 Peter's characterization of wives as "children of Sarah" (3.6), see Janette H. Ok, "You Have Become Children of Sarah: Reading 1 Peter 3.1–6 through the Intersectionality of Asian Immigrant Wives, Patriarchy, and Honorary Whiteness," *Minoritized Women Reading Race and Ethnicity: Intersectional Approaches to Constructed Identity and Early Christian Texts*, eds. Mitzi J. Smith and Jin Young Choi (Lanhan, MD: Lexington, 2020), 111–29.
[113] Michaels, *1 Peter*, 64. Michaels equates its usage to the English word "heritage" (ibid.). See, e.g., Dionysius of Halicarnassus (*Antiq. rom.* 5.48.2); Diodorus Siculus (*Bib. hist.* 4.8.5; 15.74.5; 17.2.2).

of the Christian use of the term as a polemic against paganism."[114] Rather than portray Greco-Roman paganism as being varied in its traditions and beliefs, Peter instead presents it as "as a unified whole, and more as a way of life" (ἀναστροφή) that stands in stark contrast to the way of life of God's elect people.[115] Thus, Gentile Christians have been "redeemed" or "rescued" from their former way of life through Christ's blood, which is infinitely more costly, precious, and enduring than perishable ransoms such as silver or gold (1.18–19) and which emancipates believers from their bondage to disobedience and immoral passions that characterizes their former existence and Gentile heritage (1.14; 2.1–2, 11; 4.2–4). By tracing his readers' origins to "God the Father of our Lord Jesus Christ" (1.3a), Peter secures their status as God's children in a way that enables them to subordinate themselves to Caesar, their masters, and/or their husbands without compromising their commitment to God and the household of God.

Appropriating Israel's Identity-Defining Designations for a Dislocated People

According to Daniel Boyarin, Gentile Christians as early as the end of the first century were, for whatever reason, not prepared to identify themselves as Jews and were thus faced with the dilemma of asking themselves: "What is the *Christianismos* in which we find ourselves? Is it the new *gens*, a new *ethnos*, a third one, neither Jew nor Greek, or is it an entirely new something in the world, some new kind of identity completely?"[116] Beginning with Justin Martyr, a strand of Christianity opted to present Christianity as a completely novel kind of identity and as a community defined by a certain canon of creed and conduct.[117] Boyarin argues that "this notion that identity is achieved and not given by birth, history, language, and geographical location was the novum that produced religion."[118]

The author of 1 Peter paves the way but does not fully argue for the idea that Christian identity is an *entirely* new religion that is achieved by belief in and adherence to a certain doctrine.[119] Rather, he presents Christian identity as something achieved through divine election, a new kind of birth—spiritual rebirth made possible through

---

[114] Michaels, *1 Peter*, 64. Cf. 2.12.

[115] Ibid.

[116] Daniel Boyarin, *Border Lines: The Partition of Judaeo-Christianity* (Philadelphia: University of Pennsylvania Press, 2004), 16–17.

[117] Ibid., 17.

[118] Ibid.

[119] On the connection between cultic practice and ethnic identity for Paul in 1 Corinthians, see Cavin W. Concannon, "*When You Were Gentiles*": *Specters of Ethnicity in Roman Corinth and Paul's Corinthian Correspondence*, Synkrisis: Comparative Approaches to Early Christianity in Greco-Roman Culture (New Haven: Yale University Press, 2014). Concannon reminds us that the particularly modern Protestant construct of the category *Christian*, "empties [1 Cor 12.2] of its strangeness by turning an ethnic designation into one of belief" (ibid., xi). For Paul, "to change one's cultic practices and allegiances is also a means of changing one's ethnicity, becoming no longer ἔθνη but now something else" (ibid.).

the resurrection of Christ from the dead, and a new line of descent. Believers are foreknown by God the Father, who chose them (1.1-3). Peter continues to emphasize the importance of his addressees' patrilineage, by declaring God as Father (1.2-3, 17), and pedigree, by presenting Christ's blood as legitimating their lineage to God the Father (1.18-19) and as the basis for their relationship to one another (2.4-10).

Gentile converts were confronted with a unique problem and opportunity to choose or construct a new way to understand themselves, and Peter addresses this very challenge. Rather than arguing that Gentile Christians are "neither Jew nor Greek" (cf. Gal 3.28) or that they are Jews, Peter argues instead that they are no longer Gentiles. He does this by appropriating ethnic identity language ascribed to the Jews as a means to express how Gentile Christians belong to God. He constructs Christian identity using ethnic language because ethnic categories—while they are fluid enough for him to adapt and reimagine to serve his purposes—help to fix or concretize the ways in which Gentile Christians are to cohere with one another and adhere to the behavior and values that imitate Christ (2.21) and befit their status as "a chosen race, a royal priesthood, a holy nation, and a people for [God's] possession" (2.9).

The basis for Peter's bold declaration that Christians are a γένος ἐκλεκτόν, βασίλειον ἱεράτευμα, ἔθνος ἅγιον, λαὸς εἰς περιποίησιν (2.9) is that God has chosen them to be these things from long ago (1.1-2) and has chosen Christ to make this possible from before the foundation of the earth (1.20). God's primordial election of Christ makes their elect status as God's people possible. In 2.9, Peter expresses his addressees' election in explicitly ethnic and religious language.[120] The fact that he utilizes Israel's identity-forming terminology, which is both ethnic and religious in meaning, demonstrates that he finds ethnoreligious categories helpful and important for shaping Christian self-understanding. The Gentiles have their gods, but the people of God belong to the true God. Christians are members of the people of God because of the ransoming blood of Christ in death and because of his resurrection. The fact that Gentile Christians have gone from being "not a people" to "a people of God" (2.10) assumes the mutability of their identities. Christ's blood is now the common bond that brings these particular people of God together (1.2, 18-19; 2.24; 3.18). However, Christians are not physical descendants of Christ but are elected as the people of God because of God's merciful decision to choose them to be his own heirs and children (1.3-5, 14) through Christ's resurrection from the dead, which resulted in new birth (1.3, cf. 23), and ransoming blood, which resulted in being free from the conduct inherited from their ancestors (1.18-19).

---

[120] There has been a general lack of attention given to the "emphatically ethnic" language in 2.9 (Horrell, "'Race', 'Nation', 'People,'" 134-5). For example, Eugene Boring calls 1 Pet 2.9-10 "one of the most dense constellations of ecclesiological imagery in the New Testament" (*1 Peter*, 98). Elliott reads 2.9-10 as emphasizing the communal identity of believers (*1 Peter*, 444). Achtemeier focuses on the term ἐκλεκτόν, rather than γένος, arguing that in 2.9, Peter's use of OT titles that designate Israel's elect and chosen status "points again to the fact that for our author the Christian community has now become God's elect and chosen people" (*1 Peter*, 167). In his careful study of the ethnoracial language in 2.9, Horrell argues that Peter's "uniquely dense collocation of ethnic identity language" serves as a "crucial early step in the construction of Christian identity in ethnoracial terms" ("'Race', 'Nation', 'People,'" 135).

By ethnicizing his recipients' Christian identity in order to replace their ethnic majority status as Gentiles, Peter seeks to create a stronger sense of ingroup identity and solidarity for his addressees and weaken their sense of belonging to the values of the dominant culture and the values of their family and associations. Ethnic identity and culture are closely entwined for Peter.[121] Thus, Peter detaches Christian identity from those Greco-Roman values and social associations at odds with Christian values. He does this by describing their corporate identity as an ethnic identity with its own distinctive culture. This culture is characterized by the following attributes: living hope (1.3); obedience to the Father (1.14); unity of spirit; mutual love among members of the household of God (2.5, 17; 3.8; 4.17); faithful adherence to the example of Christ—who committed no sin, spoke without guile, did not reply with insults when insulted, and did not threaten revenge though he suffered (2.21–5); and humility toward one another (5.5–6).

By constructing an ethnic identity for people who are stigmatized and suffering as consequence of their faith in Christ, Peter helps his addressees disidentify with their past and reidentify as the "people of God" (2.9–10). By describing Christians as displaced but elect resident aliens and foreigners and strangers, Peter speaks to their foreignness in society while imbuing them with a greater sense of being God's own people who belong to God's household (ὁ οἶκος τοῦ θεοῦ) (4.17; cf. 2.5 [οἶκος πνευματικός]). He does this in order to help his addressees cope with the social conflict, prejudice, and subsequent alienation and persecution resulting from their conversion and adherence to Christian religion.[122]

Cultural "Homelessness" is a major theme in the letter of 1 Peter, as John Elliott has drawn attention to in his groundbreaking book, *A Home for the Homeless*.[123] According to Elliott, the letter's addressees have experienced homelessness because of their actual sociopolitical status as πάροικοι prior to conversion.[124] Thus, for Elliott, Peter offers those who are already "homeless" or foreign a new "home"—i.e., a new sense of home and belonging. While Elliott rightly underscores the significance of the household metaphor in 1 Peter as a "major coordinating ecclesiological symbol" employed by Peter to provide a distinctive communal identity for his struggling and suffering audience,[125] he wrongly interprets πάροικοι and παρεπιδήμοι as evidence of their concrete sociopolitical identity as literal "resident aliens and visiting strangers" prior and in addition to "the religious dimension of their social strangerhood."[126]

Peter addresses his audience not as literally homeless prior to conversion but as culturally homeless as a result of their conversion. In 1.1, Peter both describes and

---

[121] By "culture," I mean way of life, conduct, values (see, e.g., 1 Pet 1.17; 2.1, 11–12) that is distinct from that of the Gentiles and from the former way of life of those born anew (1.3).

[122] On the nature of prejudice evidenced in 1 Peter, see Travis B. Williams, *Persecution in 1 Peter: Differentiating and Contextualizing Early Christian Suffering* (NovTSup 145; Leiden: Brill, 2012), 128–9. See also Horrell, *1 Peter*, 53–9 and Holloway, *Coping with Prejudice*, 4–5, 40–73.

[123] John H. Elliott, A Home for the Homeless, 165–266. Elliott, Conflict, Community, and Honor: 1 Peter in Social-Scientific Perspective (Eugene, OR: Cascade, 2007), 14.

[124] Elliott, *A Home for the Homeless*, 21–58.

[125] Ibid., 200.

[126] Ibid., 35.

prescribes his readers' exceptional relationship with God and estranged relationship with society when addressing his letter "to the elect who are living as foreigners in the diaspora." Christians are ἐκλεκτοί in the sense that they are "chosen" by God to live a life set apart for God among τὰ ἔθνη, τὰ γενή, and οἱ λαοί (2.9–10), just as God selected and gathered Israel of old from among all the races, nations, and people of the earth.[127] When taken metaphorically and in relation to ἐκλεκτός, the terms παρεπίδημος and διασπορά in 1.1 give a glimpse of the social alienation and marginalization experienced by the addressees as a result of their divinely chosen status. These terms also prescribe how Peter wants his addressees to understand and posture themselves as foreigners to the values of the surrounding world in which they formerly felt socially and culturally at home. Peter desires his addressees to understand themselves as "resident aliens and foreigners" vis-à-vis the prevailing Gentile values and way of life. They are no longer to feel at home among the Gentiles. Rather, they are to "be built into a spiritual house" and constitute the "household of God" (2.5; 4.17). They are to experience "at-home-ness" among fellow believers.

As Shively Smith sets forth, diaspora from the perspective of 1 Peter is a condition induced by "decisive and volitional consent" and "not by divine compulsion and peremptory command."[128] Diaspora is a way of life resulting from the faithful response and embrace of God's people to God's action through Christ.[129] Diaspora is thus not a social condition of displacement and estrangement[130] but rather is a social stance of religious displacement and estrangement for a people very much at home in the values of the dominant culture. In 1.1, Peter as well as James make novel use of "diaspora," appropriating a term exclusively used to describe Judaism to the Christian community.[131]

Peter speaks in metaphorical terms of the conflicts and tensions experienced by his readers with the surrounding culture while also putting their negative social circumstances in proper and positive theological and eschatological perspective. Although the language Peter uses to describe his addressees in 1.1, 17, and 2.11 is figurative, their social conflict is not. Later in the letter, it becomes more apparent that they are indeed beleaguered and beset by social hostility, conflict, slander, and persecution from their non-Christian neighbors, governors, masters, husbands, etc. (e.g., 1.6–7; 2.12, 14–15, 18–20; 3.13, 16–17; 4.1, 4, 12–16). The language of living as elect foreigners in the diaspora serves sociological purposes.[132] Through the idea that

---

[127] See 1 Chr 16.13; LXX Ps 88.4; 104.6, 43; Isa 65.9, 15, 23 for examples of God's choosing of Israel. For examples of Israel described as a particular γένος, see Exod 1.9; Josh 4.14; 11.21; Esth 2.10. For examples of Israel as an ἔθνος among ἔθνη, see Gen 12.2; 18.18; Exod 19.5–6; Lev 20.26; Deut 7.6–7; 10.15; 14.2; 26.19. For examples of Israel as God's λαός, see Exod 6.7; 7.4; 7.16; Deut 9.26, 29; 14.2, 21; 26.15.

[128] Shively T. J. Smith, *Strangers to Family: Diaspora and 1 Peter's Invention of God's Household* (Waco: Baylor University Press, 2016), 21.

[129] Ibid.

[130] Contra Elliott, *A Home for the Homeless*, 38.

[131] Ibid.

[132] On how diasporic identity is being contested and constructed in 1 Peter to form what will come to be known as Christian identity, see Kaalund, *Reading Hebrews and 1 Peter*, 111–135.

Christians are foreigners in a land in which they are no longer to feel at home and coupled with the idea that they are, in effect, an ethnic group with a common heavenly father, birth narrative, bloodline, and way of life, Peter seeks to equip believers with the theological and sociological lenses to interpret their suffering and better endure it.

Elected Group Identity

Tertullian, writing during the reign of the *collegia*-friendly Septimius Severus, describes Christians as a benign *collegium* (association) and pleads for the toleration of Christian communities on these grounds (*Apol.* 39). Justin Martyr, responding to the prevailing opinion that Christianity is a depraved *supertitio*, presents Christianity as a philosophy in order to claim that Christianity promoted genuine piety—i.e., a belief in God and a way of life appropriate with this belief (*Dial.* 8).[133] Robert Wilken explains that Justin and Tertullian identified Christians with philosophical schools and associations in the Greco-Roman world in order to provide the greatest possibility for outsiders to interpret Christianity.[134] While there were differences between Christian groups and philosophical schools and associations, the fact that these apologists saw them as analogous at least from the point of view of non-Christians points to some overlap between these groups.[135]

The voluntary nature of Greco-Roman associations was as important point of connection between various groups, and there were many types, such as *collegium*, *secta*, *faction*, *thiasos*, *eranos*, and *koinon*.[136] A majority of collegia consisted of the urban poor, slaves, and freedmen. They all had some form of formal organization, rules for entry, and standards of behavior, though their requirements and rituals varied.[137] They were primarily associated with the household,[138] formed around a common

---

[133] See Robert L. Wilkin "Collegia, Philosophical Schools, and Theology," in *The Catacombs and the Colosseum: The Roman Empire as the Setting of Primitive Christianity* (Valley Forge, PA: Judson Press, 1971). See also Robert L. Wilken, *The Christians as the Romans Saw Them* (New Haven: Yale University Press, 2003).

[134] Wilkin, "Collegia, Philosophical Schools, and Theology," 286.

[135] Stephen G. Wilson, "Voluntary Associations," in *Voluntary Associations in the Graeco-Roman World*, eds. John S. Kloppenborg and Stephen G. Wilson (London: Routledge, 1997), 1–15, 9. For an overview of various models from the Greco-Roman social environment that were available to Pauline communities, such as the household, the voluntary association, the synagogue and the philosophical or rhetorical school, see Wayne A. Meeks, *The First Urban Christians: The Social World of the Apostle Paul* (New Haven: Yale University Press, 1983), 74–85. For why and how Jewish and Christian groups sought to exploit the category of "philosophy" to explain themselves in social terms to the Greco-Roman world, see Steve Mason, "Philosophiai: Greco-Roman, Judean, and Christian," in *Voluntary Associations in the Graeco-Roman World*, 31–58. Peter's use of ethnic reasoning, as I argue, is concerned with shaping ingroup rather than outsider perception.

[136] Wilson, "Voluntary Associations," 1.

[137] Ibid., 9, 23. The fact that the Greeks and Romans used "a rather bewildering array of terms" to refer to voluntary associations makes attempts at clearly categorizing them difficult (18).

[138] It thus behooved masters and mistresses of large households to permit their slaves and freeman to organize collegia within the confines of the domos, rather than seek them outside their master's control (ibid., 23). Wilson notes the possibility that some Pauline churches began as domestic collegia (see Rom 16.5; Col 4.15; ibid.).

trade, or formed around the cult of a deity. Above all, it was the social benefits that attracted its members—i.e., the business of eating and drinking.[139] To varying degrees such conviviality required the generosity of wealthier persons, who might receive in return praise and honor in the form of inscriptions, titles, wreaths, or statues.[140] While early Christian fellowship also consisted of meals (e.g., 1 Cor 11.17–22, Gal 2.12), the goals of these communities were more concerned with salvation in a comprehensive sense and not with eating and fellowship for their own sake.[141]

Most associations did not demand the exclusive allegiance of their members and a person could be a member or patron of more than one group, though for practical and personal reasons, most chose to belong to only one association.[142] Jews and Christians, in contrast, demanded exclusive loyalty from its members, though in reality, such strict boundaries were often more porous.[143] Baptism in Christ signaled for converts "an extraordinarily thoroughgoing resocialization, in which the sect was intended to become virtually the primary group for its members, supplanting all other loyalties."[144] Whereas membership in collegia was voluntary and did not require a radical transformation of behaviors and relationships, Christian identity, as 1 Peter presents it, is the result of God the Father's election and made possible by the resurrection of Jesus Christ from the dead (1.1–3). It is formed on the basis of Christ's blood (1.18–19). Christians must choose to live into this new identity (e.g., 1.13–16; 2.1, 11–12; 4.1–2, 7; 5.6–9) and exhibit group loyalty tantamount to the kind of intimate and enduring affection expected of blood siblings (1.22; 3.8; 4.8–11, 5.12–14).[145]

Conclusion

Christians have become dislocated from the world and from their former way of living not only through election but also because they have been "born anew to a living hope" (1.3; 23). The concept of new birth serves as the point of departure for the way in which Christians are to understand their former existence. The very idea that Christians have a new identity challenges them to intensify the process of their

---

[139] Ibid., 18–19.
[140] Wayne A. Meeks, *The First Urban Christians: The Social World of the Apostle Paul* (New Haven: Yale University Press, 1983), 78.
[141] Meeks, *The First Urban Christians*, 79. See, e.g., Paul's exhortation in 1 Cor 10.31–3 (NRSV): "So, whether you eat or drink, or whatever you do, do everything for the glory of God. Give no offense to Jews or to Greeks or to the church of God, just as I try to please everyone in everything I do, not seeking my own advantage, but that of many, so that they may be saved."
[142] Wilson, "Voluntary Associations," 18–19.
[143] Ibid., 10. So also Meeks, *The First Urban Christians*, 78.
[144] Meeks, *The First Urban Christians*, 78. Meeks sees the only analogous parallel in antiquity was conversion to Judaism (ibid.).
[145] See S. Scott Bartchy, "Undermining Ancient Patriarchy: The Apostle's Vision of a Society of Siblings," *BTB* 29, no. 2 (1999): 68–78; Horrell, "From ἀδελφοί to οἶκος θεοῦ: Social Transformation in Pauline Christianity," *JBL* 120, no. 2 (2001): 293–311; Jeremy Punt, "He Is Heavy … He's My Brother: Unraveling Fraternity in Paul (Galatians)," *Neot* 46, no. 1 (2012): 153–71.

identification with Christ and disidentification from their past.¹⁴⁶ Those born anew must continue to struggle against their former lusts, values, and behaviors. The idea of being πάροικοι and παρεπιδήμοι helps believers maintain a critical distance between their former and present values and behaviors. Because there are no physical markers to clearly differentiate or set apart who they are now from the pagan people they once were, Peter portrays Christian identity in ethnic-identity language to promote a stronger sense of peoplehood and ingroup solidarity.¹⁴⁷

When Peter ascribes his beleaguered addressees with the community- and ethnic identity-forging titles and dignities of Israel in 2.9 drawn from Jewish Scriptures,¹⁴⁸ he does not do so in order to replace Israel as the "people of God" (2.10) or to incorporate them into the legacy of Israel¹⁴⁹ or to transpose the status and identity of Israel unto the Church.¹⁵⁰ Rather, as Horrell explains, Peter draws on the specific traditions of Judaism because they are "a form of ethnic identity with religio-cultural practices at its heart" that make it possible for him to construct the same form of identity for his addressees "without recourse to a specific territorial attachment or to biological (human) kinship links."¹⁵¹ Peter thus uses ethnic reasoning in his construction of Christian identity in order to provide a new way for his Gentile Christian addressees to understand themselves in relation to God the Father and to one another as a holy people who, because of divine election and new birth, share the same blood line—that of Jesus Christ.

---

[146] I am indebted to Paul Holloway for the term and concept of "disidentification" as it relates to 1 Peter (*Coping with Prejudice*, 131), which he borrows from Erving Goffman (*Stigma*, 44).

[147] In Greco-Roman antiquity, "cult defined ethnicity and ethnicity defined cult" such that ethnicity and religiosity were fundamentally intertwined (Paula Fredriksen, "Judaizing the Nations: The Ritual Demands of Paul's Gospel," *NTS* 56 [2010], 232–52, 234). This is why Fredriksen prefers to use "pagan" (which in modern parlance connotes religion) rather than "Gentile" (which connotes ethnicity) when speaking of first-century ἔθνη and to use "ex-pagan pagans" when speaking of non-Jewish members of the first-century movement around Jesus (ibid., 242n23). The idea that Gentile converts became "ex-pagan pagans" helps convey the radical transformation involved in becoming Christian for 1 Peter's addressees. As Fredriksen boldly asserts, "In a culture where what we call 'religion' was seen as an innate, not detachable, aspect of identity, this phenomenon [of conversion] scarcely made sense: it was tantamount to changing one's ethnicity" (ibid., 239).

[148] Exod 19.6 and Isa 43.20–1.

[149] Cf. Elliott, *A Home for the Homeless*, 38 and Elliott *1 Peter*, 443.

[150] Cf. Peter Richardson, *Israel in the Apostolic Church* (SNTSMS 10; Cambridge: Cambridge University Press, 1969), 172.

[151] Horrell, "'Race', Nation', 'People,'" 161.

4

Constructing Boundaries and Contesting Stigma in the Making of Ethnic Identity in 1 Peter

Introduction

In the previous chapter I showed how Peter constructs Christian identity as an ethnic identity, as opposed to other sorts of identities, such as a *collegium* or philosophical school. He does so to provide a strong, distinct, cohesive, and positive ingroup identity for his beleaguered addressees, who must endure anti-Christian hostility and subsequent persecution, maintain their social and religious distinctiveness as Christians, and remain active participants in society. By portraying Christian identity in ethnic terms, Peter helps his addressees understand not only who they *are* because of their new identities given by God in Christ, but also who they are *no longer*. Although concerned for how outsiders view his addressees (2.11–12, 3.1–2, 15–16), Peter constructs Christian identity as an ethnic group identity in order to promote ingroup solidarity and self-understanding and to prevent them from succumbing to the social pressures to revert back to their former way of life.

In this chapter, I consider how Fredrik Barth's concept of "ethnic boundaries," i.e., how boundaries erected between groups and the ways in which groups protect or breach these boundaries, can be critically and fruitfully applied to 1 Peter. Peter's construction of ethnic identity functions to sharpen differences with his readers' former identities and with those who oppose their new allegiance and way of life by creating an antithesis between the people of God and the people *not* of God. I also examine the role of stigma in 1 Peter with the help of Erving Goffman's influential study on stigma. Peter constructs Christian identity along explicitly ethnic lines as a strategy to contest and reappropriate the stigma associated with being "Christian" and to reduce the temptation for Christians to revert to their former identity. If Christians understand themselves as being people who possess not only a new present-day identity but also a new lineage through the blood of Christ, they will see an enormous distinction between being a Christian and not having been one. Although they have abandoned their old lineage, they are not left without one. Rather, Christians now possess a separate system of honor and distinct cultural identity that enables them to subvert the stigma imposed upon them by the dominant culture.

As a social anthropologist, Barth approaches ethnic group identity as a dynamic process of differentiation and negotiation between one people group and another, rather than viewing ethnic communities as primordial, a priori groups to which people naturally belong. Ethnic identity formation, Barth argues, occurs not in cultural isolation from outsiders but through social contact, conflict, compromise, and negotiation with outsiders. Ethnic labels persist even when individual members of an ethnic group cross boundaries and identify with people from outside of their ethnic group. Barth's boundary analysis in the study of ethnicity is highly compatible with Goffman's classic study on stigma, published six years earlier.[1] Both Barth and Goffman focus on the interactional level rather than on the socio-structural level of analysis, which resonates with the perspective of Peter, who does not explicitly critique the legitimacy of Rome nor consider the socioeconomic contingencies faced by the addressees of his letter. Rather, Peter focuses on the suffering experienced as a result of social prejudice.[2] Barth illuminates how boundaries and stigmas are dynamic and relational in nature and emerge from complex social interactions and processes. Boundaries, Barth maintains, are less about lines drawn between one group and another than about their symbolic power to create ingroup identity. Likewise, Goffman's study demonstrates how stigma has the power to reduce the chances of an individual or a group to survive socially but also the power to create a very strong sense of ingroup identity. I argue that Peter uses the strategy of creating an ethnic identity for his addressees in order to help his addressees cope with anti-Christian prejudice and contest the stigma associated with being Christian.

Barth on Ethnic Boundaries

In his seminal introduction to the collection of essays entitled, *Ethnic Groups and Boundaries*, published in 1969, Barth departs theoretically and empirically from then-prevailing studies on ethnicity within the field of social anthropology.[3] First, Barth rejects constructing an ideal type of an ethnic group. Further, he avoids presenting ethnic groups as empirically recurring or biologically self-perpetuating. Rather, he focuses his study on the *processes* involved in the making and maintaining of ethnic groups. In doing so, Barth sees an ethnic group as essentially a form of social organization rather than as a possessor of fixed cultural features or differences that can be described or predicted. Barth does not deny that groups share fundamental cultural

---

[1] Goffman, *Stigma*.
[2] For a presentation of the evidence that early Christians suffered as targets of "*social prejudice*," see Holloway, *Coping with Prejudice*, 40–66. In sum, "to be Christian is to be a criminal, and to be accused of being Christian is to be accused of being a criminal" (65). Although Christianity was considered a crime, the Roman government did not go out of its way to seek out Christians; the kind of persecution Christians experienced prior to the first "official" government-sponsored persecution in 250–1 CE was social prejudice (65). Social prejudice manifests to varying degrees in behaviors such as "coolness avoidance, verbal abuse, exclusion, discrimination, and of course violence" (28).
[3] Barth, *Ethnic Groups*, 9–38.

values, but he contends that a group's shared culture is "an implication or result, rather than a primary and definitional characteristic of ethnic group organization."[4]

Second, Barth emphasizes the "ascriptive" and "exclusive" nature of ethnic groups. By "ascriptive," he means that members of a group identify themselves and are identified by others as making up a category, such as "Hmong," that can be distinguished from other analogous categories, such as "Vietnamese."[5] An ethnic group's cultural features depend on the existence and maintenance of boundaries. Barth relocates the critical focus of a group's ethnic identity from the *center* of ethnic communities, where members strive to remain as exclusive and insulated as possible, to the *periphery* of ethnic communities, where members come into numerous points of contact with members of other ethnic groups. By "exclusive," he means that although the criteria for group membership may change and the cultural characteristics of its members may be transformed, "the fact of continuing dichotomization between members and outsiders" remains constant.[6] Thus ethnic groups define themselves by and against other groups. Inter-ethnic differences must be reinforced in order for ingroup identity to remain distinct and definitive.[7]

The emphasis Barth places on the boundaries of a group as the location for ethnic identity construction challenges the naïve but persistent assumptions that (1) geographical or social isolation is needed to maintain ethnic distinctiveness and diversity and (2) assimilation and acculturation occur at the geographical borders and social boundaries of a group.[8] To the contrary, Barth argues that it is the interaction between ethnic groups that leads to the persistence and maintenance of boundaries:

> Ethnic distinctions do not depend on the absence of social interaction and acceptance, but are quite to the contrary often the very foundations on which embracing social systems are built. Interaction in such a social system does not lead to its liquidation through change and acculturation; cultural differences can persist despite inter-ethnic contact and interdependence.[9]

In other words, a group maintains its ethnic identity not because its members avoid interacting with others, but precisely because its members do interact with others. Identity formation occurs when a group's members come into social contact, conflict, compromise, and negotiation with those whom they identify as outsiders. Therefore, Barth makes the often-cited point that it is "the ethnic *boundary* that defines the group, not the cultural stuff that it encloses."[10]

---

[4] Ibid., 11. Barth outlines the four typical definitions anthropologists use to describe ethnic groups on *op. cit.* 10–11. He focuses on the last description—namely that an ethnic group "has a membership which identifies itself, and is identified by others, as constituting a category distinguishable from other categories of the same order"—as being the most significant.
[5] Ibid., 14.
[6] Ibid.
[7] Ibid., 14–16.
[8] Ibid., 9.
[9] Ibid., 10.
[10] Ibid., 15.

Cultural features, cultural characteristics, and even the organization of a group can change or differ within the group, but the process of demarcating who is in and who is out is both constant and vital for a group's identity to remain intact. Take, for example, the members of a group who say they are ethnically Korean. If these Koreans are willing to be treated as Korean and allow others to interpret and judge their behavior as Korean in contrast to, say, Japanese, then Barth would insist that it makes no difference how dissimilar some Koreans actually behave from other Koreans in their overt behaviors. What matters is that those who consider themselves "Korean" willingly declare their allegiance to a shared Korean culture over against some other cultural identity.

According to Barth, ethnic groups also resist change "by being joined in stereotyped clusters as characteristics of one single identity."[11] Stereotypes then serve to unite or categorize people under one ethnic identity, despite the diversity and differences among its members. They also serve to characterize people from outside one's ethnic group as belonging to one simplistic identity. An ethnic group makes use of stereotypes in both positive and negative ways to organize the variety of activities and behaviors both of its members and of outsiders into clusters of meaning. Stereotypes function to *delimit* rather than *delineate* ethnic culture.[12]

The impact of Barth's socio-anthropological work cannot be overstated for the study of ethnicity and sociology. With the exception of Max Weber, sociologists prior to Barth did not use the term "ethnic groups" in the study of cultural difference.[13] Barth's work has been widely cited and applied to many disciplines. He effectively moved the study of "ethnicity" into the laps of sociologists with his "Copernican" insight that social interaction is the precondition for ethnic group identity.[14] His boundary analysis helped sociologists see that to be a culturally distinct ethnic group requires both group insiders to perceive themselves and outsiders to perceive them as different or as a culturally distinctive collectivity.[15] Barth universalized the understanding of ethnicity to include the dominant majority group rather than confining ethnicity to minority groups.[16] He did this by refocusing and relocating the study of ethnicity away from aspects of culture, such as language, customs, dress, religious practices, and onto the social processes and interactions with non-group members that give shape to cultural identity. Barth fleshed out how group identity is relational, not between ingroup members, as conventionally understood, but with

---

[11] Ibid., 17.

[12] Thomas Bauman, *The Pekin: The Rise and Fall of Chicago's First Black-Owned Theater* (Urbana: University of Illinois Press, 2014), xx.

[13] Weber himself never uses the word *Ethnizität* in his work, but he does discuss *ethnische Gruppen* in his analysis of race and nationality. See Max Weber, *Economy and Society: An Outline of Interpretive Sociology*, eds. Guenther Roth and Claus Wittich (Berkeley: University of California Press, 1968 [1922]). Weber defines *ethnische Gruppen* as "those human groups that entertain a subjective belief in their common descent because of similarities of physical type or of customs or of both, or because of memories of colonisation or migration" (ibid., 389).

[14] Sinisa Malesevic, *The Sociology of Ethnicity* (London: Sage 2004), 2.

[15] Malesevic, *Sociology*, 4.

[16] Ibid., 3.

non-group members.¹⁷ Thus, in order for a group to know who they are, they must know who they are not.

Barth was mostly concerned with explaining why ethnic boundaries remained stable and persisted or reproduced themselves over time despite the boundary crossings or social contact between persons of different groups and cultures. Ethnic groups remain intact even when individual members move across boundaries. In fact, the boundaries are permeable and boundary crossings can help make them durable. Although Barth himself did not explain how boundaries emerged in the first place, his analysis opened up the doors to further investigation of how and why boundaries arise and transform to include or exclude new groups, to become more nebulous and porous, and to eventually dissolve over time or persist over time.¹⁸ The enduring potential of ethnicity may be why Peter finds constructing Christian identity along ethnic lines so helpful.

Constructing Social Boundaries in 1 Peter

In 1 Peter 2.10, Peter asserts that his addressees are "now a people of God" (νῦν δὲ λαὸς θεοῦ) in contrast to their "former" existence as a "people *not* of God" (οἵ ποτε οὐ λαὸς ... θεοῦ). By οὐ λαός, Peter means that, prior to their conversion, Christians did not possess a shared communal identity. If the readers accept Peter's assertion that they are "people of God" and are willing to be treated, interpreted, and judged by themselves and by others according to this identity, then they can overcome any overt differences among them—such as class, status, gender, and ethnic identity—that would have previously prevented them from seeing each other as members of the same people group (2.9–10) and surrogate family (2.5, 17; 3.8; 4.8–10). Their declared commitment to a shared culture and status as the people of God is superordinate to any differences because they are now joined to one another not through biological bloodlines but through the ransoming blood of Christ (1.18–19). For Peter, what makes Christians who they are is the objective and unchanging fact that God has chosen them to be his people and given them a new life through the death and resurrection of Jesus Christ (1.1–3). Christians should thus ascribe to themselves the identity God has already ascribed to them.

Peter builds to this climactic contrast in 2.10 of who Christians are and who they are no longer through his rich assemblage of metaphors. He begins in 1.3 with the potent theological concept of new birth. The new birth metaphor plays an integral role in 1 Peter (1.3; 1.23) and serves as the theological foundation for the distinctively Christian identity Peter seeks to build. The concept of new birth also serves as the point

---

¹⁷ Thomas Hylland Eriksen, *Ethnicity and Nationalism: Anthropological Perspectives* (London: Pluto Press, 1993), 10. Barth's analysis, according to Erikesen, led to the realization that ethnic groups cannot be studied without also studying the majority ethnic group. Malesevic, Sinisa, *The Sociology of Ethnicity*, 3. See Richard Jenkins, *Rethinking Ethnicity: Arguments and Explorations* (London; Thousand Oaks, CA: Sage, 1997). See also Wsevolod W. Isajiw, "Approaches to Ethnic Conflict Resolution: Paradigms and Principles," *International Journal of Intercultural Relations* 24, no. 1 (2000): 105–24.

¹⁸ Wimmer, *Ethnic Boundary Making*, 4.

of departure for the way in which Christians are to understand their former existence.[19] The very idea that Christians have a new identity challenges them to intensify the process of their identification with Christ and their disidentification from their past. They are placed in a new family with longstanding and legitimate ancestral roots and promised a heavenly inheritance and future salvation that engenders confidence, even as they are "grieved" by their present hardships (1.4-9). Christians can endure their "various trials" (1.6) by tracing their existence back to the foreknowledge of God and forward to their rich and secure inheritance in heaven and their imminent and complete salvation (1.5).

Peter then builds up to an antithesis between those "who believe" and those "who do not believe" (2.7)[20] before his climactic declaration in 2.9 that Christians are a γένος ἐκλεκτόν, βασίλειον ἱεράτευμα, ἔθνος ἅγιον, λαὸς εἰς περιποίησιν. In 2.9b-10, the contrast between those who believe and those who do not believe culminates in antithesis between believers themselves whom God "has called out of darkness and into his marvelous light" and who were "once not a people but now are God's people" and who "had not received mercy but now have received mercy."[21] Here Peter reiterates the theme of God the Father's merciful act of re-begetting believers (1.3). Peter also builds upon the contrast he started to draw between their new identity as God's obedient, holy, reverent, and ransomed children and former identity as ignorant people living according to their fleshly desires and the conduct they have inherited from their ancestors (1.14-19).

In 2.11-12 and 4.3-4, Peter makes the sharpest distinction between these two groups when contrasting the exceptional and holy people of God with those whom he refers to in one sweeping, opposing category, "the Gentiles" (τὰ ἔθνη), i.e., the people *not* of God. The dichotomy between the special people of God and the rest does more than characterize, stereotype, or demonize "the other."[22] This contrast also functions to distinguish his readers' past as non-believers from their present as believers (1.3-2.8). By reminding his addressees that they used to be like these "Gentiles," Peter reveals his anxiety about the ease with which they might return to their previous identity. He also underlines God's agency in their transformation (1.3; 2.1.18-19; 2.1-10). Thus Peter's characterization of "the other" is also a characterization of "the self," as Peter depicts his addressees as those who continue to struggle to pattern themselves after Christ

---

[19] Miroslav Volf makes a similar point when he comments that new birth does not mean Christians are outsiders to their social world, but rather they are "the *insiders* who have diverted from their culture by being born again. They are by definition those who are not what they used to be, those who do not live like they used to live" ("Soft Difference: Theological Reflections on the Relation between Church and Culture in 1 Peter," *ExAud* 10 [1994]: 15-30, 18-19).

[20] Isa 28.16; LXX Psa 117.22; Isa 8.14.

[21] LXX Hos 2.25.

[22] Cf. Paul R. Trebilco who also sees Peter's use of the term "Gentiles" as a "high boundary term that strongly excludes" (*Outsider Designations and Boundary Construction in the New Testament: Early Christian Communities and the Formation of Group Identity* [Cambridge: Cambridge University Press, 2017, 270). Contra Volf, who finds it significant that 1 Peter establishes difference positively, not negatively ("Soft Difference," 20-1). The author of 1 Peter does celebrate Christian identity in positive terms (e.g., 1.3; 2.9); yet as I argue, he purposely stereotypes Gentiles as "other" as a way to help Gentile converts disassociate with their former way of life.

and to understand themselves as people who have been born anew. Rather than make a Jew/Gentile dichotomy, Peter first broadens the identification of Israel as a γένος ἐκλεκτόν, βασίλειον ἱεράτευμα, ἔθνος ἅγιον, λαὸς εἰς περιποίησιν, and λαὸς θεοῦ (2.9–10) to include his addressees and then contrasts this exceptional and holy people with the "Gentiles" (τὰ ἔθνη), i.e., the people *not* of God (2.12).[23]

To say that Christians have been given a new life and placed in a new situation due to God's past election of them and their apocalyptic hope implies that their old life with its dead hope, depreciating inheritance, and unreliable salvation no longer has any relevance.[24] This is not to say, however, that those born anew no longer struggle with their former lusts, values, and behaviors. Peter urgently and affectionately pleads in 2.11, "Beloved, I exhort [you], as resident aliens and foreigners, to disengage (ἀπέχεσθαι) from the desires of the surrounding culture, which wage war against [your] life." The verb ἀπέχω,[25] literally "hold oneself" (ἔχω) "apart from" (ἀπό), when combined with the direct object ἐπιθυμία,[26] conveys the sense of "stay clear away from," "deliberately avoid." The fact that this admonition comes immediately after Peter has spelled out in rich ethnic language who his readers are (2.9–10) reveals that who they are no longer continues to trouble them in the present.

Believers face the persistent temptation to succumb to the "desires of the surrounding culture" (αἱ σαρκικαὶ ἐπιθυμίαι) because these desires, though inappropriate for the people of God, remain powerful and prevalent among those who are not of God. Peter associates ἐπιθυμίαι in 1.14 with the cravings by which believers should no longer be shaped (μὴ συσχηματιζόμενοι). In 4.2–3, he associates them with the desires that accord with human nature but are opposed to the will of God and thus are distinctively Gentile in nature. Thus τῶν σαρκικῶν ἐπιθυμιῶν refers to the "desires that belong to the surrounding world,"[27] not only the individually oriented "desires of the flesh." In all four instances of ἐπιθυμία in 1 Peter (1.14; 2.11; 4.2, 3), the word conveys the sense of ignorant (ἐν τῇ ἀγνοίᾳ in 1.14) or senseless behavior (in association with τὴν αὐτὴν τῆς ἀσωτίας ἀνάχυσιν in 4.4).[28] Peter has already assured his addressees in 1.18–19 that Christ's "precious blood" has "ransomed" them "from the futile way

---

[23] While it is not entirely clear whether or not Peter intends for Jews to be included in the category "Gentiles," his failure to mention "Jews" at all in his letter remains very puzzling to me.

[24] Achtemeier, *1 Peter*, 95.

[25] See, e.g., Acts 15.20, 29; Thess 4.3, 5.22 for a similar use of ἀπέχεσθαι.

[26] Elliott, *1 Petery*, 462.

[27] Trans. Achtemeier, *1 Peter*, 172.

[28] Balch understands ἐπιθυμία as the passion for which Christians are caricatured, citing the description of a Christian woman in Apuleius, *The Golden Ass* 9.14 as an example for how outsiders associated Christians with sexual immorality (*Let Wives Be Submissive*, 86–7). Balch's point that pagans slandered Christians for a litany of negative vices applies more readily to 2.12, where Peter speaks of Gentiles maligning Christians as evildoers (κακοποιῶν), and to 4.15, where he lists a catalogue of vices for which Christians are being slandered. Horrell strongly asserts: "There must be no truth in the accusations of being murderers and thieves, or even 'those who meddle in others' affairs', for Christians are to be demonstrably ἀγαθοποιοί not κακοποιοί» (cf. 4.15, 19) (in "The Label Χριστιανός," 183). Contra Achtemeier, who takes the vices listed in 4.15 at face value as referring to "actual deeds" Christians could be accused of committing (*1 Peter*, 311).

of life inherited from their ancestors" that characterized and controlled their conduct prior to conversion. However, the hereditary desires of the dominant culture remain a serious threat to God's chosen people, as indicated by Peter's use of the military term στρατεύονται ("wage war"), which "figuratively depicts the devastating internal effect of Gentile-like desires upon believers."[29] Peter has already spoken of ἐπιθυμίαι in 1.14 as the cravings of their former ignorance and describes them in 2.11 as "resident aliens and foreigners" within society. Thus to render ἀπέχεσθαι as "disengage" serves to underscore how believers must do more than avoid the behaviors that are antithetical to their new life in Christ: they must stop doing them entirely.

To "disengage" from the prevailing value system does not mean Christians are to avoid contact with Gentiles. They rather set themselves apart from the desires of the dominant culture when they "maintain honorable conduct among the Gentiles" (τὴν ἀναστροφὴν ὑμῶν ἐν τοῖς ἔθνεσιν ἔχοντες καλήν; 2.12). Although the participle ἔχοντες does not fit the characteristics of an imperatival participle because of its grammatical link to ἀπέχεσθαι (v. 11), it functions as an imperative "by virtue of that same link" and "carries the main thrust of Peter's command" that he expounds upon in 2.13–4.6.[30] Disengaging from inappropriate conduct prevalent in society requires that Christians maintain appropriate boundaries with Gentiles. As Barth argues, an ethnic group creates, develops, and maintains difference only through interaction with others. Through right contact with and not isolation from Gentiles, the people of God differentiate and set themselves apart from outsiders and thereby gain a stronger sense of ingroup identity.

When Christians engage in what Peter refers to as "honorable conduct"[31] (τὴν ἀναστροφὴν ... καλήν), Gentiles may still condemn them as "evildoers" (κακοποιοί) for their refusal to participate in the behaviors and values that the latter consider appropriate (3.16-17; 4.4; 14, 16, 19) and also because Christians participate in activities that even Gentiles would consider shameful, such as behaving in lowly manner patterned after Christ (2.21-3; cf. 3.9).

Gentiles, however, may be compelled or persuaded on the day of visitation to glorify God (δοξάζω) "from observing (ἐποπτεύοντες) [their] honorable deeds" (2.12). The verb ἐποπτεύω means to pay close attention to[32] and is used in the NT only here and in 3.2 (cf. ἐπόπτης in 2 Pet 1.16). In both 2.12 and 3.2, the verb in the participle implies that Christians are under the continuous and careful scrutiny of Gentiles and that their good behavior has the potential to lead to a change in perception.[33] When observed, good Christian behavior can disprove the slander of Gentiles (2.12), "silence

---

[29] Peter similarly uses the military term ὁπλίσασθε ("arm yourself,") in 4.1.
[30] Michaels, *1 Peter*, 117; Elliott, *1 Peter*, 465. Contra Achtemeier (*1 Peter*, 177) and Joel Green (*1 Peter*, THNTC [Grand Rapids: Eerdmans, 2007], 65 n. 4), who take ἔχοντες to be an adverbial participle of means.
[31] See Elliott's discussion of the phrase τὴν ἀναστροφὴν ... καλήν and its related counterparts in 1 Peter in *1 Peter*, 465-6, 468-9.
[32] BDAG, 387.
[33] Or, as Michaels puts it, "ἐποπτεύοντες is all that comes between καταλαλοῦσιν and δοξάσωσι τὸν θεόν" (*1 Peter*, 118).

the ignorance of foolish people" (2.15), and win over unbelieving husbands "without a word" (3.2). Elliott explains, "In a culture where such great weight is laid upon visions as the ultimate arbiter of truth, this stress upon the *visibility* of Christian behavior and its empirical apprehensions makes eminent sense."[34]

The notion that Gentiles who slander Christians as "evildoers" will nevertheless observe their good deeds suggests Peter's addressees and Gentiles share some common ground in judging what is "good," as repeated in 2.14 and 3.2, even as Peter characterizes the desires and behavior of Gentiles in an entirely negative light elsewhere in the letter (e.g., 4.2-4). The possibility that Gentiles can rightly judge honorable conduct, even as they are maligned, suggests that the Gentile behaviors that Peter disparages function more as stereotypes, which, according to Barth, unite or categorize people under one ethnic identity while characterizing people from outside one's ethnic group as belonging to one simplistic identity. It also suggests that Gentiles are stereotyping Christians in a similar way and that proximity to Christians is the only way in which false ideas and claims can be corrected. Thus to disengage from the behaviors of the dominant culture does not mean that Christians must disengage from Gentiles altogether. Rather, they are to live honorably in plain sight of Gentiles, who may in turn come to see the falsity of their charges and join believers in glorifying God (cf. 1.7; 4.13, 14, 16). Their new set of values and orientation does not take them out of the world but rather puts them in more contact and conflict with it. Peter indicates in 2.12; 3.14-17; 4.12, 16; 5.9 that accusations against Christians are common and to be expected. Despite the frequency of suffering, Peter encourages Christians to participate in public life and remain in their households, even if they now belong to a spiritual household and are to understand themselves as "resident aliens and foreigners."

According to Balch, Peter in 2.12 expresses his concern for good opinion of outsiders by exhorting believers to engage in socially acceptable behavior and conform to the expectations of Hellenistic-Roman society.[35] Christians are to accommodate socially and politically not out of a missionary impulse or concern but in order to reduce the great tension Christians experience within the larger society and especially within the domestic sphere, so that non-believers would stop criticizing the new cult.[36] Balch rightly notes that Peter's emphasis in 2.12 is not on the conversion of Gentiles. However, Peter's main concern is not that believers reduce tension and unnecessary difference between Christians and Gentiles who malign them, but that believers actually live in such a way that befits the people of God (1.14-18, 2.9-10) while living *among* Gentiles. It is only when Christians disengage from the values of the dominant culture that they can engage Gentiles properly. Thus, Peter's interest lies in "conversion's *cause* ('from observing your good works') and final *result* (to 'glorify God on the day of visitation'),"[37] rather than in Gentile conversion or Christian accommodation to Gentile expectations of what is "good."

---

[34] Elliott, *1 Peter*, 468.
[35] Balch, *Let Wives Be Submissive*, 87-8.
[36] Ibid.
[37] Michaels, *1 Peter*, 118.

Peter prefaces the distinction between the people of God and Gentiles in 2.12 with the exhortation to live as social πάροικοι ("resident aliens") and παρεπίδημοί ("foreigners") in 2.11. This exhortation underscores the distinction Peter wants his addressees to make between themselves and members of the dominant culture, with whom they are no longer to identify and from whose behaviors they must struggle to disassociate. In 4.3-4, he drives a larger wedge between Gentiles and Christians in order to convince the latter that they "have already spent enough time in doing what the Gentiles like to do, living in licentiousness, passions, drunkenness, revels, carousing, and lawless idolatry" (4.3).[38] By disengaging from their former way of life, Christians behave in ways that Gentiles consider strange and astonishing: "By this they are astonished when you no longer join them in the same absurd degree of senseless behavior, and so they vilify [you]" (4.4). The reason Gentiles speak evil of (βλασφημέω) Christians has to do with the fact that Christians are no longer participating in the same profligate activities as their former pals, drinking buddies, or "erstwhile cronies"[39] (4.2-4).

Among the vices listed in 4.3, ἐπιθυμίαι have already been portrayed by Peter in a purely negative sense (1.14; 2.11; 4.2). In 1.14, ἐπιθυμίαι refer to the cravings, lusts, or impulses that exercised control in their former life. In 2.11, Peter modifies ἐπιθυμίαι with σαρκικός and describes them as dominating forces of the flesh that "wage war against [their] soul." In 4.2, Peter pits the "desires of the flesh" (ἀνθρώπων ἐπιθυμίαις) against the will of God and relegates such desires as the fuel for their former behavior. Such repetition suggests that Peter's addressees, while learning to disidentify with the ἐπιθυμίαι that dictated their behaviors prior to conversion, have not completely severed themselves from the selfish cravings or indulgences that make living into their newly begotten (1.3, 22-3), newborn-like state (2.1-3) impossible (2.1-3). Hence, in 4.1-2, Peter exhorts believers to "take up arms" (ὁπλίσασθε) against such threatening and harmful passions, suggesting that they are not as vigilant about disengaging from them as they should be. In 4.4, Peter sums up the vices in 4.3 with the phrase τῆς ἀσωτίας ἀνάχυσιν ("absurd degree of senseless activity"), which sharply contrasts the mental readiness for action, sober-mindedness, and self-control Peter calls for in 1.13, 4.7, and 5.8.

As Barth explains, stereotypes delimit rather than delineate culture and in effect function to exclude outsiders rather than accurately represent them.[40] In order to help Christians regard their new life in Christ as qualitatively different from their past life, Peter sets up exaggerated binaries between what the Gentiles and the people of God do. This helps the latter de-familiarize and disidentify from a former way of life still acutely familiar to but longer appropriate for those who have been "born anew to a living hope through the resurrection of Christ from the dead" (1.3b). Just as Gentiles stereotype Christians as evildoers (2.12), so Peter stereotypes Gentiles as the profligate "other" (4.3). This is not because Christians and Gentiles share no values in common

---

[38] NRSV.
[39] Elliott, *1 Peter*, 725.
[40] For a brief analysis of how Barth's concept of ethnic boundaries and "stereotyped clusters" applies to African Americans in the South Side of Chicago at the start of the twentieth century, see Bauman, *The Pekin*, xx.

or cannot live in contact with each other. Rather, Peter perceives the struggle among his addressees to embody their new corporate identity as a people of God in the face of hostility, slander, and persecution; and so he urges them to stop engaging in fleshly behaviors that set them *among* rather than *apart from* the Gentiles and that reinforce the negative stereotypes Gentiles have of them. Peter sharply distinguishes between ἔθνος ἅγιον and τὰ ἔθνη because he understands the tensions, hostilities, and subsequent persecutions experienced by his readers as stemming not only from the fact that they are "Christians" but also from the fact that they are no longer "Gentiles."

Disidentifying from "The Futile Conduct Inherited from Your Ancestors"

For Barth, who pioneered what later became known as "constructivism," ethnicity is not a cultural given but the product of social process; it is not ascribed through birth but is chosen depending on circumstances and "made and remade."[41] An ethnic group's culture or set of behavioral norms is not inherent to the group but results from social factors and frictions. Peter detaches Christian identity from Greco-Roman cultural values that put them at odds with Christian values by giving them a sense of a communal ethnic identity that has its own distinctive culture. This is significant for my analysis of 1 Peter because of the social location of the letter's recipients, who were formerly at home in the dominant Greco-Roman culture[42] and who must now become aliens and strangers in a land with values, customs, households, standards, and lifestyles intimately familiar to them. Peter assumes that were it not for divine intervention—i.e., the fact that they were "chosen" by God and "born anew through the resurrection of Jesus Christ from the dead" (1.1–3)—his readers would still be operating according to the "futile conduct inherited from [their] ancestors" (1.18) and the prevailing values of the broader culture around them (2.11; 4.3–4). He thus redefines their past(s) as ἔθνη, even as he gives them a new shared history (1.1–2, 10–12, 20).

Thus Peter constructs Christian identity in ethnic terms, so that his primarily Gentile readers find the means to *disidentify* from their past—i.e., their former ignorance (1.14), their inherited "futile ways" (1.18), and the litany of immoralities that once characterized their lives and that, from Peter's point of view, still characterizes the surrounding Gentile culture (4.3–4)—and *reidentify* as an entirely new people with a new history, present, and future. Peter believes that the better the people of God understand who they are no longer, the better they can live as the people they are, especially in the face of suffering that results from their new identity as Christians.

---

[41] Wimmer, "The Making and Unmaking of Ethnic Boundaries: A Multilevel Process Theory," *American Journal of Sociology* 113, no. 4 (January 2008): 971.

[42] While Greco-Roman culture cannot be summarized as one thing, I describe the dominant culture as a singular entity in my discussion of 1 Peter as a way to replicate Peter's presentation of Gentiles as belonging to one large category of those who are not a people of God (1.10). I take the same approach when describing Christians as belonging to the minority culture while recognizing that there were many "minority" cultures that had a position at the under-belly of the Roman empire.

Constrained Christian Identity

In multi-ethnic social systems, Barth sees ethnic identity as constraining people's behavior in all their activities and interactions with others in a similar way that sex and rank constrain a person's behavior.[43] Ethnic identity cannot be easily disregarded or temporarily put aside because it is "superordinate to most other statuses."[44] A Chinese American, for example, may identify as American, having been born and raised in the United States, but be treated as a "perpetual foreigner"—one who is never "American" but always ethnic.[45] This sheds light on why Peter finds the use of ethnic language to construct Christian identity so helpful. He wants to create not only a cohesive corporate identity for Christians but also a constrained identity that demarcates cultural, social, and theological differences. Christians are no longer Gentiles and must therefore no longer live like Gentiles. So Peter reasons in 4.3, "for the time that has passed [is] sufficient for carrying out the will of the Gentiles,"[46] and goes on to list examples of behaviors that should no longer characterize the people of God and that characterize and even caricature Gentiles. Peter wants Christians to be set apart through their obedience to the will of God and faithful adherence to the example of Christ because they now live according to a completely different set of values and according to a completely new eschatological orientation toward the world.

Peter thus overcommunicates and overemphasizes group differences and particularities, especially in 2.9–10 and 4.3–4, when addressing how Christians have an entirely new existence—past, present, and future—because of Christ. However, he encourages his addressees to live in an understated, undercommunicated way, so that their actions speak louder than their words.[47] Speech plays a significant role in 1 Peter as the author presents Jesus' ability to keep his mouth from speaking deceit (2.22), citing from Isaiah 53.9 as an example for Christians to follow (2.21; 3.10). Peter emphasizes Christ-like conduct in response to slandering, defiling speech (2.1, 11–12, 15, 22–3; 3.1–4, 9–10, 16). What Christians now know to be true of themselves because of Christ can help them withstand the pain of being falsely accused. References to speech in 3.9, 15–16 reveal that Peter does not endorse a verbally passive or silent strategy toward false accusations, slander, blasphemy, etc. Rather, in 3.9, he urges those who follow in the steps of Christ (2.21) to "bless" (εὐλογέω) those who inflict evil (κακός) or verbal

---

[43] Barth, *Ethnic Groups*, 17–19.
[44] Ibid., 17.
[45] The cultural stereotype of the perpetual foreigner has been persistently imposed upon ethnic minorities in the United States, particularly Asian Americans. The stereotype interrogates the identity of those who understand themselves to be as American as their European American counterparts who perceive them to be less American. See Ok, "Always Ethnic, Never 'American,'" 418–20.
[46] Trans. Elliott (*1 Peter*, 710).
[47] I owe the language of over- and under-communication to Erving Goffman, who writes, "one over-all objective of any team is to sustain the definition of the situation that its performance fosters. This will involve the over-communication of some facts and the under-communication of others" (*The Presentation of Self*, 141). In 1 Peter, Peter loudly pronounces Christian identity for his addressees through written words, while exhorting his addressees to live out this identity in deed and gentle speech (e.g., 3.15).

insults (λοιδορία) on them.[48] He thus overcommunicates difference between Gentiles and Christians in order to emphasize their new life in Christ.

In 3.15, Peter exhorts his addressees to "always be prepared to give a defense to anyone who demands of [them] a reason for the hope that is in [them]." Being ready to articulate the reason for the hope Christians possess (cf. with "living hope" in 1.3) does not mean that they should go out of their way to defend themselves or disprove false accusations through reciprocally harsh or zealous speech. Rather, Christians should go out of their way to respond with verbal "gentleness" (πραΰτης) and "reverence" (φόβος)[49] (3.16). Only those who "sanctify Christ as Lord in [their] hearts" can readily defend themselves with gentleness and respect when asked to do so.[50] Their confidence and calmness should "astonish" those who interrogate them (cf. 4.4; 12).

Construing the Gentile "Other"

By presenting an ethnic understanding of Christian identity, on the one hand, and characterizing people and practices from their former way of life as one clustered, stereotyped ethnic group (τὰ ἔθνη), on the other, Peter hopes Christians can be more resistant to reverting to their former way of life. According to Barth, the moral and social conventions concomitant with ethnic identity become more resistant to change when they are joined in "stereotyped clusters as characteristics of one single identity."[51] Peter makes great effort to particularize and concretize Christian identity from 1.1–2.10. In 2.12, he minimizes the diversity found among Gentiles by grouping them into one vague conglomerate category. In doing so, he drives a wider wedge between insiders and outsiders. The more he reduces the complexity of the people whom he groups as "Gentiles" and emphasizes the unity and singular identity of the people God, the harder he makes it for Christians to revert to Gentile ways of being.

Peter sees his addressees' former way of life as incompatible with their new life in Christ. He thus constructs a binary between the people of God and Gentiles, who are not of God, so that the former begin to see how their previous ways of behaving are now inappropriate and incompatible with their identity as Christians. Using ethnic categories enables Peter to replace his readers' previous way of life lived according to the "human desires" (ἀνθρώπων ἐπιθυμίαις) and the "will of the Gentiles" (τὸ βούλημα τῶν ἐθνῶν) with a way of life lived according to the example of Christ

---

[48] While the noun κακός denotes a less specific form of evil or harm, the noun λοιδορία denotes verbal abuse.

[49] "Φόβος" in 3.16 refers to "reverence" for God (cf. 1.17; 2.17, 18; 3.2), in contrast to the way φόβος refers to fear of hostile humans in 3.6 and abusive neighbors in 3.14 (Elliott, *1 Peter*, 625, 629).

[50] It is interesting that Peter does not instruct his addressees to be ready to defend their innocence or their conduct. Rather, he tells them to be prepared to provide a reason for the hope that is theirs. Pliny's account of his formal inquiry concerning the Christians living in Bithynia-Pontus (*Ep.*10.96) bears striking resemblance to the situation spoken of in 2.14, 3.15–16, and 4.16 and to the conflict between the letter's readers and their neighbors assumed by Peter. While serving as governor of Pontus and Bithynia around 110 CE, Pliny corresponds with Trajan on the treatment of Christians in the eastern provinces of the Roman empire, known as the Anatolian Peninsula or Asia Minor. See Holloway, *Coping with Prejudice*, 18, 40–73.

[51] Barth, *Ethnic Groups*, 17.

(2.18ff), who "suffered in the flesh" (Χριστοῦ οὖν παθόντος σαρκί) and according to the "will of God" (θελήματι θεοῦ) (4.1–3a).

Goffman on Stigma

In his classic work, *Stigma: Notes on the Management of Spoiled Identity*, Goffman identifies three forms or marks of stigma: (1) physical "abominations" or "deformities"; (2) alleged "blemishes" of individual character; and (3) "tribal" identities that can be passed from generation to generation.[52] Most germane to this study of 1 Peter is the second form of stigma, as Christians are stigmatized for what Goffman would call their blemishes of individual character, i.e., for their superstition, criminality, and anti-social, religiously exclusive atheism associated with being Christian. Peter constructs Christian identity along explicitly ethnic lines as a strategy to contest and reappropriate the stigma associated with being "Christian" and to reduce the temptation for Christians to revert to their former identity in the face of social prejudice. If Christians understand themselves as being people who possess not only a new present-day identity but also a new lineage through the blood of Christ, they will see an enormous distinction between being a Christian and not having been one. Although they have abandoned their old lineage, they are not left without one. Rather, Christians now possess a separate system of honor and a distinct ethnic identity that enable them to subvert the stigma imposed upon them by the dominant culture.

Goffman describes the term stigma as "an attribute that is deeply discrediting."[53] Stigma involves labeling, stereotyping, categorizing who is ingroup and who is outgroup, the loss of status, and discrimination.[54] Stigma itself is relational, dynamic, and relative in nature because it is a mark of disgrace that emerges from within a web of preconceived but generally unfixed notions of what is normative and abnormal, acceptable and unacceptable, etc.[55] Having a severe limp, for example, may be a stigma for an aspiring soldier because it calls into question his ability to perform the difficult physical demands required of a soldier. This person's limp then severely discredits him from being a choice candidate for military combat. But if a soldier has a similar limp resulting from his extensive military service, then the very thing that stigmatizes and discredits the young, aspiring soldier serves as badge of honor and credibility for a seasoned officer with political aspirations.

Those who impose stigma are referred to by Goffman as "normals."[56] Normals do not depart negatively from the particular expectations of a group. Rather, they

---

[52] Goffman, *Stigma*, 4–5. While the descriptive accuracy of these precise categories has been challenged, Holloway rightly notes that Goffman's essential and important point is that "virtually any type of identity marker can serve as stigma" (*Coping with Prejudice*, 34).

[53] Ibid., 3. Goffman also refers to stigma as a "failing," "shortcoming," or "handicap."

[54] See Bruce G. Link and Jo C. Phelan, "Conceptualizing Stigma," *Annual Review of Sociology* 27 (2001): 363–87.

[55] Goffman, *Stigma*, 3.

[56] Ibid., 5.

reinforce and perpetuate group expectations, which include creating the idea of what and who is "normal" and who is "abnormal." Thus when normals stigmatize a person or a group, they do so because they perceive the stigmatized as deviating from acceptable standards of normalcy. Normals ultimately believe that the person who bears a mark of stigma is somehow less human, inadequately human, or "not quite human."[57] The view of the stigmatized as inferior fuels and justifies various forms of discrimination, which reduce the stigmatized person's chances of success in life. Normals impute a variety of additional imperfections to a person on the basis of his or her original and stigmatized imperfection/failure. They construct ideology and theories to explain a stigmatized person's inferiority and the potential danger that he or she represents. In doing so, normals prevent or disqualify the stigmatized from full social acceptance at both the informal and formal level. We see this, for example, in the pejorative labeling of undocumented immigrants living in the United States as "illegal immigrants" or "illegal aliens." Criminals are by definition "illegal"; thus, the term "illegal immigrant" suggests that undocumented immigrants are criminal in nature simply by virtue of their presence in the United States. The slur is associated with other unsavory characteristics, such as being dirty, diseased, threatening to the public good, and thoroughly un-American. A Tweet sent by Donald Trump during his presidential campaign is particularly illustrative of this point: "Many of the thugs that attacked the peaceful Trump supporters in San Jose were illegals. They burned the American flag and laughed at the police."[58] Despite the fact that the Associated Press has eliminated the expression *illegal immigrants* from its stylebook because of its imprecision,[59] and opponents of the term *illegal* argue that it stigmatizes, dehumanizes, and marginalizes the very people it seeks to describe,[60] negative attitudes toward "undocumented immigrants" or "unauthorized migrants" continue to permeate public and private discourse on the subject of immigration.

Goffman underscores that not all negative or undesirable attributes result in stigma, "but only those which are incongruous with our stereotype of what a given type of individual should be."[61] That is, stigma can be imposed on persons who disrupt stereotypes or expectations. A study entitled "Prescriptive Stereotypes and Workplace Consequences for East Asians in North American" shows that people of East Asian descent (i.e., Asian Americans) are descriptively stereotyped as highly competent (i.e., qualified, capable, skilled), cold (i.e., lacking in emotion or friendliness and thus less trustworthy), and obedient and non-dominant (i.e., not assertive or attempting to take

---

[57] Ibid.
[58] Donald J. Trump (@realDonaldTrump), June 4, 2016, 6:04 AM, Tweet.
[59] Rachel Weiner, "AP Drops 'Illegal Immigrant' from Stylebook," *The Washington Post*, April 2, 2013, accessed September 23, 2017, http://www.washingtonpost.com/blogs/post-politics/wp/2013/04/02/ap-drops-illegal-immigrant-from-stylebook/.
[60] See Jose Antonio Vargas, "Immigration Debate: The Problem with the Word Illegal," *Time*, September 21, 2012, accessed September 23, 2017, http://ideas.time.com/2012/09/21/immigration-debate-the-problem-with-the-word-illegal/. See also John McWhorter, "Banning the Term 'Illegal Immigrant' Won't Change the Stigma," *Time*, April 9, 2013, accessed September 23, 2017, http://ideas.time.com/2013/04/09/viewpoint-banning-the-term-illegal-immigrant-wont-change-the-stigma/.
[61] Goffman, *Stigma*, 3.

charge).⁶² In the workplace, people disliked a dominant East Asian coworker compared to a non-dominant East Asian or dominant or non-dominant white coworker. Furthermore, dominant East Asian coworkers experienced more harassment at work than non-dominant East Asian or dominant or non-dominant white coworkers. This study suggests that non-dominance is both a descriptive stereotype, reflecting beliefs of how East Asians do behave, and a prescriptive stereotype, reflecting beliefs of how East Asians *should* behave.⁶³ As long as East Asians remain in relatively subordinate positions, they pose minimum threat to whites and are likely to be lauded as a "model minority," who justify the social system as meritocracy.⁶⁴ However, when East Asians behave assertively and take on more higher positions of leadership, they pose both economic and social threats to whites⁶⁵ and are more likely to be stigmatized as "perpetual foreigners."⁶⁶ Thus, Goffman does not equate a stereotype with stigma because a stereotype does not necessarily alienate or discredit a person, but rather a person's unwillingness to cohere with certain social expectations or the stereotypes of the dominant or normal culture does/can alienate a person who behaves in unexpected ways. Difference itself does not stigmatize a person, but rather "undesired difference" from what is anticipated stigmatizes a person.

It is generally assumed that stereotyping or profiling is usually reserved for passing strangers and that familiarity can, but may not always, reduce contempt.⁶⁷ Normals who come into more frequent and personal contact with a blind person, for example, may eventually become less put off by the disability and behave with relative normalcy around the abnormal person.⁶⁸ The stigmatized bear the brunt of the hard work of bringing others to not view one's stigma as a crucial feature of his or her identity. This "breaking through," as Fred Davis calls it, requires the stigmatized to have a special tactfulness, intimacy, and more frequent contact with normals in order to increase

---

⁶² Jennifer L. Berdahl and Ji-A Min, "Prescriptive Stereotypes and Workplace Consequences for East Asians in North America," *Cultural Diversity and Ethnic Minority Psychology* 18, no. 2 (2012): 141–52, 142.

⁶³ Ibid., 141–2.

⁶⁴ Ibid., 142–3. For discussions on the effects of the "model minority" stereotype, see, e.g., Nicholas Daniel Hartlep, *The Model Minority Stereotype: Demystifying Asian American Success* (Charlotte, NC: Information Age, 2013); Victor Bascara, *Model-Minority Imperialism* (Minneapolis: University of Minneapolis Press, 2006); Claire Jean Kim, "The Racial Triangulation of Asian Americans," *Politics & Society* 27, no. 1 (1999): 105–38; "The Effects of Seeing Asian-Americans as a 'Model Minority,'" *New York Times*, accessed April 5, 2017, https://www.nytimes.com/roomfordebate/2015/10/16/the-effects-of-seeing-asian-americans-as-a-model-minority.

⁶⁵ Berdahl and Min, "Prescriptive Stereotypes," 142.

⁶⁶ The image of the "perpetual foreigner" has also been a prevailing narrative burdening Asian Americans, one that even their "model minority" status cannot seem to mitigate. See, e.g., Sze-Kar Wan, "Asian American Perspectives: Ambivalence of the Model Minority and Perpetual Foreigner," in *Studying Paul's Letters: Contemporary Perspectives and Methods*, ed. Joseph A. Marchal (Minneapolis: Fortress, 2012), 175–90; Que-Lam Huynh et al., "Perpetual Foreigners," 133–62; Frank H. Wu, *Yellow: Race in America beyond Black and White* (New York: Basic Books, 2003); Mia Tuan, *Forever Foreigners or Honorary Whites?: The Asian Ethnic Experience Today* (New Brunswick, NJ: Rutgers University Press, 1999).

⁶⁷ Goffman, *Stigma*, 53.

⁶⁸ Ibid., 51–2.

the tolerance among normals for the defects, abnormalities, or even deviance that previously caused distance.[69]

Although stigma is imposed upon individuals and/or groups by normals, it can also be contested. The stigmatized, in some circumstances, possess the agency to challenge or disregard their devalued status.[70] Goffman notes that it is entirely possible for an individual to deviate from or fail to live up to what normals demand of her while at the same time remaining relatively untouched by this failure.[71] Those who identify with the underground punk culture, for example, may celebrate the very characteristics that the dominant culture holds against them. To be a punk is to go against the grain. "Punks" may reappropriate the stigma imposed upon them by normals as a credit to their subversive, stick-it-to-the-man mentality. Goffman asserts that social identity can be interpreted in unconventional ways.[72] Thus, those labeled as social deviants may choose to deviate yet again from standard conventions of normalcy by rejecting the idea that they are somehow inferior people.

Goffman differentiates between one's *"virtual social identity"* and *"actual social identity"* and between those who are *"discredited"* by normals and *"discreditable."*[73] Virtual social identity refers to the characteristics imputed to a person. Actual social identity refers to the characteristics and attributes that a person can prove to possess. Discredited people are those with obvious failings that cannot be easily hidden. Discreditable people, however, possess failings that can be hidden. Both the discredited and discreditable face the difficult challenge of managing their spoiled identities when coming into social contact with others.[74] The discredited, whose stigma is obvious, must manage tensions that arise as a result of their deviant trait. The discreditable, whose stigma is less obvious, must manage information that can potentially disclose their deviant trait.

André Aciman writes of his mother and her experience of being deaf: "Some men whistled when she walked by, because she was beautiful and sexy and had a way of looking you boldly in the face until you lowered your eyes. But, when she shopped and spoke with the monotone, guttural voice of the deaf, people laughed."[75] Such an example highlights what Goffman means by discreditable versus discredited and actual versus virtual social identities. As long as Aciman's mother refrained from speaking,

---

[69] Fred Davis, *Passage through Crisis: Polio Victims and Their Families* (Indianapolis: Bobbs-Merrill, 1963), 127–8 as cited by Goffman (ibid., 52).
[70] James C. Scott's work is relevant here, as he examines how subordinate groups resist the ideological hegemony of those in power through ambiguous, anonymous, "hidden" means (*Domination and the Arts of Resistance: Hidden Transcripts* [Yale University Press, 2008]). See Horrell's application of Scott's work in "Between Conformity and Resistance: Beyond the Balch-Elliott Debate towards a Post Colonial Reading of First Peter," in *Reading First Peter with New Eyes: Methodological Reassessments of the Letter of First Peter*, eds. Robert L. Webb and Betsy Bauman-Martin (LNTS 364; London and New York: T&T Clark, 2007), 111–43; 117–20.
[71] Goffman, *Stigma*, 6.
[72] Ibid., 10.
[73] Ibid., 2, 41–2.
[74] Ibid., 42.
[75] André Aciman, "Are You Listening?," *The New Yorker*, March 17, 2014, 32–5.

she could pass as a hearing woman. The moment she spoke, however, her stigma became audible and thus visible. Such vulnerability to exposure puts the possessor of a less visible stigma in the predicament of whether "to display or not to display; to tell or not to tell; to let on or not to let on; to lie or not to lie; and in each case, to whom, how, when, and where."[76] In the case of Aciman's mother, it was a matter of time before she had to display or disclose her stigma in order to participate in basic social interactions and transactions at the risk of being teased, pitied, or ostracized. In those instances, she became discredited. The onus was on her to find the resources and strategies to manage and even rise above the stigma of deafness. Even with her coping mechanisms in place, only her familiar acquaintances and intimate family and friends could differentiate between her virtual social identity (helpless, pitiable, less of a person) and actual social identity (independent but in need of help, un-self-pitying and yet lonely, and a full-fledged person with deficiencies of hearing).

In many cases, stigma is symbolic. On the one hand, a tattoo, for example, may symbolize rebellion, and darker skin may symbolize racial-ethnic inferiority. On the other hand, a Harvard class ring may symbolize prestige, and whiteness may symbolize normalcy and racial superiority. Goffman discusses the role of "stigma symbols," which function in the opposite way of "status" or "prestige symbols."[77] It is possible for the stigmatized to employ prestige symbols in ways that counter their stigma symbols because doing so may help to break up, problematize, or nuance "an otherwise coherent picture" of individuals as being less human, valuable, normal, and acceptable.[78] Prestige symbols can contest stigma symbols by casting doubt on the veracity and validity of virtual (as opposed to actual) identity imposed upon the stigmatized. Hence, Goffman refers to such symbols as "*disidentifiers.*"[79] A high-powered working woman may break up or challenge the stigma of non-femininity by wearing a wedding ring and displaying photos of her children on her desk.

Contesting and Subverting Christian Stigma in 1 Peter

Stigma can be contested or reappropriated in such a way as to reverse the negative effects of stigma and stereotypes. Peter finds the possibility of this in the way Christians are stigmatized for their allegiance to Christ. Thus, he creates an honored identity for his readers using ethnic language and concepts so that they can better understand, not only who they are no longer, but who they are now as people of God and what is in store for them in the eschatological future. The challenge of no longer living as Gentiles and the hostility arising from being associated with Jesus and Jesus' followers lead Peter to create boundaries and contest stigma. Peter seeks symbolically to draw clear lines between the people of God and the people not of God so that Christians can differentiate who they once were from who they are now as a result of their new birth. He differentiates Gentiles from the people of God in order

---

[76] Goffman, *Stigma*, 42.
[77] Ibid., 43.
[78] Ibid., 44.
[79] Ibid.

to help them overcome the very real temptation and pressure to revert to their former lifestyles, so that they can disidentify with their former existence and fully identify with their new status as a "chosen race, a royal priesthood, a holy nation, a people for [God's] possession" (2.9).

Goffman notes that stereotyping is often reserved for passing strangers. A normal (a Gentile) who comes into more frequent and personal contact with a stigmatized person (a Christian) may over time become less put off by the stigmatized person's defect and behave with relative normalcy around the abnormal person. The present participle ἐποπτεύοντες ("observing") in 2.12 implies both continuity and intent.[80] Being under the scrutinizing and careful gaze of non-believers requires a frequency and familiarity of contact that would enable Christians possibly to make the strange familiar. In other words, familiarity has the potential to reduce contempt. In the case of 1 Peter, however, the stigmatized persons are not passing strangers but people very familiar to normals. This suggests that although Christians are not literal strangers to the people who slander (2.12) and revile them (4.14), they are behaving in ways that seem strange, even to those who know them well. They are intimately acquainted with the norms, values, and practices of the dominant culture and so must all the more abstain from living in such a way that does not befit those born anew to a living hope but that continues to feel like second nature.

Goffman's insight into the double bind of stereotypes suggests that behaving in ways that both honor God and disrupt negative and false stereotypes held by the dominant culture can prove to be more problematic than beneficial and more of a liability than an asset for the addressees of 1 Peter. In 2.12, Peter shows that it is possible for Gentiles to "malign" (καταλαλοῦσιν) Christians as "evildoers" (κακοποιοί), even as Christians strive to maintain "honorable conduct" (ἀναστροφὴ ... καλή) among the Gentiles. This is due in part to the fact that Gentiles and Christians do not always see eye-to-eye on what constitutes "honorable" behavior.

While Peter does suggest the possibility that Gentiles and Christians can agree on what is "good" (ἀγαθός) behavior in 2.14, he more explicitly portrays Gentile conduct in very negative terms in 4.1–6 and provides a list of accusations as equal in negativity as those leveled against Christians in 4.16. Furthermore, while Peter expresses the consolatory hope and possibility that "honorable conduct" on the part of Christians may someday be recognized (ἵνα ... δοξάσωσι τὸν θεὸν ἐν ἡμέρᾳ ἐπισκοπῆς; 2.12),[81] he does not promise that such a radical transformation of perception and speech on the part of Gentiles will occur. Nevertheless, he enjoins Christians to behave in such a way that disrupts, contradicts, and even improves Gentile attitudes toward them and the God they worship with the hope that Gentiles will eventually perceive rightly what they now perceive wrongly: that Christians are indeed doers of good.

The comments of Roman historians Tacitus (c. 56–c. 120 CE) and Suetonius (c. 69–c. 119 CE) reflect the general mistrust, hatred, and accusation experienced

---

[80] See my earlier discussion of 2.12 on pp. 66–71.
[81] The construction ἵνα ... δοξάσωσι denotes the possibility that Gentiles who now slander Christians may praise God at a later time.

by early Christians.[82] In *Annals* (15.44), Tacitus calls Christianity a "pernicious superstition" (*extiabialis superstitio*). Nero could scapegoat Christians for the disastrous fire in Rome (64 CE) in order to suppress rumors that he himself ordered the fire to make room for his building programs precisely because the populace already held Christians in utter contempt and associated them with all sorts of shameful and immoral practices (*flagitia*). According to Tacitus, "vast numbers were convicted" not on account of arson but for "hatred of the human race" (*odio humani*).[83] In *Nero* (16.2), Suetonius also describes Nero's persecution of the Christians, explaining that "punishment by Nero was inflicted on the Christians, a class of men given to a new and mischievous superstition" (*superstitionis novae ac maleficae*). Such negative allegations and perceptions of social and religious deviance by non-Christian Roman authors correspond to the Gentile depiction of Christians as "evildoers" in 2.12 and 4.15.

While it has been the widely held view that Peter points to good works as a possible solution to such baseless slander in 2.13–3.7,[84] Peter exhorts his addressees to continue doing what is good in 2.12, not so that Gentiles may glorify God in the eschatological future but because such conduct glorifies God irrespective of Gentile praise or condemnation (3.13–17; 4.12–19).[85] He thus cautions them against reinforcing the negative allegations and perceptions that do not cohere with their identity in Christ (2.21–25) while encouraging them to endure the suffering that results from following Christ (1.6; 2.4, 7–8; 3.9, 13–18; 4.1, 12–14, 16). Christians may consider themselves "blessed" (μακάριος) when "reviled" (ὀνειδίζω) for the name of Christ and when they "suffer" (πάσχω) as Christians (4.14–16).[86] However, they are not to suffer "as a murderer, or a thief, or an evildoer" (4.15). In 4.4, Gentiles are "astonished" (ξενίζω) that believers no longer "run with" (συντρέχω) them in the same "absurd degree of senseless behavior" they once did, such as the catalogue of misconduct listed in 4.3. While Barth's insights on the function of stereotypes have helped to illuminate Peter's

---

[82] While we cannot simply take these authors living in Rome as representative of attitudes in Asia Minor at the time 1 Peter was written, they provide us with some evidence of how non-Christians perceived Christians. For discussion on the question of how Christians were perceived by pagans in the late first/early second century, see Stephen Benko, *Pagan Rome and the Early Christians*, reprint ed. (Bloomington, IN: Indiana University Press, 1986). For a portrayal of pagan criticism of Christianity from the beginning of the second century to the time of Julian in the late fourth century, see Wilken, *The Christians as the Romans Saw Them*.

[83] *Annals* 15.44.

[84] So, e.g., Achtemeier, *1 Peter*, 177; Goppelt, *A Commentary on I Peter*, 159; W. C. van Unnik, "Christianity according to 1 Peter," *ExpT* 68 (1956/57), 82.

[85] Travis B. Williams, *Good Works in 1 Peter: Negotiating Social Conflict and Christian Identity in the Greco-Roman World* (Tübingen: Mohr Siebeck, 2014) offers extensive and recent treatment on good works in 1 Peter that challenges the consensus among modern scholars that Peter sees good works as a means to accommodate to Greco-Roman society and reduce social hostility. According to Williams, "the language of good works represents a form of subaltern resistance wherein colonial mimicry is used to invert the oppressive dynamics of hegemonic discourse and social domination" (ibid., 260).

[86] Although Peter adopts Χριστιανός as "insider-facing language," the fact that it is one of a number of labels used by outsiders in an accusatory way implies that being called a Χριστιανός would lead to suffering (Paul Trebilco, *Self-Designations and Group Identity in the New Testament* [Cambridge, Cambridge University Press, 2012], 283).

use of stereotypes and exaggerated difference in 4.3-4,[87] Goffman's idea of "undesired difference"[88] helps reveal why Gentiles may perceive the radical change of behavior in Christian converts as inappropriate and offensive to the point of being blasphemed. According to Goffman, it is not a stereotype itself that necessarily alienates or discredits a person. Rather, it is a person's unwillingness to cohere with certain social expectations or the stereotypes of the dominant or normal culture that alienates a person who behaves in unexpected or shocking ways.

As stigmatized people, Christians bear the responsibility to conduct themselves with the sort of tactfulness and familiarity that concretizes, humanizes, and even possibly neutralizes and transforms the negative association with the "name of Christ" (4.14). It has been argued by Elliott that Peter takes a sectarian approach to the dominant culture.[89] The constellation of terms in 2.9 in addition to the strong household language throughout the letter certainly can be seen as sectarian when read in isolation from the rest of Peter's exhortations. Goffman, however, helps us consider how one of the perils of a strong ethnic and religious group identity is that the dominant culture can more readily stereotype Christians as a profligate other because Christians themselves are intentionally separating themselves from their husbands, relatives, friends, neighbors, and associates. However, in the household code (2.13-3.7), we see Peter's exhortation for his addressees to maintain conduct viewed as appropriate by normals insofar as it does not compromise their allegiance and obedience to Christ and commitment to one another.

Through the household ethic, Peter attempts to preserve the bonds of intimacy of the household, not only to keep societal peace but also to prevent Christians from reinforcing false and negative stereotypes that Christians are family and society haters.[90] The emphasis Peter places on being an οἶκος πνευματικὸς and οἶκος τοῦ θεοῦ provides an alternative family and household *in addition* to their unbelieving families and households. Christians must manage multiple commitments (e.g., to their masters, husbands, wives, neighbors, and associates) and must navigate multiple ideologies and pressures (e.g., how to honor the emperor without worshipping him, how to live as free people within the laws of Rome, how to worship God while living under the roof of a master or husband who worships other gods).[91] Their primary and ultimate commitment, however, is to Christ their Lord.

---

[87] See discussion on p. 21.
[88] Goffman, *Stigma*, 5.
[89] Elliott, "1 Peter, Its Situation and Strategy: A Discussion with David Balch," in *Perspectives on First Peter*, ed. Charles H. Talbert (NAPBR Special Studies Series 9; Macon, GA: Mercer University Press, 1986), 61-78. This is an expanded version of Elliott's discussion with Balch at AAR/SBL in 1982 on the theme "1 Peter: Social Separation or Acculturation?"
[90] For detailed comment on the theories regarding the traditions employed in 2.13-17, see Elliott, *1 Peter*, 503-11.
[91] Balch argues for the apologetic function of 1 Peter's household code. According to Balch, Peter addresses slaves and wives first because they faced intense social tension between the church and Roman society, since Romans believed wives and slaves to be particularly susceptible to the seduction of foreign cults, citing, e.g., from Tertullian, *Apology* 3; Apuleius, *The Golden Ass* IX.14; Dio Chrysostom, *Nicom.* 38.14 (*Let Wives Be Submissive*, 81-116, esp. 88, 96-97).

"Faith Information Control"

In their article, "Whiteness, Non-whiteness and 'Faith Information Control': Religion among Young People in Grønland, Oslo," Anders Vassenden and Mette Andersson employ Goffman's stigma analysis to explore the interplay of ethnicity, race, and religion among Christians, Muslims, and non-religious urban young people in secular Norwegian society.[92] In the dominant culture of Norway, both whiteness and non-religiosity serve as prestige symbols; non-whiteness and religiosity serve as stigma symbols to the extent that whiteness signifies secularism and non-whiteness, or "racial ethnicity," signifies religion (namely Islam).[93] Thus non-white Muslims or Christians are "discredited" because they possess the highly visible stigmas of both ethnicity *and* faith. White Christians, however, are "discreditable" because they possess the invisible stigma of faith but have the freedom to choose how much or how little of their faith to reveal.[94]

Because being secular is associated with being white, white Christians must provide a verbal or non-verbal cue or expression of their faith, such as a T-shirt with a distinctly Christian image or message on it, a cross tattoo or necklace, or the explicit verbal statement, "I am a Christian."[95] Even though white Christians interviewed in this study seldom reported the experience of direct hostility from non-Christians, they

---

[92] Anders Vassenden and Mette Andersson, "Whiteness, Non-Whiteness and 'Faith Information Control': Religion among Young People in Grønland, Oslo," *Ethnic and Racial Studies* 34, no. 4 (2011): 574–93. Scandinavia is a region where secular beliefs are normative and where being non-religious is neither taboo nor attached to stigma (ibid., 579). Race as a concept, on the other hand, is taboo in Norway, a nation with a history of racism toward its minority groups but without the infamous institutionalized racism that mires US history. Thus, Norwegians prefer using the term "ethnicity" when speaking of what Americans might refer to as "race relations" (Mette Andersson, "Colonialisation of Norwegian Space: Identity Politics in the Streets of Oslo in the 1990s," *Norsk Tidsskrift for Migrasjonsforkning* 7, no. 1 [2006]: 6–24). Andreas Wimmer takes a "dragnet approach" to ethnicity, race, and nationhood by advocating for a broad, encompassing definition of ethnicity that treats "race" and "nationhood" as special case or subtype of "ethnicity" (*Ethnic Boundary Making*, 7–8). He argues that race and ethnicity in particular, although not one and the same, are inextricably related to the extent that "there is no clear-cut line between ethnosomatic and other types of ethnicity that would justify establishing entirely separate objects of analysis to be addressed with different analytical language" (ibid., 8). In the United States, "race" is usually associated with African Americans, and "race relations" commonly refers to the interactions between blacks and whites. "Ethnicity" more commonly refers to the distinctions among different countries of origin that are neither white nor black (ibid.).

[93] Vassenden and Andersson, "Whiteness, Non-Whiteness," 575, 583.

[94] It should be noted that in Norwegian society at large, Christianity is less stigmatized than Islam. This is largely due to the country's historically homogeneous ethnic and religious social make-up of white Lutherans. High rates of formal church membership combined with secularity among white Norwegians point to the possible influence of "cultural religion" (N. J. Demerath III, "The Rise of 'Cultural Religion' in European Christianity: Learning from Poland, Northern Ireland, and Sweden," *Social Compass* 47, no. 1 [2000]: 127–39). It is may also be due to the erection of strong religious boundaries, which can find its roots in the pietistic bifurcation of saved persons from everyone else and emphasis on personal salvation and *sola fide* (Vassenden and Andersson, "Whiteness, Non-Whiteness," 578–9).

[95] Goffman calls this expression a "signs-given" (i.e., verbal or non-verbal expressions intended to give a certain impression of oneself to another) in contrast to a "signs-given off" (i.e., darker skin color or racial-ethnic identity; Vassenden and Andersson, "Whiteness, Non-Whiteness," 577).

often talked about how they downplay their faith among other whites.[96] This freedom to reveal or not reveal faith and to whom, to what extent, and in which context is a phenomenon Vassenden and Andersson refer to as "faith information control." Although it represents freedom to choose to reveal or not to reveal one's religious beliefs, it also represents a social dilemma particularly for white Norwegian Christians. Although non-white Muslims may face racial and religious discrimination, they do not experience the necessity for faith information control. Among both whites and non-whites, it is therefore unnecessary for a Pakistani Norwegian to provide a cue and say, "I am a Muslim," because it is already assumed that she is because of her signs given off (ethnicity) and, if applicable, by her signs given (hijab).[97]

In the minority context, however, stigma and prestige symbols shift. It is prestigious or honorable to be religious and taboo to be non-religious. Thus, Vassenden and Andersson's findings reiterate Goffman's assertion that stigma symbols and prestige symbols are context-dependent.[98] While non-white Muslims may engage in "impression management" among non-Muslims by trying, for example, to distance themselves from ideology that makes them appear as a fundamentalist or terrorist sympathizer, they do not downplay or deny that they are Muslims.[99] This leads Vassenden and Andersson to conclude that non-white Muslims do not experience the dichotomous faith information control of their white Christian counterparts, who must articulate their religiosity in order for it to become mutual knowledge.[100]

As discreditable people, Norwegian Christians have various options: (1) They can hide or conceal their faith so as to "pass" for a normal person. (2) They can immediately and voluntarily disclose their faith to avoid misunderstanding and anxiety or tension resulting from concealment. (3) They can gradually disclose their faith as the later part of the sequence in the process of becoming known to avoid the potential of being wholly discredited or stigmatized.[101] This "adaptive technique," which Goffman calls "covering," involves first passing as normal and then disclosing their faith (i.e., their stigma) once normalcy is established.[102] Once they reveal their faith, they are discredited but careful to avoid fulfilling the stereotypes and prejudices of peers.

Peter does not seek to conceal Christian identity but rather seeks to make Christian identity in-concealable in the way that it is for Norwegian Muslims. He thus describes Christian identity in ethnic terms and creates a separate system of honor by which he hopes to encourage his addressees to endure hostility for the time being. Peter tries to contest stigma, not simply by disrupting the coherent, reductionistic, and stereotypical

---

[96] Ibid., 581. Interestingly, a Muslim high school student interviewed spoke of how white Christians speak more openly with her about their faith than with their white atheist peers. She credits the visibility of her faith (she wears highly visible and religiously explicit hijab) as the reason why white Christians find her easy to talk to about matters of religion (ibid., 582).
[97] Ibid., 582–3.
[98] Ibid., 577–8.
[99] Ibid., 583.
[100] Ibid., 584.
[101] Ibid., 589.
[102] Ibid., 590.

picture of Christians as antisocial, atheistic, subversive evildoers, but also by turning the mark of stigma into a badge of honor.[103] By presenting Christians as belonging to an ethnic group, Peter seeks to build internal cohesion and self-understanding that prevents his readers from concealing, covering, or denying their faith in association with Christ and other Christ followers.

Stigma Reversal

In his article, "Contesting Stigma: On Goffman's Assumptions of Normative Order," Abdi Kusow reexamines Goffman's key proposition that stigma—particularly the tribal stigma of race, religion, ethnicity, and nation—is something that normals actively impose and the discredited passively bear.[104] Kusow demonstrates instead how Somali immigrants to Canada contest stigma by creating counter-social and moral positions. In doing so, the stigmatized turn the tables on the stigmatizers by refusing to consent to the values, meanings, and labels of the normative, dominant order and by not allowing the stigma to actually spoil their personal and collective identities. In Kusow's words, "through reverse stigmatization, counter devaluation, and rejection of discrimination, Somalis reveal the problematics of stigma establishment and therein raise the question of who is stigmatizing whom."[105]

What Kusow finds inadequate about Goffman's stigma theory is its focus on the experience of stigmatized groups, rather than on the social contingencies or the historical, social, and individual contexts in which stigma-normal processes are determined.[106] While Goffman does recognize the importance of a stigmatized group's history, political development, and current policies and place in the social structure for understanding its members' face-to-face experiences and encounters, Kusow argues that he does not emphasize enough the way in which deviant-normal processes can be defined differently depending on the groups and social classes that make up society.[107] Contrary to Goffman, Kusow does not assume the existence of a normative order. With Goffman, Kusow agrees that the stigmatized have the agency to reverse stigma and redefine who are normals and who are deviants and provides an actual example of such stigma reversal within a particular community.[108]

In his research on the Somali immigrant population in Toronto, Kusow found that Somalis based their understanding of ethnicity and social differentiation on clan

---

[103] So Elliott, *Conflict, Community, and Honor*, 39; Horrell, "'Race,' 'Nation,' 'People,'" 143.

[104] Abdi M. Kusow, "Contesting Stigma: On Goffman's Assumptions of Normative Order," *Symbolic Interaction* 27, no. 2 (2004): 179–97.

[105] Ibid., 179.

[106] Ibid., 181.

[107] Ibid., 182. Kusow takes issues not so much with Goffman, but with the way in which most recent research on stigma focuses solely on what Goffman had to say about stigma management, which is the focus on Goffman's work, rather than on Goffman's insight into the importance of social factors and historical, cultural, and individual contexts in influencing the ways stigma and normalcy are conceived. Such research overlooks Goffman's critical caveat that "in some instances, individuals and groups who are normatively regarded as stigmatized, in fact, perceive the 'normals' as the stigmatized ones" (Goffman, *Stigma*, 6).

[108] Kusow, "Contesting Stigma," 182.

affiliation and not at all on race or skin color.[109] They possessed no analogy in Somalia for the color-based, racial categories that factored so heavily in North American identity discourse. It was only after coming to Canada when Somali immigrants became increasingly aware of the possibility that they could be stigmatized on the basis of their skin color. They caught on quickly to ways in which the mass media portrayed blackness as an undesirable, inferior identity category.[110] Therefore, Somalis were resistant to being categorized as black, since they understood themselves to be Somalis, in general, and from a certain tribe in Somalia, in particular. While some Somali immigrants learned through experience that color-based stigma was a real issue, most respondents to Kusow's interviews perceived the reasons for their stigmatization as resulting from their immigrant or refugee status or from their Muslim religious values—not from the blackness of their skin and the stereotypes associated with being black.[111]

Even though most immigrants interviewed perceived being black, immigrant, and refugee as carrying a certain degree of stigma, not all immigrants accepted the devalued way in which white Canadians viewed them. Somali immigrants, who grew up in a culture of non-racialized cultural identities, contested these stigmas by creating a separate system of honor by doing the following:

1. limiting social interaction;
2. rejecting Canadian identities;
3. rejecting the existence of discrimination—i.e., discrimination based along color lines/based on color categories; and
4. stigma reversal.[112]

Kusow concludes from the data collected that Somali immigrants acknowledge that cultural and value differences exist between themselves and mainstream white Canadians. However, they do not acknowledge or perceive that they are stigmatized on the basis of their skin color, since no persons in their homeland are categorized, stereotyped, and/or stigmatized based on color-based identities.[113] By differentiating themselves from white Canadians based on culture and values, Somali immigrants "construct the boundaries of stigma on the basis of symbolic attributes rather than skin color. The construction of stigma boundaries on this basis allows Somali immigrants to impose their own stigma on mainstream white Canadians."[114] In other words, Kusow's research suggests that it is possible for those who are normally stigmatized to perceive the "normal" as the stigmatized ones. Because the Somali immigrants failed to comprehend the dominant Canadian perspective on the nature and source of color- or race-based stigma, they could disavow it and impose their own understanding of

---

[109] Ibid., 186.
[110] Ibid., 187.
[111] Ibid.
[112] Ibid., 189–92.
[113] Ibid., 192.
[114] Ibid.

social stratification that was based not on color-based racial characteristics but on class differences or what anthropologists have referred to as a "segmentary lineage structure."[115]

Honorary Ethnics

By asserting moral and cultural difference, Somali immigrants construct a morally superior "symbolic boundary" through the use of moral discourse.[116] They construct a separate system of honor that rejects the stigma of race/skin-color imposed upon them. This serves as a case in point for Goffman's discussion of the role of "stigma symbols," which function in the opposite way of "status" or "prestige symbols."[117] Somalis in Kusow's study employ prestige symbols in order to contrast their stigma symbols because doing so may help to break up, problematize, or nuance "an otherwise coherent picture" of individuals as being less human, valuable, normal, and acceptable.[118]

In Goffmanian terms, the Somalis "disidentify" with the very categories and symbols intended to make them feel inferior to white Canadians and identify instead with their own categories and symbols that make them feel superior to white Canadians.[119] They stigmatize those who attempt to stigmatize them, but they do so based on cultural rather than racial criteria. Such are the cultural categories that they grew up with and brought with them from Somalia.[120] They do this, however, not in order to change perceptions of white Canadians but rather to turn the tables on them by refusing to passively bear the stigma of blackness. Somalis understand themselves as an ethnic and religious people, not only as black people. They maintain moral value of their identity and even assert that they are morally and culturally superior to white Canadians, whom they portray as lacking cohesive cultural, ethnic, and religious identity and moral fiber. In doing so, Somalis reject stigma imposed on them, impose stigma on white Canadians, and impute prestige to themselves.

In the case of the Somali immigrants living in Toronto, the deviant group and those who label them operate on the basis of two different cultural systems.[121] The same can be said about the deviant group (Christian) and labeling group (Gentiles) in 1 Peter. When reversing the order of Kusow's argument, one can see why Peter finds ethnic identity construction so helpful. Peter rejects the stigma imposed upon them by Gentiles. In turn, he imposes stigma upon Gentiles and imputes an honored ethnicity on Christians, thereby reversing the idea of who is stigmatizing whom. As honorary ethnics, Peter exhorts Christians to disassociate themselves from the values of the dominant culture while maintaining relationships with members of this culture, and develop a sense of familial, ethnic, and spiritual community. Stigma reversal in the

---

[115] Ibid., 182, 184
[116] Ibid., 193.
[117] Goffman, *Stigma*, 43.
[118] Ibid., 44.
[119] See ibid.
[120] Kusow, "Contesting Stigma," 194.
[121] Ibid.

fullest sense is promised as a future, not present reality. As exiles and resident aliens, Christians can contest stigma by rejecting the validity of the stigma and by seeing themselves as superior to those who stigmatize them (1.13–19; 2.4–12; 4.3).

Conclusion

Using similar strategies to the Somali immigrants in Kusow's study based on Goffman's stigma analysis, Peter attempts to create a separate system of honor for believers by constraining social interaction, rejecting their former Gentile identities, and by reversing stigma. Barth sees ethnic identity as constraining people's behavior in all their activities and interactions with others, shedding light on why Peter finds the use of ethnic language to construct Christian identity so helpful. Peter wants to create not only a cohesive corporate identity for Christians but also a constrained identity that demarcates cultural, social, and theological differences.

Whereas Somali immigrants in Toronto and Pakistani immigrants in Oslo find it impossible to blend into white culture by virtue of their non-whiteness and because of their discredited identities as black people (in the case of Somalis) and religious people (in the case of Pakistanis), the Christians addressed in 1 Peter who live in Asia Minor find it very possible to allow their Christian identities to go unnoticed. Thus, Peter exhorts Christians to erect boundaries, to see themselves as an elect, holy, and ethnic people, to behave in ways that please God first and foremost, and others only insofar as it is possible. Peter wants Christians to believe they are as marked by Christ as Somalis in Toronto are marked by their blackness and as Pakistanis in Oslo are marked by their religiousness, and finds ethnic language critical to shaping an inextricably inconcealable Christian self-understanding. Because there are no easy physical markers, the author of 1 Peter seeks to inscribe fictive genetic markers in order to help his readers understand themselves as possessing a distinct, honored ethnic identity that cannot be denied, renounced, or hidden. Without the immediate visibility of physical difference to set them apart, Peter exhorts Christians to be so marked by Christ—even at the risk of being discredited, stigmatized, and persecuted—in their theology, self-understanding, communal relationships, and behavior that those who knew them before they became Christian can hardly recognize them.

5

Conclusion: Reinforcing Christian Distinctiveness through Bonds of Blood

There is something about shared blood that enables people to have an enduring sense of collective identity even across borders. At the historic summit of South and North Korea on April 27, 2018, President Moon Jae-In, leader of South Korea, and Kim Jung Un, leader of North Korean, held hands as they crossed the border that divides the two warring countries. In their joint declaration, in which they both solemnly declared that there would be no more war on the Korean Peninsula, they stated that the first aim of inter-Korean peace is to "reconnect the blood relations of the people."[1] The division of Korea between North and South, which took place in 1945 at the end of the Second World War, created a clear-cut line—the DMZ—between the two nations along the thirty-eighth parallel. However, it apparently did not create a clear-cut ethnic line between the two Koreas. The notion of kinship, or "having the same blood" (*homaimon*), remains central to both ancient and modern perceptions of ethnicity. Such realities remind us that 1 Peter's construction of Christian identity as an ethnic identity has strong community-building and cohering-potential for people who are stigmatized as a consequence of their faith in Christ.

The role of ethnicity in 1 Peter's construction of "Christian" identity has been the driving force of this study, as I have examined the ways Peter creates, in effect, a shared ethnicity as he seeks to forge a distinct, cohesive, and positive group identity for his beleaguered addressees who must endure anti-Christian hostility and subsequent persecution. I treat ethnicity as a social construction that revolves around a set of markers or characteristics, which Anthony D. Smith has summed up as including shared genealogies, history and culture, common territory or homeland, and an internal feeling of solidarity.[2]

Herodotus effectively employs such ethnic indicators—common blood (real or perceived), common language, shared religious practice, and shared customs (8.144.2)—as a rhetorical strategy to galvanize a sense of peoplehood among those who do not necessarily see themselves as belonging to one common group identity. He does this not only to provide a compelling definition of "Greekness," but also to make

---

[1] "Declaration of North and South Korean Summit," April 27, 2018, *CNN*, https://www.cnn.com/2018/04/27/asia/read-full-declaration-north-south-korea/index.html?ofs=fbia.
[2] Smith, *Ethnic Origins*, 22–31.

a desperate plea for members of competing Greek cities to rise up and rally against a common Persian enemy at a critical juncture in the Greek war effort. It was the military threat of the non-Greek, barbarian "other" that fortified a collective sense of identity. Furthermore, Herodotus' portrayal of the Ionians as having a fictive, self-constructed—rather than primordial—ethnic identity suggests how a group can self-identify as an ethnic group by making claims of common kinship, history, geography, and customs, even if such bonds are not "real."[3] Their shared sense of history and descent enabled Greeks to come to terms with their subjugation to the seemingly limitless power of the Romans, who were neither Greek nor barbarian. During the first two centuries of the Roman empire, Greeks attempted to define themselves according to their glorious heritage rooted in their unique ancestry, even as their political and cultural influence in the present diminished.

Peter also employs the similar strategy of appealing to the past (election and birth story) and to common descent (shared patrilineage and blood ties) to define for his addressees what it means to be Christian in a society hostile to this identity. By ethnicizing his recipients' Christian identity in order to replace their ethnic majority status as Gentiles, he attempts to create a stronger sense of ingroup identity and solidarity for his addressees and weaken their sense of belonging to the values of the dominant culture and the values of their family and associations. The letter of 1 Peter constructs an ethnicity for its predominantly Gentile audience in primarily five ways by:

1. establishing their relationship to God and to one another, not along shared biological bloodlines or territorial attachments but through election, new birth, and the ransoming blood of Christ;
2. instructing them to live according to a new culture characterized by obedience and holiness;
3. linking them with a heavenly homeland and as members of an eschatological household of God by depicting them as a diaspora people who are dislocated from mainstream society;
4. drawing on Israel's identity-defining designations to describe his addressees as a rhetorical strategy to construct Christian identity as an ethnoreligious identity—i.e., as a divinely engendered people characterized by religio-cultural practices patterned after the example of Christ; and
5. lastly, by strengthening their sense of communal identity as Χριστιανοί, so that when they suffer as a result of this identity, they do so for the right reasons and in the right ways.

Fredrik Barth conceives of ethnic groups in a way that fits well with Herodotus' perceptions of ethnicity and sheds light on the rhetorical strategy of Peter. Ethnic identity formation occurs not in cultural isolation from outsiders but through social contact, conflict, compromise, and negotiation with outsiders. Barth does not dismiss

---

[3] See *Hist* 1.143, 146, 147.

the importance of cultural difference itself in defining a group's identity, but he sees the boundary maintenance between one group and another as the critical factor in defining the ethnic group.[4] Boundaries are drawn primarily by social behavior and expressed through the delineation of differences. While a group's identity is not solely the result of difference or opposition to another group, Barth argues that the features that make up a group's ethnic identity receive greater clarification in relation to other ethnic groups.

When applied to 1 Peter, Barth's analysis helps illuminate the way in which Peter's construction of ethnic identity functions to sharpen differences between his readers' former identities and that of those who oppose their new allegiance and way of life by creating an antithesis between the people of God and the people *not* of God. First Peter's use of ethnic reasoning helps construe this new religious identity as superordinate to all others. By emphasizing new birth and patrilineage, the shared blood of Christ, and the common practices concomitant with being obedient children of God, the letter's author urges his readers to undergo the equivalent of a transfer of ethnic membership from the broad category of "Gentiles" to the particular and peculiar identity as God's people. Peter's strategy points to the durability and resilience of the sense of belonging that is rooted in the belief of common ancestry and shared culture (belief, behavior, practice) especially for those who seem to be experiencing the crisscrossing, conflicting, and intersecting pull of multiple social identities.

Barth's boundary analysis in the study of ethnicity is highly compatible with Erving Goffman's classic study on stigma. Goffman demonstrates how stigma has the power to reduce the chances of an individual or a group to survive socially but also the power to create a very strong sense of ingroup identity. His analysis helps support the argument I make that Peter uses the strategy of creating an ethnic identity for his addressees in order to help his addressees cope with anti-Christian prejudice and contest the stigma associated with being Christian. As stigmatized people, Christians bear the responsibility to conduct themselves with the sort of tactfulness and intimacy that concretizes, humanizes, and even possibly neutralizes and transforms the negative association with the "name of Christ" (4.14). Furthermore, because there are no easy physical markers that set his addressees apart from Gentiles, Peter seeks to inscribe in them biological markers in the form of shared patrilineage of God the Father and the shared blood of Jesus Christ with the hope that they will understand themselves as possessing a distinct, honored, ethnic identity that cannot be denied, renounced, or hidden.

In *Coping with Prejudice*, Paul Holloway demonstrates how the author of 1 Peter spends the majority of his letter trying to advise his readers on how best to cope with the social prejudice of their neighbors. Christians suffered prejudice in the form of hostile sentiments and damaging stereotypes, which only fueled more public animosity against them. Christians in Peter's letter faced persecution sporadically by their neighbors and possibly even suffered court-mandated punishment. However, they experienced the "ever-present threat" of social prejudice at a constant level, which

---

[4] Barth, *Ethnic Groups*, 14.

is why Peter seeks to console them in their suffering and equip them with strategies to endure it.⁵ The social situation described by Holloway is one that I imagine for the addressees of 1 Peter. While I agree that Peter consoles his addressees and equips them with strategies for how to cope with prejudice, I argue that he also provides them with a resilient sense of ingroup identity that assures them that who they once were no longer defines them.

By constructing an ethnic identity for people who are stigmatized as a consequence of their faith in Christ, Peter helps his addressees disidentify with their past and reidentify as the "people of God" (2.9–10). By describing Christians as displaced but elect foreigners and strangers, Peter speaks to their foreignness in society, while imbuing them with a greater sense of being God's own people, who belong to God's household. He does this in order to help his addressees cope with the social conflict, prejudice, and subsequent alienation and persecution resulting from their conversion and adherence to Christian religion.

Further Implications of This Study

Asian American Studies

The potential effectiveness of Peter's strategy can be considered in light of recent scholarship on ethnicity. According to a psychological study conducted by Que-Lam Huynh et al.,

> American ethnic minorities who feel that they are frequently perceived as foreigners and denied their in-group status may feel conflicted about their national identity and have a sense of cultural homelessness, which in turn can lead to poorer overall psychological adjustment.⁶

These findings may have implications for the ways in which ethnic minority groups participate in American civic society. Research based on social dominance theory⁷ suggests that being a member of an ethnic minority can decrease one's sense of belonging to the nation and mainstream American culture because such belonging is more strongly and positively associated with members of the dominant group than with members of subordinate ethnic groups.⁸

My study on the role of ethnicity in 1 Peter has further implications.⁹ Peter's strategy to describe Christian identity in ethnic terms promotes, in effect, the idea that Christians are perpetual foreigners in mainstream society. Research describing

---

⁵ Holloway, *Coping with Prejudice*, 234.
⁶ Que-Lam Huynh et al., "Perpetual Foreigners in One's Own Land," 157.
⁷ See, e.g., Jim Sidanius and Felicia Pratto, *Social Dominance: An Intergroup Theory of Social Hierarchy and Oppression* (Cambridge: Cambridge University Press, 1999).
⁸ Huynh et al., "Perpetual Foreigners," 137.
⁹ See Ok, "Always Ethnic, Never 'American,'" 424–25.

the psychological impact of the perpetual foreigner stereotype on Asian Americans suggests it is the awareness among Asian Americans that they are perceived and treated as perpetual foreigners that contributes to their seeing their own ethnic and national identities as dissimilar and even incompatible. This dissonance often results in the increased struggle to form a unified and integrated identity. By virtue of having two contrasting and often conflicting identities, Asian Americans are forced to maintain a more complex social identity, which may lead to depressive symptoms, a decreased sense of hope and life satisfaction, and a lower level of civic participation relative to white Americans.

Peter's strategy thus may be problematic when applied to Asian American Christians, who already experience the perpetual foreigner stereotype by virtue of their ethnic identities. The addressees in 1 Peter must also maintain contrasting and often conflicting identities as former Gentiles who are to see themselves as entirely new people who belong to a new ethnic group with a new culture. However, unlike Asian Americans who struggle to belong to the dominant culture because they are perceived as perpetual foreigners, the Christians in 1 Peter face social hostility and persecution because they seek and are encouraged to disassociate and disengage from the values and behaviors of the dominant society and conceive of themselves as temporary foreigners (1.6, 17). Peter is at pains to help his addressees see themselves as culturally homeless and socially different, so that they live as people born anew to a living, eschatological, and heavenly hope—while remaining in Kansas, so to speak.

How does the impact of the perpetual foreigner stereotype ironically provide evidence for the potential effectiveness of the Petrine author's strategy for employing ethnicity as a theological category in order to construct an ethnic identity for his addressees? How then can the letter of 1 Peter offer any sort of exhortation or consolation to Asian Americans Christians, who wish to shed the stereotype of the perpetual foreigner and be seen as a vital and integral part of the national identity while maintaining their ethnic identities? Such are the questions that I am continuing to explore.

Canonical Studies

First Peter has long been recognized as a letter saturated with words and images from the Jewish scriptures, especially 2.4–10. Commentators have noted the importance of 2.9–10 as an appropriation of Israel's identity for the Church.[10] However, less attention has been paid to the way in which the Petrine author constructs Christian identity using ethnic terms. David Horrell has persuasively argued that the "uniquely dense" cluster of ethnic identity language in 2.9 initiates a discourse about ethnicity and race in early Christian writing, as the verse functions as an "crucial early step in the construction

---

[10] Esp. the phrase βασίλειον ἱεράτευμα (because of its influence of Reformation doctrine of the priesthood of all believers).

of Christian identity in ethnoracial terms."[11] Ethnicity's durable and "real" and yet fluid and malleable aspects made it possible for New Testament writers to contest, negotiate, and shape Christian identity through ethnic discourse.[12] The fact that early Christian authors understood or perceived ethnicity and religious practice as mutually constitutive made ethnic reasoning a valuable rhetorical strategy for incorporating Gentile Christians into long narrative of God's unique dealings with God's chosen, covenant people, Israel.[13] To varying degrees, ethnic articulations of identity also provide for 1 Peter's author and other NT writers the language of belonging.

It would take another book to demonstrate how Peter's particular mode of ethnic reasoning and ethnic identity construction compares to that found in other New Testament texts, such as Acts, Romans, Galatians, the Corinthian correspondence, the Johannine literature, James, Philippians, or Colossians. Such a comparative study is beyond the scope of this book. However, based on what I have discovered about 1 Peter and know about other NT texts, I wish to suggest that what sets 1 Peter apart from other articulations of identity construction is how its author develops the idea of what it means to be Christian with an intensity marked by nuanced, pastoral, on-the-ground sensitivity. The writer of 1 Peter employs ethnicity metaphors to give addressees the common language which defines them over against other groups and their former selves. This language encourages them to see their bonds of kinship to another and to the God the Father who has called them as his elect and holy people and obedient children as inextricably linked through the blood of Christ. This way of self- and group-understanding has the potential to create a resilient and enduring sense of social cohesion. Thus 1 Peter's construction of Christian identity as an ethnic identity promotes an entirely new social, cultural, and ethnoreligious group identity for Gentile believers, even as they continue to live among and interact with unbelievers.[14]

This study has implications for how 1 Peter can be situated within the NT canon. Peter employs descriptively thick and socially and theologically meaningful metaphors to describe and shape what Christian community looks like and how its members are

---

[11] Horrell, "'Race', 'Nation', 'People,'" 135, 154. Jeremy Punt understands 1 Peter as demonstrating how "early Jesus communities negotiated a new identity, rather than insisting on incorporating many ethnicities into a distinct agglomeration, a non-ethnic or race-less obliqueness" ("He Is Heavy ... He's My Brother," 161 n. 38). Cf. Buell, "Rethinking the Relevance of Race for Early Christian Self-Definition," *HTR* 94, no. 4 (2001): 449–76, 473.

[12] For examples of more recent scholarship that have applied a contested and contestable understanding of ethnicity to their analysis of New Testament and early Christian texts, see Buell, *Why This New Race*; Hodge, *If Sons, Then Heirs*; Barreto, *Ethnic Negotiations*; Sechrest, *A Former Jew*; Horrell, "'Race', 'Nation', 'People'"; Concannon, "*When You Were Gentiles*"; Balch, *Contested Ethnicities and Images: Studies in Acts and Arts* (WUNT 345; Mohr Siebeck, 2015); and Christopher Stroup, *The Christians Who Became Jews: Acts of the Apostles and Ethnicity in the Roman City* (New Haven: Yale University Press, 2020). Identity is a prominent concern in the New Testament, not to be understood as the sole preoccupation of scholarship in recent decades or as disconnected from theological concerns. So Punt ("He Is Heavy ... He's My Brother," 161 n. 37).

[13] Buell, "Rethinking the Relevance of Race," 459; Richard N. Longnecker, "Paul's Vision of the Church and Community Formation," in *Community Formation in the Early Church and in the Church Today*, ed. Richard N. Longnecker (Peabody, MA: Hendrickson, 2002), 73–88, 75.

[14] See Barth, *Ethnic Groups*, 9, 14.

to relate to one another and those outside the community. This leads me to ask how much the development of the NT canon was influenced by the relative "success" of most, if not all, of the twenty-seven documents in contributing to the social cohesion and sense of new identity of the Christ followers. Did the documents that eventually formed the canon perhaps do so because they proved to be most helpful in reinforcing the various bonds that kept the new Christian communities and the generations of such communities down into the early fourth century from collapsing under pressure from blood families and then from imperial persecution? What linguistic strategies did other early Christian documents employ to create, reinforce, and sustain a new sense of identity, even though they did not "make the cut"?[15] I wish to explore such questions, building on the work of other scholars with regard to ethnicity and early Christian documents and in conversation with those who have argued for stronger canonical presence of the Catholic Epistles based on its compositional and theo-literary impact.[16] Perhaps the emphasis on community and identity formation that Peter reveals and its subsequent impact may be more determinative for what constituted the books of the NT canon than previously understood.

---

[15] For example, the *Didache*, 1 Clement, the authentic Letters by Ignatius, *the Shepherd of Hermas*, and other "Apostolic Fathers." I am indebted to Scott Bartchy for engaging in stimulating conversations on this topic that helped me form these questions.

[16] See, e.g., David R. Neinuis, *Not by Paul Alone: The Formation of the Catholic Epistle Collection and the Christian Canon* (Waco, TX: Baylor University Press, 2007); Nienhuis and Robert W. Wall, *Reading the Epistle of James, Peter, John, and Jude as Scripture: The Shaping and Shape of a Canonical Collection* (Grand Rapids: Eerdmans, 2013); Jörg Frey et al., eds., *Between Canonical and Apocryphal Texts: Processes of Reception, Rewriting, and Interpretation in Early Judaism and Early Christianity* (WUNT 419; Tübingen: Mohr Siebeck, 2019).

Bibliography

Achtemeier, Paul J. *1 Peter: A Commentary on First Peter*. Hermeneia. Minneapolis: Augsburg Fortress, 1996.
Achtemeier, Paul J. "Newborn Babes and Living Stones: Literal and Figurative in 1 Peter." In *To Touch the Text: Biblical and Related Studies in Honor of Joseph Fitzmyer, S.J.* Edited by Maurya P. Horgan and Paul J. Kobelski. New York: Crossroad, 1989.
Achtemeier, Paul J. "Suffering Servant and Suffering Christ in 1 Peter." In *The Future of Christology: Essays in Honor of Leander E. Keck.* Edited by Abraham J. Malherbe and Wayne A. Meeks. New York: Crossroad, 1993, 176–88.
Aciman, André. "Are You Listening?" *The New Yorker*, March 17, 2014.
Agnew, Frances H. "1 Peter 1:2—An Alternative Translation." *CBQ* 45 (1983): 68–73.
Anderson, Benedict. *Imagined Communities: Reflections on the Origin and Spread of Nationalism*. London: Verso, 1983.
Andersson, Mette. "Colonialisation of Norwegian Space: Identity Politics in the Streets of Oslo in the 1990s." *Norsk Tidsskrift for Migrasjonsforkning* 7, no. 1 (2006): 6–24.
Balch, David L. *Contested Ethnicities and Images: Studies in Acts and Arts*. WUNT 345. Mohr Siebeck, 2015.
Balch, David L. *Let Wives Be Submissive: The Domestic Code in I Peter*. Chico, CA: Society of Biblical Literature, 1981.
Barreto, Eric D. *Ethnic Negotiations: The Function of Race and Ethnicity in Acts 16*. WUNT 294. Tübingen: Mohr Siebeck, 2010.
Bartchy, S. Scott. "Undermining Ancient Patriarchy: The Apostle's Vision of a Society of Siblings." *BTB* 29, no. 2 (1999): 68–78.
Barth, Fredrik, ed. *Ethnic Groups and Boundaries: The Social Organization of Culture Difference*. Bergen, Oslo: Universitetsforlaget, 1969.
Bascara, Victor. *Model-Minority Imperialism*. Minneapolis: University of Minneapolis Press, 2006.
Bauman, Thomas. *The Pekin: The Rise and Fall of Chicago's First Black-Owned Theater*. Urbana: University of Illinois Press, 2014.
Baumann, Gerd. *The Multicultural Riddle: Rethinking National, Ethnic and Religious Identities*. New York: Routledge, 1999.
Beare, Francis Wright. *The First Epistle of Peter: The Greek Text with Introduction and Notes*. 3rd ed. Oxford: Blackwell, 1970.
Bechtler, Steven. *Following in His Steps: Suffering, Community, and Christology in 1 Peter*. SBLDS 162. Atlanta: Scholars Press, 1998.
Benko, Stephen. *Pagan Rome and the Early Christians*. Reprint ed. Bloomington: Indiana University Press, 1986.
Berdahl, Jennifer L., and Ji-A Min. "Prescriptive Stereotypes and Workplace Consequences for East Asians in North America." *Cultural Diversity and Ethnic Minority Psychology* 18, no. 2 (2012): 141–52.
Bernal, Martin. *Black Athena: Afroasiatic Roots of Classical Civilization*. Vol. 1. 3 vols. New Brunswick, NJ: Rutgers University Press, 1987.

Bernal, Martin. *Black Athena: Afroasiatic Roots of Classical Civilization*. Vol. 2. 3 vols. New Brunswick, NJ: Rutgers University Press, 1991.
Best, Ernest. *1 Peter*. New Century Bible. London: Oliphants, 1971.
Bigg, Charles A. *Critical and Exegetical Commentary on the Epistles of St. Peter and St. Jude*. ICC. New York: Scribner's Sons, 1901.
Boring, M. Eugene. *1 Peter*. ANTS. Nashville: Abingdon, 1999.
Boyarin, Daniel. *Border Lines: The Partition of Judaeo-Christianity*. Philadelphia: University of Pennsylvania Press, 2004.
Brown, Raymond E. *The Gospel According to John*. AB. Vol. 29–29A. Garden City, NY: Doubleday, 1966.
Brubaker, Rogers. *Ethnicity without Groups*. Cambridge: Harvard University Press, 2006.
Brubaker, Rogers, and Frederick Cooper. "Beyond 'Identity.'" *Theory and Society* 29, no. 1 (2000): 1–47.
Buell, Denise Kimber. "Constructing Early Christian Identities Using Ethnic Reasoning." *Ann. Storia Dellesegesi* 24, no. 1 (2007): 87–101.
Buell, Denise Kimber. *Why This New Race: Ethnic Reasoning in Early Christianity*. New York: Columbia University Press, 2005.
Buell, Denise Kimber. "Rethinking the Relevance of Race for Early Christian Self-Definition." *HTR* 94, no. 4 (2001): 449–76.
Burkert, Walter. *Greek Religion: Archaic and Classical*. Translated by John Raffan. Oxford: Blackwell, 1985.
Burstein, Stanley. "Greek Identity in the Hellenistic Period." In *Hellenisms: Culture, Identity, and Ethnicity from Antiquity to Modernity*. Edited by Katerina Zacharia. Burlington, VT: Ashgate, 2008.
Cartledge, Paul. *The Greeks: A Portrait of Self and Others*. Oxford: Oxford University Press, 1993.
Clackson, James, and Geoffrey Horrocks. *The Blackwell History of the Latin Language*. Malden, MA: Wiley-Blackwell, 2010.
Concannon, Cavin W. *"When You Were Gentiles": Specters of Ethnicity in Roman Corinth and Paul's Corinthian Correspondence*. Synkrisis: Comparative Approaches to Early Christianity in Greco-Roman Culture. New Haven: Yale University Press, 2014.
Davids, Peter H. *The First Epistle of Peter*. NICNT. Grand Rapids: Eerdmans, 1990.
Davis, Fred. *Passage through Crisis: Polio Victims and Their Families*. Indianapolis, IN: Bobbs-Merrill, 1963.
Deissmann, Adolf. *Light from the Ancient East: The New Testament Illustrated by Recently Discovered Texts of the Graeco-Roman World*. Translated by Lionel R. M. Strachan. London: Hodder and Stoughton, 1911.
Demerath, N. J., III. "The Rise of 'Cultural Religion' in European Christianity: Learning from Poland, Northern Ireland, and Sweden." *Social Compass* 47, no. 1 (2000): 127–39.
deSilva, David A. *Honor, Patronage, Kinship & Purity: Unlocking New Testament Culture*. Downers Grove, IL: InterVarsity, 2000.
Dionysius of Halicarnassus. *The Roman Antiquities of Dionysius of Halicarnassus*. Translated by Earnest Cary. 7 vols. LCL. Cambridge: Harvard University Press, 1937.
Duncan-Jones, Richard. *Conflict, Community, and Honor: 1 Peter in Social-Scientific Perspective*. Eugene, OR: Cascade, 2007.
Duncan-Jones, Richard. *The Economy of the Roman Empire: Qualitative Studies*. Cambridge: Cambridge University Press, 1982.
Elliott, John H. *1 Peter: A New Translation with Introduction and Commentary*. AB 37B. New York: Anchor Bible, 2001.

Elliott, John H. "1 Peter, Its Situation and Strategy: A Discussion with David Balch." In *Perspectives on First Peter*. Edited by Charles H. Talbert, 61–78. NAPBR Special Studies Series 9. Macon, GA: Mercer University Press, 1986.

Elliott, John H. *A Home for the Homeless: A Sociological Exegesis of 1 Peter, Its Situation and Strategy*. Philadelphia: Fortress Press, 1981.

Elliott, John H. *Conflict, Community, and Honor: 1 Peter in Social-Scientific Perspective*. Eugene, OR: Cascade, 2007.

Eriksen, Thomas Hylland. *Ethnicity and Nationalism: Anthropological Perspectives*. London: Pluto Press, 1993.

Eriksen, Thomas Hylland. "Ethnicity, Race and Nation." In *The Ethnicity Reader: Nationalism, Multiculturalism, and Migration*. Edited by Montserrat Guibernau and John Rex. 2nd ed. Cambridge; Malden, MA: Polity, 2010.

Esler, Philip F. *Conflict and Identity in Roman: The Social Setting of Paul's Letter*. Minneapolis: Augsburg Fortress, 2003.

Fearon, James D. "What Is Identity (As We Now Use the Word)?" Stanford University, November 3, 1999.

Feldmeier, Reinhard. "Der Erste Brief Des Petrus." THNT 15, no. 1. Leipzig: Evangelische Verlagsanstalt, 2005.

Fenton, Steve. "Debate Explaining Ethnicity." *Journal of Ethnic and Migration Studies* 30, no. 4 (2004): 831–5.

Fenton, Steve. *Ethnicity*. Cambridge; Malden, MA: Polity, 2010.

Fredriksen, Paula. "Judaizing the Nations: The Ritual Demands of Paul's Gospel," *NTS* 56 (2010): 232–52.

Frey, Jörg, Claire Clivaz, and Tobias Nicklas, eds. *Between Canonical and Apocryphal Texts: Processes of Reception, Rewriting, and Interpretation in Early* Judaism *and* Early Christianity. WUNT 419. Tübingen: Mohr Siebeck, 2019.

Furnish, Victor Paul. "Elect Sojourners in Christ: An Approach to the Theology of 1 Peter." *PSTJ* 28, no. 3 (1975): 1–11.

Gabba, Emilio. *Dionysius and the History of Archaic Rome*. Sather Classical Lectures Vol. 56. Berkeley: University of California Press, 1991.

Gaventa, Beverly Roberts. *From Darkness to Light: Aspects of Conversion in the New Testament*. Philadelphia: Fortress, 1986.

Gellner, Ernest. *Nations and Nationalism*. Oxford: Blackwell, 1983.

Georges, Pericles. *Barbarian Asia and the Greek Experience*. Baltimore: Johns Hopkins University Press, 1994.

Glazer, Nathan, and Daniel P. Moynihan, eds. *Ethnicity: Theory and Experience*. 1st ed. Cambridge: Harvard University Press, 1975.

Gleason, Maud W. *Making Men: Sophists and Self-Presentation in Ancient Rome*. Princeton: Princeton University Press, 1995.

Gleason, Philip. "Identifying Identity: A Semantic History." *The Journal of American History* 69, no. 4 (1983): 910–31.

Goffman, Erving. *Stigma: Notes on the Management of Spoiled Identity*. Englewood Cliffs, NJ: Prentice-Hall, 1963.

Goffman, Erving. *The Presentation of Self in Everyday Life*. New York: Anchor, 1959.

Goppelt, Leonhard. *A Commentary on I Peter*. Edited by Ferdinand Hahn. Translated by John E. Alsup. Grand Rapids: Eerdmans, 1993.

Goppelt, Leonhard. *Der Erste Petrusbrief*. Edited by Ferdinand Hahn. KEK 12/1. Göttingen: Vandenhoeck & Ruprecht, 1978.

Green, Joel. *1 Peter*. THNTC. Grand Rapids: Eerdmans, 2007.

Green, Peter. *From Ikaria to the Stars: Classical Mythification, Ancient and Modern.* Austin: University of Texas Press, 2004.

Gruen, Erich S. "Herodotus and Persia." In *Cultural Identity in the Ancient Mediterranean.* Edited by Erich S. Gruen. Issues & Debates. Los Angeles: Getty Research Institute, 2011.

Gruen, Erich S. *Rethinking the Other in Antiquity.* Martin Classical Lectures. Princeton: Princeton University Press, 2011.

Guibernau, Montserrat, and John Rex, eds. "Introduction." In *The Ethnicity Reader: Nationalism, Multiculturalism, and Migration.* 2nd ed. Cambridge; Malden, MA: Polity, 2010.

Hall, Edith. *Greek Tragedy: Suffering under the Sun.* Oxford: Oxford University Press, 2010.

Hall, Edith. *Inventing the Barbarian: Greek Self-Definition through Tragedy.* Oxford: Clarendon Press, 1989.

Hall, Jonathan M. "Contested Ethnicities: Perceptions of Macedonia within Evolving Definitions of Greek Identity." In *Ancient Perceptions of Greek Ethnicity.* Edited by Irad Malkin. Center for Hellenic Studies Colloquia 5, 159–86. Cambridge: Harvard University Press, 2001.

Hall, Jonathan M. *Ethnic Identity in Greek Antiquity.* Cambridge: Cambridge University Press, 1997.

Hall, Jonathan M. *Hellenicity: Between Ethnicity and Culture.* Chicago: University of Chicago Press, 2002.

Hartlep, Nicholas Daniel. *The Model Minority Stereotype: Demystifying Asian American Success.* Charlotte, NC: Information Age, 2013.

Hartog, François. *The Mirror of Herodotus: The Representation of the Other in the Writing of History.* Translated by Janet Loyd. Berkley: University of California Press, 1988.

Herodotus. *Herodotus.* Translated by A. D. Godley. London; New York: W. Heinemann; G.P. Putnam's Sons, 1921.

Herodotus. *Herodotus: The History.* Translated by David Grene. Chicago: University of Chicago Press, 1988.

Hillyer, Norman. *1 and 2 Peter, Jude.* Peabody, MA: Hendrickson, 1992.

Himes, Paul A. *Foreknowledge and Social Identity in 1 Peter.* Eugene, OR: Wipf and Stock, 2014.

Hobsbawm, E. J. *Nations and Nationalism since 1780.* Cambridge: Cambridge University Press, 1990.

Hobsbawm, Eric, and Terence Ranger, eds. *The Invention of Tradition.* Cambridge: Cambridge University Press, 1983.

Hodge, Caroline Johnson. *If Sons, Then Heirs: A Study of Kinship and Ethnicity in the Letters of Paul.* Oxford: Oxford University Press, 2007.

Hoffmann, Michol. "Sociolinguistic Interviews." In *Research Methods in Sociolinguistics: A Practical Guide.* Edited by Janet Holmes and Kirk Hazen, 25–41. Malden, MA: Wiley-Blackwell, 2014.

Holloway, Paul A. *Coping with Prejudice: 1 Peter in Social-Psychological Perspective.* Tübingen: Mohr Siebeck, 2009.

Holmberg, Bengt, and Mikael Winninge, eds. *Identity Formation in the New Testament.* WUNT 227. Tübingen: Mohr Siebeck, 2008.

Holmes, Janet, and Kirk Hazen, eds. *Research Methods in Sociolinguistics: A Practical Guide.* Malden, MA: Wiley-Blackwell, 2014.

Hornblower, Simon. "Greek Identity in the Archaic and Classical Periods." In *Hellenisms: Culture, Identity, and Ethnicity from Antiquity to Modernity*. Edited by Katerina Zacharia. Burlington, VT: Ashgate, 2008.

Hornblower, Simon. *The Greek World 479–323 BC*. 2nd ed. London: Routledge, 1991.

Horrell, David G. *1 Peter*. NTG. London: T&T Clark, 2008.

Horrell, David G. "Aliens and Strangers? The Socio-Economic Location of the Addressees of 1 Peter." In *Becoming Christian: Essays on 1 Peter and the Making of Christian Identity*. LNTS 394, 100–32. London: T&T Clark, 2013.

Horrell, David G. *Becoming Christian: Essays on 1 Peter and the Making of Christian Identity*. LNTS 394. London: Bloomsbury T&T Clark, 2013.

Horrell, David G. "Between Conformity and Resistance: Beyond the Balch–Elliott Debate towards a Postcolonial Reading of First Peter." In *Reading First Peter with New Eyes: Methodological Reassessments of the Letter of First Peter*. Edited by Robert L. Webb and Betsy Bauman-Martin. LNTS 364, 111–43. London: T&T Clark, 2007.

Horrell, David G. "Ethnicisation, Marriage and Early Christian Identity: Critical Reflections on 1 Corinthians 7, 1 Peter 3 and Modern New Testament Scholarship." *NTS* 62 (2016): 439–60.

Horrell, David G. "From ἀδελφοί to οἶκος θεοῦ: Social Transformation in Pauline Christianity," *JBL* 120, no. 2 (2001): 293–311.

Horrell, David G. "'Race', 'Nation', 'People': Ethnoracial Identity Construction in 1 Pet. 2.9." In *Becoming Christian: Essays on 1 Peter and the Making of Christian Identity*. LNTS 394, 133–63. London: Bloomsbury T&T Clark, 2013.

Horrell, David G. "The Label Χριστιανός (1 Peter 4:16): Suffering, Conflict, and the Making of Christian Identity." In *Becoming Christian: Essays on 1 Peter and the Making of Christian Identity*. LNTS 394, 164–210. London: T&T Clark, 2013.

Hort, Fenton John Anthony. *The First Epistle of St. Peter: I.1–II.17: The Greek Text with Introductory Lecture, Commentary, and Additional Notes*. London: Macmillan, 1898.

Hutchinson, John, and Anthony D. Smith. "Introduction." In *Ethnicity*. Edited by John Hutchinson and Anthony D. Smith, 3–14. Oxford: Oxford University Press, 1996.

Huynh, Que-Lam, Thierry Devos, and Laura Smalarz. "Perpetual Foreigners in One's Own Land: Potential Implications for Identity and Psychological Adjustment." *Journal of Social and Clinical Psychology* 30, no. 2 (2011): 133–62.

Isajiw, Wsevolod W. "Approaches to Ethnic Conflict Resolution: Paradigms and Principles." *International Journal of Intercultural Relations* 24, no. 1 (2000): 105–24.

Isaac, Benjamin. *The Invention of Racism in Classical Antiquity*. Princeton: Princeton University Press, 2004.

Jáuregui, Miguel Herrero de, Ana Isabel Jiménez San Cristóbal, Eugenio R. Luján Martínez, Raquel Martín Hernández, Marco Antonio Santamaría Álvarez, and Sofía Torallas Tovar, eds. *Tracing Orpheus: Studies of Orphic Fragments*. Berlin: Walter de Gruyter, 2011.

Jenkins, Richard. *Rethinking Ethnicity: Arguments and Explorations*. London; Thousand Oaks, CA: Sage, 1997.

Jenkins, Richard. *Social Identity*. 4th ed. London: Routledge, 2014.

Jobes, Karen H. *1 Peter*. BECNT. Grand Rapids, MI: Baker Academic, 2005.

Jones, Christopher P. *Plutarch and Rome*. Oxford: Clarendon, 1971.

Kaalund, Jennifer T. *Reading Hebrews and 1 Peter with the African American Great Migration: Diaspora, Place, and Identity*. LNTS. London: Bloomsbury T&T Clark, 2019.

Keener, Craig S. *The Gospel of John: A Commentary*. Peabody, MA: Hendrickson, 2003.

Kelly, J. *A Commentary on the Epistles of Peter and of Jude*. New York: Harper & Row, 1969.

Kennedy, Rebecca F., C. Sydnor Roy, and Max L. Goldman, eds. *Race and Ethnicity in the Classical World: An Anthology of Primary Sources in Translation*. Indianapolis: Hackett, 2013.

Kim, Claire Jean. "The Racial Triangulation of Asian Americans." *Politics & Society* 27, no. 1 (1999): 105–38.

Konstan, David. "To Hellênikon Ethnos: Ethnicity and the Construction of Ancient Greek Identity." In *Ancient Perceptions of Greek Ethnicity*. Edited by Irad Malkin. Center for Hellenic Studies Colloquia 5. Cambridge: Harvard University Press, 2001.

Kraftchick, Steven J. "Reborn to a Living Hope: A Christology of 1 Peter." In *Reading 1-2 Peter and Jude: A Resource for Students*. Resources for Biblical Study 77, 83–98. Atlanta: Society of Biblical Literature, 2014.

Kusow, Abdi M. "Contesting Stigma: On Goffman's Assumptions of Normative Order." *Symbolic Interaction* 27, no. 2 (2004): 179–97.

Lau, Lisa Irene. *Moral History from Herodotus to Diodorus Siculus*. Edinburgh: Edinburgh University Press, 2016.

Lieu, Judith M. *Christian Identity in the Jewish and Graeco-Roman World*. Oxford: Oxford University Press, 2004.

Lieu, Judith M. "'Impregnable Ramparts and Walls of Iron': Boundary and Identity in Early 'Judaism' and Christianity." *NTS* 48 (2002): 297–313.

Lieu, Judith M. *Neither Jew nor Greek? Constructing Early Christianity*. Edinburgh: T&T Clark, 2002.

Link, Bruce G., and Jo C. Phelan. "Conceptualizing Stigma." *Annual Review of Sociology* 27 (2001): 363–87.

Longnecker, Richard N. "Paul's Vision of the Church and Community Formation." In *Community Formation in the Early Church and in the Church Today*. Edited by Richard N. Longnecker, 73–88. Peabody, MA: Hendrickson, 2002.

Luraghi, Nino. "The Study of Greek Ethnic Identities." In *A Companion to Ethnicity in the Ancient Mediterranean*. Malden, MA: Wiley-Blackwell, 2014.

Mackie, Hilary. *Talking Trojan: Speech and Community in the Iliad*. Lanhan, MD: Rowman & Littlefield, 1996.

MacMullen, Ramsay. *Romanization in the Time of Augustus*. New Haven: Yale University Press, 2000.

Malesevic, Sinisa. *The Sociology of Ethnicity*. London: Sage, 2004.

Malkin, Irad, ed. *Ancient Perceptions of Greek Ethnicity*. Center for Hellenic Studies Colloquia 5. Cambridge: Harvard University Press, 2001.

Martin, S. Rebecca. "Ethnicity and Representation." In *A Companion to Ethnicity in the Ancient Mediterranean*. Edited by Jeremy McInerney. Malden, MA: Wiley-Blackwell, 2014.

Martin, Troy W. *Metaphor and Composition in 1 Peter*. SBLDS 131. Atlanta: Scholars Press, 1992.

Mason, Steve. "Philosophiai: Greco-Roman, Judean, and Christian." In *Voluntary Associations in the Graeco-Roman World*. Edited by John S. Kloppenborg and Stephen G. Wilson. London: Routledge, 1997.

Mazurek, Carl. "*Agricola* and the Flavian Romanization of Britain." *Hirundo* VI (2007): 41–7.

Mbuvi, Andrew Mūtūa. *Temple, Exile, and Identity in 1 Peter*. LNTS 345. London: T&T Clark, 2007.

McInerney, Jeremy. "Ethnicity: An Introduction." In *A Companion to Ethnicity in the Ancient Mediterranean*. Edited by Jeremy McInerney. Malden, MA: Wiley-Blackwell, 2014.

McInerney, Jeremy. "Ethnos and Ethnicity in Early Greece." In *Ancient Perceptions of Greek Ethnicity*. Center for Hellenic Studies Colloquia 5. Cambridge: Harvard University Press, 2001.

McWhorter, John. "Banning the Term 'Illegal Immigrant' Won't Change the Stigma." *Time*, April 9, 2013. http://ideas.time.com/2013/04/09/viewpoint-banning-the-term-illegal-immigrant-wont-change-the-stigma/.

Meeks, Wayne A. *The First Urban Christians: The Social World of the Apostle Paul*. New Haven: Yale University Press, 1983.

Mellor, Ronald. "*Graecia Capta*: The Confrontation between Greek and Roman Identity." In *Hellenisms: Culture, Identity, and Ethnicity from Antiquity to Modernity*. Edited by Katerina Zacharia, 79–125. Burlington, VT: Ashgate, 2008.

Michaels, J. Ramsey. *1 Peter*. WBC 49. Waco, TX: Word, 1988.

Mitchell, Lynette G. "Greeks, Barbarians and Aeschylus' 'Suppliants.'" *Greece Rome* 53, no. 2 (2006): 205–23.

Mitchell, Stephen. *Anatolia: Land, Men, and Gods in Asia Minor. Vol I: The Celts and the Impact of Roman Rule*. Oxford: Clarendon, 1993.

Momigliano, Arnaldo D. *Alien Wisdom: The Limits of Hellenization*. Cambridge: Cambridge University Press, 1975.

Moy, Russell G. "Resident Aliens of the Diaspora: 1 Peter and Chinese Protestants in San Francisco." *Semeia* 90, no. 91 (2002): 51–67.

Munson, Rosaria Vignolo. "Herodotus and Ethnicity." In *A Companion to Ethnicity in the Ancient Mediterranean*. Edited by Jeremy McInerney, 341–55. Malden, MA: Wiley-Blackwell, 2014.

Murray, A. T. *Iliad*. Vol. 1. 2 vols. Cambridge: Harvard University Press, 1924.

Nagy, Gregory. *Pindar's Homer: The Lyric Possession of an Epic Past*. Baltimore: Johns Hopkins University Press, 1990.

Neinuis, David R. *Not by Paul Alone: The Formation of the Catholic Epistle Collection and the Christian Canon*. Waco, TX: Baylor University Press, 2007.

Nienhuis, David R., and Robert W. Wall. *Reading the Epistle of James, Peter, John, and Jude as Scripture: The Shaping and Shape of a Canonical Collection*. Grand Rapids: Eerdmans, 2013,

Ok, Janette H. "Always Ethnic, Never 'American': Reading 1 Peter through the Lens of the 'Perpetual Foreigner' Stereotype." In *T&T Clark Handbook to Asian and Asian American Biblical Hermeneutics*. Edited by Seung Ai Yang and Uriah Y. Kim, 417–26. New York: T&T Clark, 2019.

Ok, Janette H. "You Have Become Children of Sarah: Reading 1 Peter 3: 1–6 through the Intersectionality of Asian Immigrant Wives, Patriarchy, and Honorary Whiteness." In *Minoritized Women Reading Race and Ethnicity: Intersectional Approaches to Constructed Identity and Early Christian Texts*. Edited by Mitzi J. Smith and Jin Young Choi, 111–29. Lanhan, MD: Lexington, 2020.

Page, Sydney H. T. "Obedience and Blood-Sprinkling in 1 Peter 1:2." *WTJ* 72, no. 2 (2010): 291–8.

Papadodima, Efi. "Ethnicity and the Stage." In *A Companion to Ethnicity in the Ancient Mediterranean*. Edited by Jeremy McInerney, 256–69. Malden, MA: Wiley-Blackwell, 2014.

Pike, Kenneth L. *Language in Relation to a Unified Theory of the Structure of Human Behavior*. 2nd ed. Mouton: The Hague, 1967.

Pliny the Elder. *The Blackwell History of the Latin Language*. Translated by James Clackson and Geoffrey Horrocks. Malden, MA: Wiley-Blackwell, 2010.

Pliny the Younger. *Pliny the Younger Complete Letters*. Translated by P. G. Walsh. Oxford: Oxford University Press, 2006. Trans. James Clackson and Geoffrey Horrocks, *The Blackwell History of the Latin Language* (Malden, MA: Wiley-Blackwell, 2010), 229.

Price, S. R. F. *Rituals and Power: The Roman Imperial Cult in Asia Minor*. Rev. ed. Cambridge: Cambridge University Press, 1985.

Punt, Jeremy. "He Is Heavy … He's My Brother: Unraveling Fraternity in Paul (Galatians)." *Neot* 46, no. 1 (2012): 153–71.

Richard, Earl J. *Reading 1 Peter, Jude, and 2 Peter: A Literary and Theological Commentary*. Macon, GA: Smyth & Helwys, 2000.

Richardson, Peter. *Israel in the Apostolic Church*. SNTSMS 10. Cambridge: Cambridge University Press, 1969.

Ross, Shawn A. "Barbarophonos: Language and Panhellenism in the *Iliad*." *Classical Philology* 100, no. 4 (2005): 299–316.

Roymans, Nico. *Ethnic Identity and Imperial Power: The Batavians in the Early Roman Empire*. Amsterdam: Amsterdam University Press, 2004.

Saïd, Suzanne. "The Discourse of Identity in Greek Rhetoric from Isocrates to Aristides." In *Ancient Perceptions of Greek Ethnicity*. Center for Hellenic Studies Colloquia 5, 275–99. Cambridge: Harvard University Press, 2001.

Sargent, Benjamin. *Written to Serve: The Use of Scripture in 1 Peter*. LNTS 547. London: Bloomsbury T&T Clark, 2015.

Scott, James C. *Domination and the Arts of Resistance: Hidden Transcripts*. New Haven: Yale University Press, 2008.

Scott, James M. *Adoption as Sons of God: An Exegetical Investigation into the Background of ΥΙΟΘΕΣΙΑ in the Pauline Corpus*. WUNT 2. Vol. 48. Tübingen: J. C. B. Mohr (Paul Siebeck), 1992.

Scott, Robert. *An Intermediate Greek-English Lexicon: Founded upon the Seventh Edition of Liddell and Scott's Greek-English Lexicon*. Edited by H. G. Liddell. Oxford: Benediction Classics, 2010.

Sechrest, Love L. *A Former Jew: Paul and the Dialectics of Race*. LNTS 410. London: T&T Clark, 2009.

Selwyn, Edward Gordon. *The First Epistle of St. Peter: The Greek Text with Introduction, Notes and Essays*. London: Macmillan, 1958.

Sherwin-White, A. N. *The Roman Citizenship*. 2nd ed. Oxford: Clarendon, 1973.

Sidanius, Jim, and Felicia Pratto. *Social Dominance: An Intergroup Theory of Social Hierarchy and Oppression*. Cambridge: Cambridge University Press, 1999.

Smith, Anthony D. *The Ethnic Origins of Nations*. Oxford: Oxford University Press, 1986.

Smith, Shively T. J. *Strangers to Family: Diaspora and 1 Peter's Invention of God's Household*. Waco, TX: Baylor University Press, 2016.

Snodgrass, A. M. *The Dark Age of Greece: An Archaeological Survey of the Eleventh to the Eighth Centuries BC*. Edinburgh: Edinburgh University Press, 1971.

Sommerstein, Alan H., ed. *Aeschylus I. Persians, Seven against Thebes, Suppliants, Prometheus Bound*. Translated by Sommerstein, Alan H. LBL 145. Cambridge: Harvard University Press, 2008.

Steiger, Wilhelm. *Exposition of the First Epistle of Peter*. Translated by Patrick Fairbairn. Edinburg: T&T Clark, 1836.

Stoler, Ann Laura. "Racial Histories and Their Regimes of Truth." *Political Power Social Theory* 11 (1997): 183–206.

Stroup, Christopher. *The Christians Who Became Jews: Acts of the Apostles and Ethnicity in the Roman City*. New Haven: Yale University Press, 2020.

Suetonius. *Suetonius: The Lives of the Twelve Caesars; An English Translation, Augmented with the Biographies of Contemporary Statesman, Orators, Poets, and Other Associates.* Edited by J. Eugene Reed. Translated by Alexander Thomson M.D. Vol. 6. Philadelphia: Gebbie & Co., 1889.

Swain, Simon. *Hellenism and Empire: Language, Classicism, and Power in the Greek World, A.D. 50–250.* Oxford: Clarendon, 1996.

Taylor, Charles. *Sources of the Self: The Making of the Modern Identity.* Cambridge: Harvard University Press, 1989.

"The Effects of Seeing Asian-Americans as a 'Model Minority.'" *New York Times.* Accessed April 5, 2017. Https://www.nytimes.com/roomfordebate/2015/10/16/the-effects-of-seeing-asian-americans-as-a-model-minority.

Thomas, Rosalind. "Ethnicity, Genealogy, and Hellenism in Herodotus." In *Ancient Perceptions of Greek Ethnicity.* Center for Hellenic Studies Colloquia 5. Cambridge: Harvard University Press, 2001.

Thomas, Rosalind. *Herodotus in Context: Ethnography, Science and the Art of Persuasion.* Cambridge: Cambridge University Press, 2000.

Thurén, Lauri. *Argument and Theology in 1 Peter: The Origins of Christian Paraenesis.* JSNTSup 114. Sheffield: Sheffield Academic Press, 1995.

Tite, Philip. "The Compositional Function of the Petrine Prescript: A Look at 1 Pet 1: 1-3." *JETS* 39, no. 1 (1996): 47–56.

Trebilco, Paul. *Self-Designations and Group Identity in the New Testament.* Cambridge: Cambridge University Press, 2012.

Tuan, Mia. *Forever Foreigners or Honorary Whites?: The Asian Ethnic Experience Today.* New Brunswick, NJ: Rutgers University Press, 1999.

Tucker, J. Brian, and A. Baker Coleman, eds. *T&T Clark Handbook to Social Identity in the New Testament.* London: Bloomsbury, 2014.

VanGemeren, Willem A. "'Abbā' in the Old Testament." *JETS* 31, no. 4 (1988): 385–98.

van Unnik, W. C. "Christianity according to 1 Peter." ExpT, 1957 1956, 79–83.

Vassenden, Anders, and Mette Andersson. "Whiteness, Non-Whiteness and 'Faith Information Control': Religion among Young People in Grønland, Oslo." *Ethnic and Racial Studies* 34, no. 4 (2011): 574–93.

Volf, Miroslav. "Soft Difference: Theological Reflections on the Relation Between Church and Culture in 1 Peter," *ExAud* 10 (1994): 15–30.

Wan, Sze-Kar. "Asian American Perspectives: Ambivalence of the Model Minority and Perpetual Foreigner." In *Studying Paul's Letters: Contemporary Perspectives and Methods.* Edited by Joseph A. Marchal. 175–90. Minneapolis: Fortress, 2012.

Weber, Max. *Economy and Society: An Outline of Interpretive Sociology.* Edited by Guenther Roth and Claus Wittich. Berkeley: University of California Press, 1968 [1922].

Weiner, Rachel. "AP Drops 'Illegal Immigrant' from Stylebook." *The Washington Post,* April 2, 2013. http://www.washingtonpost.com/blogs/post-politics/wp/2013/04/02/ap-drops-illegal-immigrant-from-stylebook/.

Wilken, Robert L. "Collegia, Philosophical Schools, and Theology." In *The Catacombs and the Colosseum: The Roman Empire as the Setting of Primitive Christianity.* Valley Forge, PA: Judson Press, 1971.

Wilken, Robert L. *The Christians as the Romans Saw Them.* New Haven: Yale University Press, 2003.

Williams, Travis B. *Good Works in 1 Peter: Negotiating Social Conflict and Christian Identity in the Greco-Roman World.* Tübingen: Mohr Siebeck, 2014.

Williams, Travis B. *Persecution in 1 Peter: Differentiating and Contextualizing Early Christian Suffering.* NovTSup 145. Leiden: E. J. Brill, 2012.
Wilson, Stephen G. "Voluntary Associations." In *Voluntary Associations in the Graeco-Roman World*. Edited by John S. Kloppenborg and Stephen G. Wilson, 1–15. London: Routledge, 1997.
Wimmer, Andreas. *Ethnic Boundary Making: Institutions, Power, Networks.* Oxford; New York: Oxford University Press, 2013.
Wimmer, Andreas. "The Making and Unmaking of Ethnic Boundaries: A Multilevel Process Theory." *American Journal of Sociology* 113, no. 4 (January 2008): 970–1022.
Windisch, Hans. *Die Katholischen Briefe*. 3rd ed. HNT 15. Tübingen: Mohr (Siebeck), 1951.
Witherington, Ben, III. *Letters and Homilies for Hellenized Christians Volume II: A Social-Rhetorical Commentary on 1-2 Peter*. Downers Grove, IL: Intervarsity Press, 2007.
Wong, Sam. *Exploring Unseen Social Capital in Community Participation.* Amsterdam: Amsterdam University Press, 2007.
Woolf, Greg. "Becoming Roman, Staying Greek: Culture, Identity and the Civilizing Process in the Roman East." *Proceedings of the Cambridge Philosophical Society* 40 (1994): 116–43.
Woolf, Greg. *Becoming Roman: The Origin of Provincial Civilization in Gaul*. Cambridge: Cambridge University Press, 1998.
Wu, Frank H. *Yellow: Race in America beyond Black and White*. Reprint ed. New York: Basic Books, 2003.
Yonge, C. D., trans. *The Works of Philo: Complete and Unabridged*. Peabody, MA: Hendrickson, 1995.
Zacharia, Katerina. "Herodotus' Four Markers of Greek Identity." In *Hellenisms: Culture, Identity, and Ethnicity from Antiquity to Modernity*. Edited by Katerina Zacharia, 21–36. Burlington, VT: Ashgate, 2008.
Zacharia, Katerina. "Introduction." In *Hellenisms: Culture, Identity, and Ethnicity from Antiquity to Modernity*. Edited by Katerina Zacharia, 1–18. Burlington, VT: Ashgate, 2008.

Scripture Index

Old Testament

Genesis
12.2; 18.18	57 n.127

Exodus
1.9	57 n.127
4.22–3	40 n.29
6.6	46
6.7	57 n.127
7.4	57 n.127
7.16	57 n.127
12.5	47 n.73
12.46	47 n.73
19.5–6	57 n.127
19.6	60 n.148
24.3, 7	40
24.3–8	40
24.7	40
29.39	47 n.72
LXX 24.8	40

Leviticus
1.10; 3.6	47 n.71
17.7	50 n.99
19.2	52
20.26	57 n.127
25.33	46

Numbers
6.14	47 n.72
27.7–11; 32.18	52 n.106
28–9	47 n.73

Deuteronomy
7.6–7	57 n.127
7.8	46
9.26	46
9.26, 29	57 n.127
10.15	57 n.127
14.2	57 n.127
14.2, 21	57 n.127
15.15	46
21.18	46
24.18	46
26.15	57 n.127
26.19	57 n.127
32.4, 7–14, 36–43	40 n.29
32.5–6, 14–35	41 n.29
32.6	40 n.29
32.18	41, 42 n.43

Joshua
4.14; 11.21	57 n.127
13.14	52 n.106
13.28	52 n.106
15.20	52 n.106
16.5	52 n.106
18.20, 28	52 n.106
19.1, 8–9, 16, 23, 31, 39, 47	52 n.106

Ezra
9.12	52 n.106

Judith
9.6	38 n.12

Esther
2.10	57 n.127

1 Samuel
25.32	41 n.30

2 Samuel
7.14	40 n.29
7.23	46
8.144	5

1 Kings
1.48	41 n.30

Scripture Index

Psalms
2.7   41
68.5; 89.26   40 n.29
71.14   46
88.4; 104.6, 43   57 n.127
103.13–14   41 n.29
LXX 117.22   66 n.20

Proverbs
8.25   41
13.22   52 n.106

Wisdom
2.16   40 n.29
4.12   43 n.50

Isaiah
8.4   45 n.61
8.14 (2.8)   66 n.20
28.16 (2.7)   66 n.20
41.8–9   45 n.58
42.6   45 n.58
43.1   45 n.58
43.20–1   60 n.148
45.3   45 n.58
45.13   46
46.11   45 n.58
48.12, 15   45 n.58
52.3   46
53   46 n.69
53.9   72
63.16; 64.8   40 n.29
65.9, 15, 23   57 n.127

Jeremiah
3.4, 19   45 n.61
3.4, 19; 31.9   40 n.29
8.19; 10.15   50 n.99

Hosea
11.1   40 n.29
11.1–8   40 n.29
LXX 2.25   66 n.21

Malachi
1.6   41 n.29
1.6; 2.10   40 n.29

New Testament

Matthew
3.9   44 n.56
20.28   46 n.69
26.41   47 n.77

Mark
10.45   46 n.69

Luke
3.8   44 n.56
22.15   43 n.49
24.21   46

John
3.3   42
3.3–8   37 n.10, 41
3.4   42
3.5   42
3.31; 19.11; cf. 8.23   42
6.63   47 n.77
19.36   47 n.73

Acts
2.23   38 n.12
8.32   47 n.73
11.26   8
14.15   50
15.20, 29   67 n.25
16   51 n.102
20.28   47 n.71
26.23   45 n.62
26.28   8

1 Chronicles
16.13   57 n.127
17.13; 22.10; 28.6   40 n.29
29.10   41 n.30

2 Chronicles
6.4   41 n.30

Romans
1.4; 6.5   45 n.62
1.24   43 n.50

3.24	46 n.69	1 Timothy	
4	51 n.101	2.6	46 n.69
4.17	47 n.78		
8.1–17	47 n.77	Titus	
8.11	47 n.78	2.1–10	53 n.110
8.15–17; 23	37 n.9	2.9	53 n.110
11	51 n.101	2.14	46
12.2	44	3.5–7	42 n.37
16.5	58 n.138		
		Hebrews	
1 Corinthians		9.11f	47 n.73
5.7	47 n.73	9.11–14	47 n.71
10.31–3	59 n.140	9.12; 15	46 n.69
11.17–22	59	9.14	47 n.72
12.2	54 n.119	9.15	40
15.12, 21	45 n.62		
15.22, 36, 45	47 n.78	James	
		1.14–15	43 n.50
2 Corinthians			
1.3	40	1 Peter	
		1.1	56–7
Galatians		1.1–2	37, 40, 42–3,
2.12	59		48 n.80, 49, 53,
3–4	51 n.101		55, 71
3.28	55	1.1–2.10	73
4.1–7	37 n.9	1.1–3	41, 53, 55, 59,
5.16–25	47 n.77		65, 71
		1.1–5	44 n.56
Philippians		1.1, 14	44
1.23	43 n.49	1.1, 17	57
3.10	45 n.62	1.14–16	10 n.47
		1.2	38–9, 40, 45,
Thessalonians			51, 55
2.13	38 n.18	1.2 (cf. 1.15, 22)	39
4.3, 5.22	67 n.25	1.2 (cf. 1.20)	38 n.15
		1.2a	37–8
Ephesians		1.2b	38–40, 48
1.3	40	1.2c	40
1.3–6	37 n.9	1.2, 3, 14, 17	50
1.7	46 n.69	1.2–3, 17	55
3.21–6.9	53	1.2, 14	51
4.17	50 n.99	1.2, 20	38 n.16
5.21–33	53 n.111	1.3	37 n.10, 40–3,
			45, 47–8, 52–3,
Colossians			56, 65–6, 66
3.18–4.1	53		n.22, 70, 73
3.18–19	53 n.111	1.3, cf. 23	55
4.15	58 n.138	1.3a	54

1.3b	37, 70	1.18	10, 49, 50 n.99,
1.3c	40, 47		51, 53, 71
1.3–2.8	66	1.18; 2.9–10	37
1.3–4	42	1.18–19	2, 40, 44–8,
1.3–5	39 n.24		46 n.69, 50,
1.3–5, 14	55		54–5, 59, 65, 67
1.3, 14, 17, 23	37	1.19	46–8
1.3, 18, 2.22–4	37	1.19–20	60
1.3, 23	41, 49, 53, 59	1.20	38, 51, 55
1.4a	47	1.22	50, 59
1.4–5	52–3	1.23	41, 53, 65
1.4–9	66	1.23–5	51
1.5	38 n.16, 66	2.1–2	35 n.1
1.5b	47	2.1–2, 11	51, 54
1.5–9; 1.17; 5.4, 6, 10	42	2.1–3	70
1.6	35 n.1, 66, 80	2.1, 5, 9–10, 24bc	42
1.6–7	44 n.56, 57	2.1, 11–12	56 n.121
1.6–9	50	2.1, 11–12, 15, 22–23	72
1.6, 17	93	2.1.18–19	66
1.7	69	2.21–25	46 n.69
1.7, 13	44 n.56	2.4	50
1.9–10	38	2.4, 6	46
1.10	38, 38 n.12, 71 n.42	2.4, 7–8	80
	38	2.4–10	55, 93
1.10–12	38	2.4–12	87
1.10–12, 20	42, 51 n.103	2.5	57
1.12	38	2.5; cf. 4.17	37
1.13	70	2.5; 4.17	38
1.13–19	87	2.5, 9	39 n.22
1.13–21	44, 45 n.60, 51	2.5, 9–10	51
1.14	10, 38, 44, 49, 53–4, 56, 67–8, 70–1	2.5, 17	56, 65
		2.7	66
		2.7–8	44
1.14b	43	2.9	8, 36 n.4, 42,
1.14–15, 18	8		45, 55, 60, 66,
1.14–17	44, 46, 53		66 n.22, 79, 81,
1.14–18	8, 69		93
1.14–19	66	2.9–10	11–12, 42,
1.15	44–5		52–3, 56–7, 67,
1.15; 2.21	45		69, 72, 92, 93
1.15–16; cf. 1.1–5	44	2.9b-10	41, 66
1.15, 16, 19, 22	39 n.22	2.9, 12; 4.3	11
1.15, 17	46	2.9, 21	38 n.12
1.16	52	2.10	10, 37, 55, 60, 65–6
1.17	44–5, 44 n.56, 56 n.121	2.10, 25; 4.2–4; cf. 1.18–19	42
1.17;cf. 1.20	45	2.11	43, 45, 57, 59, 67–8, 70–1

2.11; 4.2–4	44	4.1, 12–14, 16	80
2.11–12	51, 66	4.2	43, 70
2.11–12, 25, 19	61	4.2, 3	67
2.12	11, 57, 67–70, 73, 79–80	4.2; 3a	74
		4.2–3	67
2.12; 4.4	10	4.2–4	54, 69–70
2.13–3.7	80–1	4.3	11, 70, 72, 80, 87
2.13–4.6	68		
2.14	69, 79	4.3–4	10, 47, 66, 70–2, 81
2.15	69		
2.16	46	4.4	67, 70
2.18ff	74	4.4; 12	73
2.18, 3.1–7	50	4.4; 14, 16, 19	68
2.18–25	50	4.7	44 n.56, 70
2.19	35 n.1	4.8–10	65
2.21	45, 55, 72	4.8–11	59
2.21–2	47	4.12	35 n.1, 59
2.21–3; cf. 3.9	68	4.12–16	50
2.21–5	35 n.1, 56	4.12, 16	69
2.21–25	80	4.12–19	80
2.22	47, 72	4.13	44 n.56, 47
2.24	51, 55	4.13, 14, 16	69
3.1–2, 15–16	61	4.14	79, 81, 91
3.1–4, 9–10, 16	72	4.14–16	80
3.15	39 n.22	4.14–17	50
3.1–6	50, 53 n.112	4.15	67 n.28, 80
3.2	68–9	4.15, 19	67 n.28
3.6	51, 53 n.112	4.16	8, 10, 79
3.7	51, 53 n.110	4.17	44, 44 n.56, 50, 56–7
3.8	56, 59, 65		
3.9	35 n.1, 38 n.12, 45, 72	4.17; cf. 2.5	56
		4.17–18	44 n.56
3.9, 13–18	80	4.19	44 n.56
3.9–14	50	5.1–5	53 n.110
3.10	72	5.5–6	56
3.13	57	5.7, 10	44 n.56
3.13–17	80	5.8	44 n.56, 70
3.14–16	44 n.56	5.8–10	35 n.1
3.14–17	50, 69	5.9	69
3.14, 17	10	5.10	38 n.12, 45
3.15	73	5.12–14	59
3.16	73	5.13	52 n.107
3.16–17	68	5.22.1	24–5
3.18	48, 55	9–10	92
3.18–22 (cf. 2.24–5)	47	10–11	2 n.4, 36 n.6, 63 n.4
3.21	43, 47		
4.1	35 n.1, 74	10–12; 20	71
4.1–2	70	12–16	57
4.1, 4	57	13–16	35 n.1
4.1–6	8, 10, 79	14–15	57

14–16	35 n.1	Cicero	28
14–17	35 n.1	*Pro Sestio*	110 29
16–17	57		
18–19	55	Dionysius of Halicarnassus	33–4
18–20	57	*Antiquitates romanae*	
22–3	70	1.89.1	33
		1.89.3–4	34 n.141
Haustafel		5.48.2	53 n.113
2.18–3.7	53		
		Diodorus Siculus	41
2 Peter		*Bibliotheca historica*	
1.16	68	3.62.6	41 n.36
1 John		Herodotus	5, 13–14, 16, 19, 22, 24–7, 31, 33–6, 89–90
5.1	42 n.43		
Pseudepigrapha		*Histories*	
1 Maccabees		4.8.5; 15.74.5; 17.2.2	53 n.113
1.22	43 n.50		
4.11	46	1.1.1	13
		1.57	26
3 Maccabees		1.131.1	23
5.7	40 n.29	1.145–6	24
		1.146	24
Classical and Ancient Christian Literature		1.146–7	24
		1.151.2	25
Aeschylus	16, 20–2, 59	1.210.2	25 n.93
		2.4.1	29
Persians	20–1, 20 n.53, 21 n.60, 22	5.22.1	24
		5.22.1–2	24
70–80	21	5.49.3	25
93–114	21 n.62	7.35.1	22
176–99	21 n.64	7.35.2	22
441–4	21 n.62	8.137–9	25
723–5	21 n.62	8.142.5	25
1–19	21	8.144	5, 13–14, 23
		8.144.1	25
Suppliants		8.144.2	23, 25, 89
22	n.68	9.122	23 n.79
Aristotle		Homer	
Politics		*Iliad*	
7.1327b	19	2.530	17
		2.802–6	18
Apuleius' *The Golden*		2.867	19
Ass 9.14	67 n.28	2.867–69	18
		2.91	5 n.21
Chrysostom, Dio		3.32	5 n.21
A Libyan Myth		7.115	5 n.21, 17
5.16	43 n.50		

11.72	5 n.21	10.80	29 n.115
22.256–9	19	10.96	73 n.50
		10.117	30
Justin			
Dialogue with Trypho		Plutarch	31 n.127
8	58	*Pompey*, 68.2	49 n.88
Juvenal		Seneca	
Satires		*De vita beata*	
3.85–110	30	13.2	29
Panegyricus		Strabo	15 n.16, 30
37.2–5	32 n.135		n.122
Philodemus	41	Suetonius	32 n.135, 79
De pietate	41 n.35	*Nero*	
		16.2	80
Pliny the Elder	28		
Natural History		Tacitus	29, 32, 79
3.39	28, 32	*Agricola 21*	32 n.136
		Annals	
Pliny the Younger	30	15.44	80
Epistulae			
5.20	29 n.115	Tertullian	
8.24	29, 29 n.117	*Apology*	
10.79	29 n.115	39	58

Subject Index

ἀναστροφή 8
ἀναγεννά 37, 37 n.10, 41, 43 n.47
ἀλλόθροος 20 n.52
ἀναγεννωμένη 41
ἀναβιόω 41
ἀνθρώπων 43
ἀλλά 44
αἷμα 45
ἄμωμος 47
αἷμα 48
ἀναστροφή 50 n.99, 54
ἀπέχω 67
αἱ σαρκικαί ἐπιθυμίαι 67
ἀπέχεσθαι 67–8
ἀνθρώπων ἐπιθυμίαις 70, 73

βαρβαρόφωνοι 19–20, 19 n.44
βάρβαρος 20, 20 n.54
βασίλειον ἱεράτευμα 93 n.10

Χριστιανός 8–9
χρόνος 45
Χριστιανός 80 n.86
Χριστιανοί 90

δι' ὑμᾶς 38
διά 40
δι' ... Ἰησοῦ Χριστοῦ 41
δι' ἀναστάσεως Ἰησοῦ Χριστοῦ 48
διασπορά 57

ἔθνος 2, 5, 7, 13
ἔργα μεγάλα τε καὶ θωμαστά 13
ἐκλεκτός 37
ἔθνος ἑταίρων 17
εἰς ὑμᾶς 38, 39 n.24
ἐν ἁγιασμῷ πνεύματος 38–9, 38 n.18
εἰς ὑπακοὴν καὶ ῥαντισμὸν αἵματος Ἰησοῦ Χριστοῦ 39
ἐξ ἀρχῆς νέον γεννηθῆναι 41

ἐπιθυμία 43
ἐλυτρώθητε 45–6
ἐκ νεκρῶν 48
ἐκλεκτοί 57
ἐκλεκτός 57
ἐπιθυμία 67, 67 n.28
ἐπιθυμίαι 68
ἔχοντες 68
ἐποπτεύω 68
ἐπιθυμίαι 70
ἔθνος ἅγιον 71

γένος 2, 7
γεννά 41
γεγόνασιν ἀρκηγέται τοῦ ἔθνους 49
γνησιωτέρας 49
γένος ἐκλεκτόν, βασίλειον ἱεράτευμα, ἔθνος ἅγιον, λαὸς εἰς περιποίησιν 55

κατὰ πρόγνωσιν θεοῦ πατρός 37
κατασκεδάννυμι 40
κληρονομία 52
κακοποιῶν 67 n.28
κακός 73 n.48

λυτρόομαι 40
λυτρόω 45
λύτρον 46
λυτρόομαι 46, 51
λοιδορία 73, 73 n.48

ματαία 50 n.99
μάταιος 51
μὴ συσχηματιζόμενοι 67

νόμος 23

οἶκος πνευματικός 37
ὅμαιμον 25
ὁ θεὸς καὶ πατὴρ τοῦ κυρίου ἡμῶν Ἰησοῦ Χριστοῦ 40

ὁ ἔθνος 49
ὁ οἶκος τοῦ θεοῦ 56
οὐ λαός 65
ὁπλίσασθε 68, 70
οἶκος πνευματικὸς 81
οἶκος τοῦ θεοῦ 81
ὡς ἀμνοῦ ἀμώμου καὶ ἀσπίλου 47

προεγνωσμένου 38
πρόγνωσις 38, 38 n.12, 38 n.16
προγινώσκω 38 n.16
παλιγγενεσία 42 n.37
πατροπαράδοτος 46, 50 n.99
προεγνωσμένου μὲν πρὸ καταβολῆς κόσμου 51
πατροπαράδοτος 53
πάροικοι 56, 60, 70
παρεπιδήμοι 56, 60, 70
παρεπίδημος 57
τῆς ἀσωτίας ἀνάχυσιν 70
Πανέλληνες 17
φύσις 26

ῥαντισμὸν αἵματος Ἰησοῦ Χριστοῦ 40

σαρκικῶν 43
συσχηματίζομαι 44
στρατεύονται 68
σαρκικός 70

τὸ Ἀττικὸν ἔθνος 26
τό γένος 26
ταῖς πρότερον ... ἐπιθυμίαις 43
τὸν καλέσαντα ὑμᾶς ἅγιον 45
τέκνα ὑπακοῆς 45
τιμίῳ αἵματι 45
τίμιος 46
τέκνα ὑπακοῆς 52
τῶν υἱῶν Ισραηλ 52
τέκνα 53
τὰ ἔθνη 66-7, 71, 73
τῶν σαρκικῶν ἐπιθυμιῶν 67
θανατόω 47
Τέκνον 52
Τίκτω 52-3

υἱοθεσία 37, 37 n.9
ὑμῖν 38

Abraham 44 n.56, 49-51
Achaeans 18-19, 24. *See also* Trojans
Achilles (in Trojan War) 19
Achtemeier, Paul J. 39 n.24, 43 nn.47-8, 55 n.120, 67 n.28
Aciman, André 77-8
actual social identity 77-8. *See also* virtual social identity
Aeschylus 14
  Persians 16, 20-2, 20 n.53
  Suppliants 22 n.68
Agnew, Francis H. 39-40, 40 n.25
Agricola 32
Alexander of Macedonia (Alexander I) 24-6, 24 n.85
American ethnic minorities 92-3
Anatolian Peninsula 73 n.50
ancestors/ancestry 5-9, 12, 21, 24, 26, 37, 47-8, 50-2, 50 n.99, 55, 66, 68, 91.
  See also common descent
Andersson, Mette 82-3
anthropology/anthropologists 15-17, 62, 63 n.4, 86
anti-Christian prejudice 3 n.10, 11, 61-2, 89, 91
Apostle Paul 50
Apuleius, *The Golden Ass* IX.14 67 n.28
Asia Minor 10, 33 n.140, 37, 73 n.50, 80 n.82
Asian Americans 4, 8 n.37, 11, 92-3
Athens/Athenians 14-16, 20-5, 28
  Herodotus on 26

Balch, David L. 67 n.28, 69, 81 n.91
baptism 40 n.26, 43, 43 nn.46-7, 47, 59
barbarian(s) 13-23, 20 n.54, 22 n.68, 25, 28, 28 n.110, 30, 32-4, 90. *See also* Greeks/Greek ethnicity
Barreto, Eric D. 51 n.102, 94 n.12
Bartchy, S. Scott 95 n.15
Barth, Fredrik 9, 11, 17, 68, 70, 80, 90-1
  on ethnic boundaries 6, 11, 61-74, 91
    constrained Christian identity 72-3
    constructing social boundaries in 1 Peter 65-71
    Gentile "Other" 73-4
  on ethnic group identity 61-2, 63 n.4, 87
  Ethnic Groups and Boundaries 62

Subject Index

Beare, Francis Wright, *The First Epistle of Peter: The Greek Text with Introduction and Notes* 38 n.16, 40 n.28
Bechtler, Stephen 11
begetting anew, God's 41, 45
behavior 8 n.37, 50 n.99, 64, 67–8, 70–2, 79–1, 87
    Christian 68–9, 81
    Gentiles 69
    Greek 30
Bithynia-Pontus 29 n.115, 30, 73 n.50
blackness 85–7
blood of Christ 2, 9, 37, 39–40, 40 n.26, 43, 52, 54–5, 91, 94
    and new birth 45–8
    ransoming 2, 36–7, 45–8, 50, 50 n.98, 51, 55, 65, 67
Boring, Eugene 55 n.120
born anew 1–2, 4, 11, 34, 37, 43, 47–8, 53, 70–1, 79, 93
Boyarin, Daniel 54
Buell, Denise 8, 51
    ethnic reasoning 9
    Why This New Race 7

Caesar, Julius 29, 30 n.126, 54
    patrilineal descent 48–51, 49 n.88
Carians 19, 24
Cartledge, Paul, *The Greeks: A Portrait of Self and Others* 16 n.21
children of God 52–4
    obedient 43–5, 44 n.56, 49, 56, 66, 91
Chinese American 72
Christian identity 1–3, 8–9, 11–12, 35–6, 47, 50–1, 53–6, 55 n.120, 59–61, 65–6, 66 n.22, 71–4, 83, 89–90, 92. *See also* non-Christian
Christianismos 54
Christianity 54, 58, 62 n.2, 80, 80 n.82, 82 n.94. *See also* Islam
Cicero 29 n.121
    civilizing mission of Rome 28
    on Greeks 29
    to Quintus 27–8
collective identity 15–16, 23, 26, 84, 89–90
collegium (association) 58–9, 61

common blood (real or perceived) 5, 13, 15, 25–6, 33, 89
common descent 1, 11, 16–17, 31, 34, 90. *See also* ancestors/ancestry
common identity 5, 15
communal identity 9, 36, 65, 71
Concannon, Cavin W. 54 n.119, 94 n.12
constructivism 71
corporate identity 56, 71–2
cultural religion 82 n.94

death of Christ 40, 46–8, 55, 65. *See also* resurrection of Christ
democracy 14, 22, 25 n.93
Demosthenes 24 n.86
deSilva, David A. 50
desires 46, 67, 69–70
    hereditary 68
    human 70, 73
    for Peter 43–4, 57
diaspora 10 n.47, 36, 57, 57 n.132, 90
Diodorus Siculus 41
Dionysius of Halicarnassus 33–4, 41
discredited people 77–8, 82–4, 87
disidentification 60, 60 n.146, 66
divine foreknowledge 38 n.16. *See also* foreknowledge
domestic code in Titus 53 n.110
dominance at workplace (East Asian) 76
dominant culture 3 n.10, 45, 56–7, 61, 68–70, 71 n.42, 74, 81–2, 90, 93
Dorian 21, 24
Douglas, Mary 16
dragnet approach 82 n.92
Duncan-Jones, Richard, *The Economy of the Roman Empire: Qualitative Studies* 27 n.102

Elliott, John H. 2 n.5, 46 n.69, 55 n.120, 69, 81
    A Home for the Homeless 56
    social-scientific criticism of NT 3 n.10
emic 8 n.37
ethnic boundaries 6, 11, 61–74, 70 n.40, 91
ethnic groups 1, 4, 6, 8, 14, 17, 35, 50, 61–5, 68, 73, 84, 90–1, 93
    ascriptive 63
    Asian Americans 4

Barth on 63, 63 n.4
exclusive 63
Fenton on 6
Smith on (*ethnie*) 36
works on 26 n.94
ethnic identity 1–2, 4–6, 8–12, 16–17, 26,
    27 n.102, 35–6, 48, 51, 56, 60–1, 64,
    72–4, 89–92, 94
ethnicity 5, 7–8, 7 n.32, 8 n.37, 11, 17,
    48, 51–2, 62, 64–5, 71, 82, 82 n.92,
    89–90, 93–4. *See also* race/racism
    and culture 56
    derivation/definition of 5 n.26, 6
    fluid and fixed nature of 9
    for Gentile by Peter 36
    Greek (*see* Greeks/Greek ethnicity)
ethnic language 55 n.120, 72, 78
ethnic reasoning 9, 11–12, 35, 51–2, 60,
    91, 94
ethnic-religious. *See* religious-ethnic
    identity
ethnie/pre-national ethnic groups 16
ethnoracial identity 7, 94
ethnos 5 n.26, 8, 35, 54
etic 8 n.37
evildoers 10, 67 n.28, 68–70, 79–80
exile(s) 10 n.47, 42, 46, 87
Exodus 40, 51

father-child relationship 53, 53 n.110
Fatherhood. *See* God as Father
Fearon, James D.
    on identity (social and personal) 4
    "What Is Identity?" 4 n.18
Fenton, Steve 5
    on race, nation, and ethnic group 6
foreigners 56–8, 67–70, 92–3. *See also*
    perpetual foreigners; resident aliens
foreknowledge 37–8, 38 n.15, 43, 66. *See
    also* divine foreknowledge
Fredriksen, Paula 60 n.147
free people 46, 81

Galatians 51, 94
genealogy 37, 48
genos 8, 35
Gentiles/Gentile Christians 1 n.1, 2, 5, 8,
    10–11, 11 n.50, 34, 37, 41, 44, 46,
    50, 50 n.98, 52–6, 60, 60 n.147, 66,
66 n.22, 67 n.23, 67 n.28, 68–74,
78–80, 86–7, 90–1, 93. *See also*
Jews/Jewish
God as Father 37–44, 40 n.29, 48, 51–3,
    55, 66, 91, 94
God Father 45 n.61
Goffman, Erving 9, 60 n.146, 72 n.47
    covering technique 83
    and Kusow 84, 84 n.107
    signs-given/signs-given off 82 n.95
    *Stigma: Notes on the Management of
    Spoiled Identity* 74
    stigma theory 11, 61–2, 74–87, 91
        Christian stigma in 1 Peter 78–81
        color-based stigma 85
        faith information control 82–4
        honorary ethnics 86–7
        normals/abnormals 74–9, 81
        stigma reversal 84–6
    on undesired difference 81
Goppelt, Leonhard 38 n.12, 40 n.26
Greco-Roman 43, 49, 54, 56, 58, 58 n.135, 58
    n.137, 60 n.147, 71, 71 n.42, 80 n.85
Greek–Persian conflicts 13–15, 20 n.53,
    26, 34
Greeks/Greek ethnicity 11, 21–6, 25 n.93,
    31, 34, 89–90. *See also* non-Greeks
    and barbarian (binary) 16–17, 24
    criteria/markers for (blood, language,
        religion, and customs) 5, 13–14, 23,
        25, 31, 33–6
    Dorian 21, 24
    ethnic consciousness 14–16, 19
    Ionians 24–5
    language 31, 31 n.127
    and Olympic Games 14, 14 n.4, 18, 24
    Panhellenic identity 14–15, 17–20, 23
    polis 14, 19, 26
    under Roman rule 26–7
    study of 15–17
    subgroups 24 n.82
Green, Joel B. 39 n.19, 42, 44, 51, 51 n.103
group identity 1–2, 12, 16–17, 26, 35,
    58–9, 63–4, 89, 91
group-understanding 12, 94. *See also* self-
    understanding
Gruen, Erich S. 14 n.11, 17, 21–2
    Rethinking the Other in Antiquity 21
    n.61

Hall, Edith 19–20
  Inventing the Barbarian 15–17
  on *Persians* 21
Hall, Jonathan 17, 17 n.30, 25, 37
  Ethnic Identity in Greek Antiquity 16, 25 n.93
  Hellenicity 18 n.38
  on shared descent 25–6
Hartog, François, *The Mirror of Herodotus: The Representation of the Other in the Writing of History* 16–17
Hebrew Scriptures 47
Hellene/Hellenic identity 16, 19–20, 22–4, 26–7, 69
Hellenization 27, 30. *See also* Romanization
Hellenized Jews 10 n.47. *See also* Jews/Jewish
Herodotus 5, 14, 14 n.11, 16, 19, 22–4, 23 n.79, 25 n.89, 25 n.93, 34, 89–90
  on Alexander's lineage 24–5
  on Arisba people 25
  on Athenians 26
  Greekness 23–4, 26, 33, 36
  Histories 13, 25
  same blood 25
Himes, Paul A., *Foreknowledge and Social Identity in 1 Peter* 38 n.15
Hodge, Caroline J. 37 n.9, 48, 50
holiness and obedience 34, 36, 39, 39 n.23
Holloway, Paul A. 3 n.10, 60 n.146, 74 n.52
  Coping with Prejudice 91
  social prejudice 35 n.1, 92
homaimon 89
Homer 5, 17–20
  Iliad 18–19, 18 n.38
  linguistic diversity 18
  Odyssey 18 n.35, 19
honorable conduct 51, 68–9, 79
honorary ethnics 86–7
Hornblower, Simon 15 n.15, 20 n.54
Horrell, David 8, 35 n.1, 55 n.120, 60, 67 n.28, 93
household 19, 36, 58, 58 n.138, 81
  of God 44, 50, 54, 56–7, 92
  household codes 53 n.111, 81, 81 n.91
  spiritual 4, 69
Huynh, Que-Lam 92–3

identity 2 n.6, 3–4, 9–10, 66, 87, 94 n.12
  collective 15–16, 23, 26, 84, 89–90
  common 5, 15
  communal 9, 36, 65, 71
  corporate 56, 71–2
  cultural 32, 61, 64, 85
  ethnic (*see* ethnic identity)
  ethnoracial 7
  group 1–2, 12, 16–17, 26, 35, 58–9, 63–4, 89, 91
  ingroup 56, 61–3, 68, 92
  nation/national 5–6, 93
  in New Testament studies 2
  personal 4–5, 84
  social 2 n.7, 4, 12
immigrants
  Pakistani 87
  Somali 84–7
  undocumented/illegal 75
immortal gods (*diis immortalibus*) 48
ingroup identity 56, 61–3, 68, 92
inheritance 34, 43 n.46, 47, 50–2, 66
inter-Korean peace. *See* South and North Korea summit, 2018
Ionians/Ionic ethnic identity 19, 24–5, 90
Islam 82, 82 n.94. *See also* Christianity
Isocrates 26
Israel 36–7, 52, 52 n.107, 60, 90, 93–4
  God's love for 40–1 n.29
  identification of 67
  identity-forming language 2, 11, 54–8
  slavery 46, 51

Jenkins, Richard 4
  Social Identity 3 n.12
Jesus Christ 41–2, 48, 52, 54, 60, 65
  blood of (*see* blood of Christ)
  death of 47–8
  election of 55
  faith in 56–7, 72, 84
  resurrection of (*see* resurrection of Christ)
Jews/Jewish 1 n.1, 2, 10, 11 n.50, 12, 42, 52, 55, 59, 67 n.23. *See also* Gentiles/Gentile Christians; Hellenized Jews
  in Asia Minor 10
  Scriptures 60
John 41–2

John the Baptist 44 n.56
Josephus 10 n.47, 41
Judaism 57

Kaalund, Jennifer T. 10 n.47
Keener, Craig S. 42 n.41
Kelly, J. A. 43 n.46
  foreknowledge 38 n.15
kinship 5 n.26, 16–17, 22, 60, 89, 94
  natural 48
Korean 8 n.37, 63–4. *See also* South and North Korea summit, 2018
Kusow, Abdi 84 n.107, 86–7
  "Contesting Stigma: On Goffman's Assumptions of Normative Order" 84

letter of 1 Peter 1, 1 n.1, 3, 10–11, 35 n.1, 36–7, 43 n.48, 91
  cultural homelessness in 56
  Haustafel 53
Lieu, Judith M. 2 n.8
lineage 17, 22, 25, 47, 49–52, 55, 61, 74, 86
Luke 8, 44 n.56

Mackie, Hilary, *Talking Trojan: Speech and Community in the* Iliad 18 n.40
MacMullen, Ramsey, *Romanization in the Time of Augustus* 27 n.106
Martyr, Justin 54, 58
Mbuvi, Andrew M. 40 n.26
McInerney, Jeremy 15
Mellor, Ronald, "*Graecia Capta*" 27 n.106
Michaels, J. Ramsey 38 n.12, 42, 42 n.43, 53
minority groups 10 n.47, 64, 71 n.42, 82 n.92, 92
model minority 76, 76 n.64, 76 n.66
Moses 40, 52
myth(s) of shared descent 1, 16–17, 25–6, 34, 36–7

Nagy, Gregory 18–19
nation/national identity 5–6, 93
nation-state 6–7
new birth 9, 36, 39 n.24, 40–3, 65, 66 n.19, 91
  and Christ's ransoming blood 45–8
New Testament (NT) 5, 41, 46, 53, 68, 94–5

Elliott's social-scientific criticism of 3 n.10
  household codes 53 n.111, 81
New Testament studies (NTS) 3 n.8, 8 n.38
  identity 2
Nicodemus 37 n.10, 41–2
non-Christian 1, 1 n.1, 12, 43, 57, 80 n.82, 82. *See also* Christian identity
non-Greeks 13, 15, 17, 19–20, 26, 31, 90. *See also* Greeks/Greek ethnicity
non-Muslims 83
non-white(ness) 82–3, 87
Norway 82, 82 n.92
Norwegian Christians 8, 82–3
Norwegian Muslims 8, 83

Old Testament (OT) 40 n.29, 52, 55 n.120
"other" 6, 9, 11, 15–17, 19, 22–3, 34, 66, 73–4

pagan/paganism 50 n.99, 54, 60, 60 n.147, 80 n.82
  ex-pagan pagans 60 n.147
Pakistani Norwegian 83
Panhellenism/Panhellenic identity 14–15, 17–20, 23
patrilineal descent 48–52, 54, 91
Paul 37, 37 n.9, 44, 54 n.119
Pelasgian 26
Peloponnesian War 23
peoplehood 5–6, 9, 12–13, 15, 35, 49, 60, 89
people of God 2, 4, 11, 37, 52, 55–6, 60–1, 65–73, 78, 91–2
perpetual foreigners 72, 72 n.45, 76 n.66, 92–3. *See also* foreigners
Persians 13–14, 17, 20–5, 25 n.93, 27
Persian Wars 14–17, 14 n.11, 19, 20 n.53, 23, 26, 33
personal identity 4–5
Petrine authorship of 1 Peter 1 n.1, 46
Philo 10 n.47, 49
Philodemus 41, 41 n.35
Phrynichus 20 n.55
Pike, Kenneth L. 8 n.37
Pliny the Elder 32
  Natural History 28
Pliny the Younger, *Epistles* 29, 29 n.115
Plutarch 31 n.127, 49 n.88

Pompey 29, 49 n.88
prestige symbols 78, 82–3, 86. *See also* stigma symbols
prophet Jeremiah 38 n.16
proto-Hellenism 18, 18 n.38
punk culture 77
Punt, Jeremy 94 n.11

race/racism 6–9, 52, 82, 93. *See also* ethnicity
  color-based stigma 85–6
  race relations 82 n.92
  racial ethnicity 82
refugee 85
religious-ethnic identity 2, 10–11, 36, 60, 60 n.147, 91
resident aliens 10 n.47, 56–7, 67–70, 87. *See also* foreigners
resurrection of Christ 2, 34, 37, 40–2, 47–8, 52, 55, 59, 70–1. *See also* death of Christ
rhetorical strategy of Peter 1, 9–11, 36, 90
Romanization 27, 27 n.106, 30–3. *See also* Hellenization
  in Britain 32, 32 n.136
  MacMullen on 27 n.106
  Woolf on 27 n.106
Romans/Rome 15, 34, 50 n.98, 51, 62, 69, 80, 80 n.82, 81 n.91, 90
  citizenship 30, 30 n.126, 32 n.135
  civilizing mission of 27–30
  Greek ethnicity under 26–7
  humanitas 28, 31, 33
  material culture 32–3
  mores 31–2
  restriction of wearing toga 32 n.135
Ross, Shawn A. 18
  "Barbarophonos: Language and Panhellenism in the *Iliad*" 18 nn.38–9

Salamis 20–1
salvation 38 n.18, 43 n.47, 47, 59, 66–7
Sargent, Benjamin, *Written to Serve: The Use of Scripture in 1 Peter* 38 n.14
Scandinavia 82 n.92
Scott, James C. 77 n.70
Scripture in 1 Peter 3
Scythians 16

Sechrest, Love L. 36 n.4, 94 n.12
secular/secularism 82
segmentary lineage structure 86
self-definition 2 n.8, 7, 13, 17, 26–7, 31, 33
self-identify 4, 90
self-understanding 3, 8, 26, 34, 52, 61, 84, 87, 94. *See also* group-understanding
Selwyn, Edward G. 50 n.99
Seneca 29
Septuagint (LXX) 5, 41, 46, 50 n.99, 53
Severus, Septimius 58
shared descent 5–6, 8, 25–6, 33, 37
Sherwin-White, A. N., *The Roman Citizenship* 30 n.126, 32 n.135, 33 n.140
sin 47, 51
slave/slavery 25, 46–7, 51, 58 n.138
Smith, Anthony D. 89
  The Ethnic Origins of Nations 16
  on *ethnies* (ethnic groups) 36
Smith, Shively 57
Snodgrass, A. M. 18
social alienation 2, 2 n.5, 3 n.10, 57
social dominance theory 92
social identity 2 n.7, 4, 12, 77, 93. *See also specific social identities*
social prejudice 35 n.1, 62, 62 n.2, 74, 91
social scientific methodology 3 n.10
solidarity 2, 23, 26, 36, 56, 60–1, 89–90
South and North Korea summit, 2018 89. *See also* Korean
Sparta/Spartan 14, 23, 25
speech 72
  uncouth speech 19 n.44
spiritual birth 53–4
stereotypes 15, 25 n.93, 64, 66 n.22, 69–71, 75–6, 79, 81, 83, 93
  of perpetual foreigner 72 n.45, 93
stigma symbols 78, 82–3, 86. *See also* prestige symbols
Strabo 15 n.16, 30 n.122
Stroup, Christopher 94 n.12
Suetonius 32 n.135, 79
  Nero 80
system of honor. *See* honorary ethnics

Tacitus 29, 32, 79
  Annals 32 n.135, 80

Taylor, Charles, *Sources of the Self: The Making of the Modern Identity* 3 n.11
Tertullian 58
Thomas, Rosalind 25 n.93
Thucydides 23
Tite, Philip 48 n.80
Titus 42 n.37, 53 n.110
Trajan 29 n.115, 30, 35 n.1
transformation 9, 32 n.135, 42–3, 47, 59, 60 n.147, 66, 79
tribes 49
Trojans 18–19, 18 n.39. *See also* Achaeans
Trojan War 19
Trump, Donald 75

unauthorized migrants 75
undocumented immigrants 75
The United States
    Asian Americans 72 n.45
    Chinese American 72
    race in 82 n.92
    undocumented/illegal immigrants 75

Vassenden, Anders 82–3
Virgil 29 n.121
virtual social identity 77–8. *See also* actual social identity
Volf, Miroslav 66 n.19, 66 n.22

wage war 67–8, 70
Weber, Max 64
    ethnische Gruppen 64 n.13
Wilken, Robert L. 58
Williams, Travis B., *Good Works in 1 Peter: Negotiating Social Conflict and Christian Identity in the Greco-Roman World* 80 n.85
Wimmer, Andreas 7, 82 n.92
Woolf, Greg
    Becoming Roman: The Origin of Provincial Civilization in Gaul 27 n.106, 30 n.126, 33 n.138
    on Roman culture 32–3

King Xerxes 21–2, 25

www.ingramcontent.com/pod-product-compliance
Lightning Source LLC
Chambersburg PA
CBHW070644300426
44111CB00013B/2246